The Politics of Nation-Build

Making Co-Nationals, Refugees, and Minorities

What drives a state's choice to assimilate, accommodate, or exclude ethnic groups within its territory? In this pathbreaking work on the international politics of nation-building, Harris Mylonas argues that a state's nation-building policies toward non-core groups – any aggregation of individuals perceived as an unassimilated ethnic group by the ruling elite of a state – are influenced by both its foreign policy goals and its relations with the external patrons of these groups. Through a detailed study of the Balkans, Mylonas shows that the way a state treats a non-core group within its own borders is determined largely by whether the state's foreign policy is revisionist or cleaves to the international status quo, and whether it is allied or in rivalry with that group's external patrons. Mylonas explores the effects of external involvement on the salience of cultural differences and the planning of nation-building policies. *The Politics of Nation-Building* injects international politics into the study of nation-building, building a bridge between international relations and the comparative politics of ethnicity and nationalism. This is the first book to explain systematically how the politics of ethnicity in the international arena determine which groups are assimilated, accommodated, or annihilated by their host states.

Harris Mylonas is an Assistant Professor of Political Science and International Affairs at George Washington University. He completed his PhD in Political Science at Yale University and is a Scholar at the Harvard Academy for International and Area Studies.

Problems of International Politics

Series Editors
Keith Darden, *Yale University*
Ian Shapiro, *Yale University*

The series seeks manuscripts central to the understanding of international politics that will be empirically rich and conceptually innovative. It is interested in works that illuminate the evolving character of nation-states within the international system. It sets out three broad areas for investigation: (1) Identity, security, and conflict; (2) Democracy; and (3) Justice and distribution.

Titles in the Series

Şener Aktürk, *Regimes of Ethnicity and Nationhood in Germany, Russia, and Turkey*

Donald Horowitz, *Constitutional Change and Democracy in Indonesia*

Steven Levitsky and Lucan A. Way, *Competitive Authoritarianism: Hybrid Regimes After the Cold War*

The Politics of Nation-Building

Making Co-Nationals, Refugees, and Minorities

HARRIS MYLONAS

George Washington University

CAMBRIDGE
UNIVERSITY PRESS

CAMBRIDGE UNIVERSITY PRESS
Cambridge, New York, Melbourne, Madrid, Cape Town,
Singapore, São Paulo, Delhi, Mexico City

Cambridge University Press
32 Avenue of the Americas, New York, NY 10013-2473, USA

www.cambridge.org
Information on this title: www.cambridge.org/9781107661998

© Harris Mylonas 2012

First published 2012
Reprinted 2013 (twice)

A catalog record for this publication is available from the British Library.

Library of Congress Cataloging in Publication Data

Mylonas, Harris, 1978–
The politics of nation-building : making co-nationals, refugees, and minorities /
Harris Mylonas.
    p. cm. – (Problems of international politics)
Includes bibliographical references and index.
ISBN 978-1-107-02045-0 (hardback) – ISBN 978-1-107-66199-8 (pbk.)
 1. Nation-building – Balkan Peninsula – History.   2. Minorities – Government policy –
Balkan Peninsula.   3. Ethnic groups – Government policy – Balkan Peninsula.   4. Balkan
Peninsula – Ethnic relations.   5. Balkan Peninsula – Foreign relations.   6. Ethnicity –
Political aspects – Balkan Peninsula.   7. Nationalism – Balkan Peninsula.   I. Title.
JN97.A38M557   2012
327.1´1–dc23   2012011707

ISBN 978-1-107-02045-0 Hardback
ISBN 978-1-107-66199-8 Paperback

Cover image: Artist: Udo J. Keppler, 1872–1956.
Caption: At present he works Bulgaria. A continuous performance since Peter, the Great.
Summary: Illustration shows a puppeteer labeled "Russia" with marionettes labeled
"Bulgaria" and "Macedonia" engaged in a sword fight; the Bulgarian puppet is about to cut
the head off the Macedonian puppet, who has dropped his sword. Hanging on the side of
the theater, to the left, are three puppets labeled "Roumelia, Servia, [and] Roumania."
Date created/published: New York: J. Ottmann Lith., 7 October 1903.
Source: Library of Congress Prints and Photographs Division, Washington, D.C. Available at:
http://www.loc.gov/pictures/item/2010652307/.

To my parents Eleni and George, and my sister Sophia

Contents

List of Figures, Maps, Tables, Graph, and Illustrations

TABLES

GRAPH

ILLUSTRATIONS

Acknowledgments

I would like to thank Stathis Kalyvas, who turned me into a social scientist. Keith Darden, Ivo Banac, Juan Linz, Ioannis Evrigenis, Bill Foltz, Nicholas Sambanis, and Andreas Wimmer were all there when I felt I had run out of inspiration. This book would not have been written without their support and guidance. George Mavrogordatos has been and remains my mentor for more than fifteen years now. He has helped me in innumerable ways.

I was also fortunate to discuss and receive feedback on specific chapters and in some cases on the whole manuscript from Robert Adcock, Dia Anagnostou, Ana Arjona, Gina Bateson, Carles Boix, Deborah Boucoyannis, Zeynep Bulutgil, Tim Crawford, Rafaela Dancygier, Martin Dimitrov, Kristin Fabbe, Jocelyn Friedlander, John Glavinas, Basil Gounaris, Adi Greif, Sheena Chestnut Greitens, Eric Grynaviski, Gabor Gyori, Casiano Hacker-Cordon, Jennie Han, Sandy Henderson, Erin Jenne, Stephen Kaplan, Jeehye Kim, Adria Lawrence, Pantelis Lekkas, Meghan Lynch, Nikos Marantzidis, Iakovos Michailidis, Christopher Muller, Elias Nikolakopoulos, Liz Perry, Pavel Petrov, Andrew Radin, Maurice Richter, Nasos Roussias, Elizabeth Saunders, Jonah Schulhofer-Wohl, John Sides, Abbey Steele, Manny Teitelbaum, Monica Toft, Konstantinos Tsitselikis, Constantine Tsoukalas, Elpida Vogli, Tristan Volpe, Lisa Wedeen, Libby Wood, and Yael Zeira.

I would like to thank my colleagues Martha Finnemore, James M. Goldgeier, Hope Harrison, Jim Lebovic, Marc Lynch, Cynthia McClintock, and Mike Mochizuki, who participated in an extremely helpful book incubator organized by Susan Sell. I would also like to thank Jorge Dominguez, Michael Hechter, Mark Kramer, Terry Martin, Tim Snyder, and Susan Woodward, who participated in my author's conference – organized by Larry Winnie and Kathleen Hoover at the Harvard Academy – their comments helped me sharpen my argument. These events were critical in both improving the content and shaping the final structure of the book. The insicive comments made by the two anonymous reviewers of the book for Cambridge University Press significantly improved my argument and the presentation of the empirics. It was at this stage of that Daphne Halikiopoulou, Henry Hale, and Matt Kocher read the manuscript and gave me incredibly helpful comments. I can't thank them enough for that.

Very important was also the role of many experts who helped me conduct independent coding of my dataset on nation-building policies in the post–World War I Balkans: Sener Akturk, Erol Ulker, Holy Case, Petre Opris, Peter Wien, Eleftheria Manta, Fuat Dundar, and Irina Culic. I would like to thank Wilder Bullard, Justin Caton, Katarina Montgomery, Seok Joon Kim, Diane Kuhn, Lisel Hintz, Rory Schacter, Anthony Staccone, and Edlira Nasi for being excellent research assistants.

I also want to thank the personnel at The Museum of the Macedonian Struggle in Thessaloniki, the Archive of Eleftherios Venizelos at the Benaki Musuem in Athens, the British National Archives, the Gennadius Library, the General State Archives of Macedonia in Thessaloniki, the Archive of the Hellenic Ministry of Foreign Affairs in Athens, the General State Archives of Florina, the General State Archives of Kozani, and The Hellenic Literary and Historical Archive in Thessaloniki.

This is the appropriate place to also thank MIT Press for allowing me to use parts of a chapter they previously published, the Carnegie Endowment for International Peace for giving me permission to reprint selected maps from their *Report of the International Commission to Inquire into the Causes and Conduct of the Balkan Wars*, and the Library of Congress for providing me with amazing illustrations.

The following institutions have supported my graduate-level education and my research for this book: the Georg W. Leitner Program in International and Comparative Political Economy, the European Union Studies Grant, the John F. Enders Research Grant, the Stavros Niarchos Foundation, the MacMillan Center for International and Area Studies at Yale, the Fulbright Foundation, Yale University, The University of Chicago, and the National Scholarship Foundation of Greece. I thank them for their generosity.

For making my life during my graduate school years at Yale significantly better, I would like to thank Mina Alaghband, Farhad Anklesaria, Julia Averbuck, David Epstein, Ileana Alkistis Giannakoura, Sara Goldblatt, Jeanne Hefez, Vasilis Kalogeridis, George Kontos, Angeliki Louvi, Panos Manologlou, Thomas Meaney, Theo Michael, Andreas Papadakis, Thodoris Prodromidis, and Nik Vlahos. I would also like to thank Andreas Akaras, Demetra Atsaloglou, Steven Bloomfield, Stefania Malamatina, Konstantina Karterouli, Artemis Seaford, George Skoulakis, Alexandros Yannis, and Marilena Zackheos for the long discussions we have had on nation-building and other topics. And of course it would be inappropriate not to thank my parents George and Eleni, my sister Sophia, and the rest of the family for tolerating me. This book is dedicated to them.

My sincere thanks, penultimately, to the community at the Harvard Academy for International and Area Studies and the Political Science department at George Washington University for creating such a great environment in which to finish my book. Finally yet importantly, I would like to thank the editorial and production teams at Cambridge University Press – especially Anne Lovering Rounds, Mark Fox, Hillary Ford, and Stephanie Sakson – and in particular Lewis Bateman, who ensured a smooth and constructive process, the outcome of which is in your hands. Of course all errors remain my responsibility.

List of Abbreviations

AEV	Archive of Eleftherios Venizelos
APK	Arheion Pavlou Kalliga
ASEAN	Association of Southeast Asian Nations
AYE	Archive of the Hellenic Ministry of Foreign Affairs
AU	African Union
CCP	Chinese Communist Party
CIA	Central Intelligence Agency
ELIA	The Hellenic Literary and Historical Archive
EU	European Union
FO	British Foreign Office
GAK/Florinas	General State Archives of Florina
GAK/Kozanis	General State Archives of Kozani
GAK/Makedonias	General State Archives of Macedonia, Thessaloniki
G.L.	Gennadius Library
IMRO	Internal Macedonian Revolutionary Organization
KSCS	The Kingdom of Serbs, Croats and Slovenes
MP	Member of Parliament
NGOs	Non-Governmental Organizations
OSCE	Organization for Security and Co-Operation in Europe
PRC	People's Republic of China
UN	United Nations
U.S.	United States of America
USIP	United States Institute for Peace
U.S.S.R.	Union of Soviet Socialist Republics

Preface

My paternal grandfather arrived in Greece in the early 1920s from the Black Sea region. His last name was "Değirmenci," which translates as "Miller" in Turkish; hence my name "Mylonas," which means "Miller" in Greek. Themistocles Mylonas was fluent in both Turkish and Pontic Greek. His Orthodox Christian background made him a prime candidate for the obligatory population exchange of 1923 between Greece and Turkey. His wife, also a refugee, came from Novorossiysk in Russia and spoke only Russian when she first arrived in the harbor of Thessaloniki (Salonica) following the Bolshevik Revolution in 1917. She was confused on her arrival by the presence of black soldiers along the shore. The Senegalese troops in the French Army of the Orient did not conform to her expectations about Greece.

My maternal grandfather was from Crete. During World War II, he fought as an officer of the Greek army against the Italians on the Albanian front. After the armistice of April 1941, he had no money to travel back to Crete and decided to stay in the north of the country. He settled in a rural area and married a refugee from Pontos.

The Ottoman Empire targeted the Pontic Greek population with exclusionary policies during World War I and the Turkish state continued these policies during the Greek-Turkish war (1919–1922). These policies led to the ultimate "repatriation" of my paternal grandfather and maternal grandmother to Greece. While my grandparents were targeted by the Turkish state with exclusionary policies, my parents were targeted by the Greek state with assimilationist policies. The two families settled in nearby villages in central Macedonia. In 1969, having already served in the Greek Army as a reserve officer, my father moved to my mother's town and started an automotive dealership. Their respective backgrounds did not prevent them from getting married three years later. Their children – my sister and I – consider themselves Greek nationals; neither speaks the languages that their parents or grandparents spoke; and neither identifies strongly with any subnational ethnic identity. These policies facilitated my parents' marriage, which would have otherwise been controversial, and the successful assimilation of my sister and myself into the Greek national identity.

My family's story is far from unique, but it gives rise to several questions of broader interest about the making of co-nationals, refugees, and minorities. How do states attempt to attain social order in multicultural environments? In particular, under what conditions does a state target a non-core group[1] with assimilationist policies rather than granting it minority rights, or eliminating it through deportation or mass killing? What is the underlying logic of political elites in pursuing these different "nation-building" policies? These questions are at the center of this book.

Many journalists, academics, and policy commentators have recently used the term "nation-building" in place of what the U.S. Department of Defense calls "stability operations."[2] In other words, by "nation-building" they mean "third-party state-building." They use the term to describe efforts to build roads and railways, enforce the rule of law, and improve the infrastructure of a state.[3] I part ways with this recent usage and I use the term "nation-building" as it has been used in the political science literature for the past five decades.[4] Nation-building, sometimes used interchangeably with national integration, is the process through which governing elites make the boundaries of the state and the nation coincide.[5] In my framework, state elites employ three nation-building policies: accommodation, assimilation, and exclusion.[6]

Accommodation refers to the ruling elites' option to retain the non-core group in the state, but grant the group special minority rights. Under accommodation, the governing elites respect and even reproduce certain "differences" of the non-core group through a legal structure and relevant institutions. Alternatively, governing elites can pursue educational, cultural, occupational, matrimonial, demographic, political, and other policies aimed at getting the non-core group to adopt the core group's culture and way of life. This is assimilation. Finally, the ruling elites can physically remove the non-core group through population exchange, deportation, or even mass killing. This is exclusion.[7] These processes have produced "minorities," "co-nationals," and "refugees."

---

[1] In this book, instead of "ethnic group" or "minority," I will use the term "non-core group" to refer to any aggregation of individuals that is perceived as an unassimilated ethnic group (on a linguistic, religious, physical, or ideological basis) by the ruling political elite of a country. I reserve the term "minority" only for groups that have been granted *minority rights* by their host state. For a more elaborate justification of the use of this term over the alternatives, see the relevant section in Chapter 2.

[2] Dobbins et al. 2003, 2005, and 2007: v; Donohoe 2004; Fukuyama 2004 and 2006.

[3] Darden and Mylonas 2012.

[4] Bendix 1969; Connor 1972; Deutsch and Foltz 1963; Eisenstadt and Rokkan 1973. For a discussion of the two definitions, see Hippler 2005; Stephenson 2005.

[5] Gellner 1983.

[6] Private efforts that contribute to the nation-building process are important but are outside the scope of this book. For an important example of this kind, see Glazier 1998.

[7] Listing both "mass killing" and "population exchange" under the term "exclusion" is controversial; however, my definition wants to capture all policies aiming at the physical removal of a population from a state's territory. It is only in this sense that such different policies (practically and ethically) are listed together.

Exclusionary policies, such as ethnic deportations and mass killings, remain a part of the repertoire of state elites around the world. Consider the recent events in Sudan, Iraq, Somalia, Congo, Rwanda, and Bosnia. At the same time, in western democratic states such as Canada and the United States, policies accommodating difference are well established; such policies of accommodation also exist in less stable states such as Lebanon. Today, assimilationist policies are more controversial than policies of accommodation. Scholars and policy makers alike tend to discuss assimilationist policies less openly since the end of the Cold War. They often resort to the term "integration" instead of "assimilation." Human rights activists tend to equate assimilationist policies with "cultural genocide" and often ask governments to apologize for past instances of assimilation. The most recent example is the public apology by Canadian Prime Minister Stephen Harper "to tens of thousands of indigenous people who as children were ripped from their families and sent to boarding schools."[8] Still, the ranks of the assimilated are many. All policy choices are with us today, although exclusion appears to be improbable in the developed world.

Naturally, the social science literature has focused primarily on the decision calculus behind the most violent state policies, such as genocide and ethnic cleansing. As a result, scholars often end up overaggregating the different "peaceful" outcomes under the residual category of "non-violent." Yet the conditions under which states pursue less violent policies such as assimilation or accommodation remain undertheorized. This book develops a theory of nation-building that focuses equally on violent and non-violent policies. Moreover, while extensive work exists on the success or failure of the various nation-building policies, there is relatively little analysis of how governments decide to pursue such policies in the first place. Scholars focus on policy outcomes not policy outputs. My theory makes predictions about policy outputs, the *selection* of policies, and specific plans for assimilation, accommodation, or exclusion.

Modernization theories, constructivist arguments, and primordialist notions are valuable but incomplete since they cannot account for important shifts in nation-building policies across space and over time. In my framework, the emergence of nationalism is the result of an interaction between strategic choices made under the structural conditions of international competition within the Westphalian system of states, technological innovations, and intellectual currents that emerged during the Enlightenment. This interaction produced what Michael Hechter has called "state-building nationalism." In my view, nationalism is more a contingent outcome of a strategic response by statesmen to modern conditions of geopolitical competition than the product of industrialization or print capitalism per se.

[8] Brown 2008. For a comparison of these policies in Australia, Canada, and New Zealand, see Armitage 1995.

The Politics of Nation-Building moves beyond explanations that emphasize ethnic hatred between groups, the importance of different understandings of nationhood, the focus on kin states, or various versions of the modernization theories to identify the geostrategic conditions under which certain policies become more likely with respect to different types of non-core groups. Ethnic group relations vary widely over time, countries with the same understandings of nationhood do treat similar groups differently, a homeland may or may not act as a homeland toward its ethnic kin, and a great or regional power may decide to act as an external backer for a group it shares no attributes with. In my account, it is the politics of ethnicity in the international arena, rather than ethnic attributes per se, that structures nation-building choices.

This book asks the reader to make a conceptual leap from the misused term "minority" to that of "non-core group," from focusing on "homelands" as the only external actor to the more inclusive concept of "external power," and from the dichotomous – and narrow – conceptualizations of nation-building policies such as "inclusion/exclusion" or "violent/non-violent" to that of "assimilation, accommodation, and exclusion." I focus on a novel dependent variable – the selection of nation-building policies – and in my effort to explain the observed variation I straddle the divide between not only history and political science, but also between comparative politics and international relations. The empirical sections of the book rely, as much as was feasible, on archival material and sources that allow me to get as close as possible to elite perceptions of and intentions toward non-core groups. This focus on elite perceptions and intentions is a conscious attempt to incorporate constructivist principles about ethnicity into my data collection process and to bring *intentions* back to political science. To be sure, the realities on the ground are messy and nonlinear; moreover, information on state policies toward non-core groups is often twisted and ambiguous. But what is at stake is an important choice: infer the intentions from the observation of behavior *or* attempt to get as close as possible to an understanding of the intentions themselves. Whenever I could I chose the latter path.

In writing this book I have three goals: first, to explore the effects of external involvement on the politicization of cultural differences; second, to broaden and deepen our understanding of the logic of state-planned nation-building policies toward non-core groups and generate a conversation that spans disciplines and geography; and third, to develop a set of policy recommendations to prevent the occurrence of ethnic cleansing while highlighting the trade-offs between policies of accommodation and assimilation. A rethinking of the process of nation-building is much needed today: continuous migration flows, increasingly protectionist tendencies in global markets, and inefficient international institutions can potentially undermine the accommodationist consensus that exists – at least among academic circles – in the developed world and unleash exclusionary policies in many developing countries. If these sorts of possibilities are to be avoided, we need to rethink the incentive structure of ruling political elites with homogenizing tendencies governing over multiethnic states. The accommodation consensus may have blinded our eyes to the unintended consequences and the hazards involved in uncritically pursuing certain norms by supporting non-core groups against governments that do not share the West's understanding of human rights.

Harris Mylonas
Washington, D.C.
September 2012

I

Introduction

Why were the Armenians living in the Ottoman Empire accommodated until 1875, but targeted with exclusionary policies thereafter, including mass killings? This empirical puzzle from the last decades of the Ottoman Empire remains unresolved. For most of the nineteenth and early twentieth century, the Ottomans still occupied significant parts of Southeastern Europe, North Africa, and the Middle East. During the early nineteenth century, the Tanzimat reform institutionalized the pre-existing accommodation of religious difference within the context of the Empire through the *millet* (religious community) system. However, external involvement by the Great Powers and the diffusion of nationalist ideas put pressure on the Ottoman way of managing diversity, undermining its multiethnic character and pushing it toward homogenization.

Armenians and Turks had lived in relative harmony in the Ottoman Empire for centuries. The Ottoman administrators treated the Armenians as the "most loyal *millet*" in the Empire. This was justified, since many different peoples in the Empire had already rebelled during the nineteenth century (e.g., the Greeks, Serbs, and Bulgarians), while the Armenians had not. By the 1890s, however, the Ottoman ruling elite's views had changed significantly, and systematic persecution of the Armenians began. Two decades later, during World War I, the Young Turks[1] – then ruling over the Ottoman Empire – perceived the Armenians as being used as a fifth column[2] and thus threatening their country's security and

---

[1] Hanioğlu 2001.

[2] According to Encyclopædia Britannica, a fifth column is a "clandestine group or faction of subversive agents who attempt to undermine a nation's solidarity by any means at their disposal.... A cardinal technique of the fifth column is the infiltration of sympathizers into the entire fabric of the nation under attack and, particularly, into positions of policy decision and national defense. From such key posts, fifth-column activists exploit the fears of a people by spreading rumours and misinformation, as well as by employing the more standard techniques of espionage

targeted them with mass killings and deportations. The result was the Armenian genocide.[3]

This puzzle gives rise to a broader question: What explains variation in state policies to manage social diversity and attain order? Despite the voluminous literature on more or less successful national integration histories,[4] as well as theories explaining a state's choice to exclude or include non-core groups,[5] there is no theory that accounts for the conditions under which a state is likely to assimilate, accommodate, or exclude a non-core group. Different paths to national integration have been proposed,[6] but no systematic theory that accounts for variation in nation-building policies.

Since World War II, modernization theorists have discussed national integration as a by-product of industrialization, urbanization, and political development.[7] According to these scholars, national sentiments were the result of people's residence/location as well as increased social mobilization, which linked peripheries to metropolitan centers.[8] Over time, it is argued, the initial passive identification turns into a more conscious and active one.[9]

Early modernization theorists have devoted little attention to direct state involvement in the process of nation-building. For example, according to the "melting pot" theory, members of the non-core group choose assimilation for material reasons. Thus, assimilation is a byproduct of economic development and does not require much state intervention.[10]

These theories do not specify who pursues nation-building policies and in what fashion. As Smith puts it, in this set of theories "the role of the state is simply to act as a handmaid of history, whose goal is a world of large-scale nation-states or regions."[11] Another problem with this set of theories is that they cannot account for the cases of non-core groups that are targeted with assimilation campaigns in states that are not undergoing modernization, or for cases of non-core groups that are kept segregated or are deported instead of assimilated in modernizing states. Moreover, these theories – developed primarily with the U.S. context in mind – were focused on the factors that may determine the success or failure of

---

and sabotage." Accessed on 06 Apr. 2009: http://www.britannica.com/EBchecked/topic/206477/fifth-column.

[3] For more, see Akcam 2006; Dündar 2010; Hovannisian 1986; Melson 1986; Suny et al. 2011.

[4] Deutsch and Foltz 1966; Eisenstadt and Rokkan 1973; Snyder 2003; Weber 1976.

[5] Bulutgil 2009; Downes 2008; Mann 2005; Naimark 2001; Rae 2002; Snyder 2010, Straus 2006, Valentino 2004, Wimmer 2002.

[6] Greenfeld 1993.

[7] Anderson 1983; Bendix 1969; Huntington 1968; Anderson et al. 1967.

[8] Deutsch 1965.

[9] The diffusionist theory of social integration makes similar predictions with the other modernization theories with respect to state preferences toward non-core groups. This theory was proposed by Parsons, Eisenstadt, and Smelser. According to them the culture of the core group trickles down to the people at the periphery. Part of Deutsch's argument captures this process with social communication doing the work (1965).

[10] Alba and Nee 2003; Glazer and Moynihan 1970; Gordon 1964.

[11] 1986: 232.

state policies. My argument, presented below, focuses instead on explaining the initial selection of policies, not their successes or failures.

Later generations of social scientists provided microfoundations for the various modernization theories.[12] These studies also embraced the unplanned character of national integration strategies posited by the modernization theorists. Their work, inspired by methodological individualism, provided microfoundations focusing on the calculations individuals make with respect to identity choices.[13] But individual level decisions are always structured within the context of state policies. Without a theory that accounts for variation in state-planned policies toward non-core groups, we cannot have a complete theory of nation-building; the "supply side" of the phenomenon is undertheorized. This book provides such a theory.

Most arguments by contemporary comparative politics scholars focus on domestic dynamics to explain state policies toward non-core groups. Group size, territorial concentration, and especially rootedness have been suggested as crucial characteristics on which governments focus when they plan their nation-building policies.[14] The logic is that large, territorially concentrated, and indigenous groups are more likely to demand autonomy or even fight for self-determination than small, dispersed, and recently settled groups. Moreover, countries with more such groups are less likely to accommodate them than countries with fewer such groups.[15]

Primordialist arguments hold that a state's treatment of non-core groups is based on cultural differences. The larger the perceived difference between the culture or race of the non-core group and the core group, the more likely it is that the non-core group will be excluded.[16] Conversely, if the groups are similar, then the non-core group will be targeted for assimilation. Scholars in this camp have also emphasized the importance of past relations between the core and the non-core group.[17] I incorporate some of these findings in my theory but with a twist, namely injecting external involvement by interested powers in the mix.

According to ethnic antipathy and status reversal theories, past relations between the dominant group and the non-core group condition state policies. Groups are constantly competing for status and self-esteem. A previously disadvantaged group is likely to target the previously advantaged group with exclusionary policies once the roles are reversed.[18] However, such arguments

---

[12] Gellner 1983; Hechter 1975; Laitin 1995 and 1998.

[13] Laitin 1998. According to this account, populations adapt to the hegemonic constitutive story in order to secure upward social mobility. Thus we should not observe any group-specific assimilation policies since people will gradually integrate. The basic incentive structure should suffice. Laitin's theory largely neglects the supply side. But often individuals are not even given the option to assimilate, while others are given incentives to do so. Laitin does address the supply side with respect to Jews and Roma in his article "Marginality: A Microperspective" (1995).

[14] Brubaker 1993; Toft 2003.

[15] Van Evera 1994; Walter 2009.

[16] Armstrong 1982; Isaacs 1975; Kaplan 1993.

[17] Horowitz 1985; Kaufman 2001; Van Evera 1994: 23–25.

[18] Horowitz 1985; Petersen 2001 and 2002.

cannot account for variation in the treatment of the same non-core group/state dyad over time.

An equally prominent theory in sociology focuses on a state's understandings of nationhood, civic versus ethnocultural.[19] According to this argument, elites in states with a civic understanding of nationhood are more likely to target all non-core groups with assimilationist policies. In contrast, elites in states with an ethnic understanding of nationhood will exclude any group that does not fit the ethnocultural criteria for nationhood.[20] However, while this argument may capture important country level differences, it cannot account for the important subnational variation that exists in most states.

Scholars studying genocide and ethnic cleansing have also advanced explanations underlining the importance of domestic political considerations, arguing that insecure regimes are likely to target certain non-core groups with exclusionary policies as a way to consolidate their power. In certain cases, this is an argument that emphasizes security threats coming from the non-core groups.[21] In other cases, the groups have not challenged their government but are just scapegoats.[22] Although such arguments illuminate certain cases they do not make any predictions with respect to assimilation or accommodation.

International dynamics have also been considered in the literature by sociologists and political scientists alike. Michael Mann and Jack Snyder, among others, have highlighted structural international factors such as the spread of democracy to account for variation in nation-building policies.[23] According to this logic, structural transformations at the international level produce societal frictions when they are introduced. Again, these country-level factors are important to understand broader trends, but they are not calibrated enough to account for subnational group-specific variation.

Finally, other scholars have drawn attention to the impact of the non-core group having a national homeland on nation-building.[24] They argue that elites in a national homeland make credible commitments to their co-ethnics abroad.[25] This commitment in turn makes the non-core group assertive toward the state they live in and can lead to a secessionist war.[26] The implicit prediction with respect to nation-building policies is that non-core groups with national homelands are likely to escalate their demands and thus are more likely to be targeted with exclusionary policies by the state whose sovereignty they challenge. The shortcomings of the various versions of the homeland argument have to do with the emphasis on the ethnic affinity between the external power and the

[19] Brubaker 1992.
[20] Brubaker's theory builds on the older distinction between 'ethnic' and 'civic' nationalism, see Kohn 1945.
[21] Gagnon 2004; Harff 1987; Straus 2006.
[22] Brass 1997; Martin 2001; Snyder 2000.
[23] Mann 2005; Snyder 2000.
[24] Brubaker 1996; Weiner 1971.
[25] Jenne 2007; Salehyan 2009; Van Houten 1998.
[26] Thyne 2009.

non-core group and the inability to account for the variation in the behavior of the "homeland" over time. Many external powers supporting non-core groups have no ethnic ties with the non-core group and, as King and Melvin have pointed out, many homelands do not act as homelands today but may do so tomorrow.[27]

THE ARGUMENT

My argument builds on existing explanations but focuses on the importance of international and geostrategic concerns for nation-building policies. It accounts for the variation in nation-building policies as a result of the interaction between host states and external powers rather than non-core groups and host states.[28]

In the stylized presentation of my argument there are three actors: a host state, a non-core group, and an external power. The ruling political elites of a host state want to reproduce their power and ensure the sovereignty of their national state. Non-core groups want to maximize their well-being and avoid state repression. Moreover, depending on how salient the non-core group's identity is the group members may also seek anything from recognition and basic minority rights all the way to autonomy or even independence. External powers often cultivate relations with non-core groups in other states to destablilize them, to increase their bargaining power, or because of ethnic ties. External powers usually – but not always – choose to support non-core groups that reside in geopolitically important areas, are large, territorially concentrated, and close to the borders.

I posit that this external involvement, whether clandestine, covert, or overt, drives not only the mobilization and politicization of the non-core group's identity, but also the host state's perception of the non-core group and the state's nation-building policies toward the group. Hence, the foreign policy goals of the host state and its interstate relations with external powers drive a host state's choices of nation-building policies toward non-core groups.

The interstate relations between the host state and the external power supporting the non-core group can take the form of rivalry or alliance.[29] These

---

[27] King and Melvin 1999/2000.

[28] The term "host state" in my framework is shorthand for the political elites ruling in the name of the core group. I use the term "host state" to distinguish it from the external power that supports the group that is more often than not also a state. The term "host" is used to signify the state where a non-core group resides and it does not imply anything about the legitimacy of the core group rights over the land versus the rights of a non-core group. In fact, often non-core groups are indigenous to the land they reside when core groups are not. For more on the definitions of the actors in my argument, see the relevant section in Chapter 2.

[29] I follow Walt's (1997: 157) definition of alliance: "An alliance is a formal or informal commitment for security cooperation between two or more states. Although the precise arrangements embodied in different alliances vary enormously, the defining feature of any alliance is a commitment for mutual military support against some external actor(s) in some specified set of circumstances."

relations in turn are influenced by – but are independent from – international alliance blocs. The nature of these interstate relations ultimately structures the relationship between the non-core group and the host state.

Domestic factors matter as well. The foreign policy goals of the host state are of great importance. A host state may have revisionist or status quo foreign policy goals.[30] The elites of a state can come to adopt revisionist goals because the military and economic power of their state is rapidly increasing relative to their competitors, because of ideological convictions, or because they have lost territories in a recent war and want to regain them. Regardless of the causes of a state's revisionism, the foreign policy goals of the ruling political elites are focused on overturning the international status quo. Alternatively, state elites may favor the international status quo. This, again, might be because their power is declining relative to their competitors, because their ideological convictions have changed because of a defeat or exhaustion, or because they have recently expanded their territory and want to consolidate it.

There is a significant debate in the international relations literature over whether all states,[31] no states,[32] or some states are revisionist.[33] My argument falls in the third camp, recently baptized "neoclassical realism,"[34] but it comes with a twist. In contrast to neoclassical realism, where domestic incentives affect a state's foreign policy behavior,[35] I suggest a reversed-neoclassical realism, where foreign policy goals interact with the nature of interstate relations with the external patrons of non-core groups to condition nation-building policies. Revisionism in my framework refers to a state's *ex ante* stated foreign policy goals, not necessarily its behavior.[36]

Four configurations that lead to different policy choices flow from a set of assumptions I discuss in Chapter 2, and have so far been neglected in the literature. First, a policy of assimilation toward that non-core group is likely if a group has no external support. Second, a host state is likely to pursue assimilation through internal colonization if the state favors the status quo and an enemy is supporting the non-core group. Third, a host state is likely to accommodate a non-core group if an ally is supporting that group. Finally, a host state is likely to exclude a non-core group when the state has revisionist aims and an enemy is supporting that group.

[30] Wolfers 1962: 90, 92.
[31] Mearsheimer 2001.
[32] Waltz 1979.
[33] Schweller 2004 and 2006.
[34] See Lobell et al. 2009; Rathbun 2008; Rose 1998.
[35] Many studies of neoclassical realism focus on the importance of domestic variables in explaining foreign policy outcomes. Jack Snyder shows the role of compact interest groups on expansionist foreign policy (1991); Jason Davidson shows that fascist Italy's revisionism in the interwar years was driven by domestic political opportunities (in Davidson 2002). Taylor Fravel (2008) argues that internal threats can account for China's policy with respect to territorial disputes.
[36] Davidson 2002.

My argument is applicable to cases that satisfy the following conditions. First, the ruling political elites represent a core group that is well defined and there is a clear criterion of inclusion – a "national type" in the age of nationalism.[37] Second, part of the population has not yet been successfully assimilated and there is no "caste structure" in place.[38] Third, the state has the capacity to directly rule the population.[39] In other words, my argument would require modification to account for variation in states that do not have a well-defined core group – maybe because they are ruled by a multiethnic coalition or their organization is based on an organizing principle that defies such definition; states where there are no non-core groups; states where there is a hierarchical ethnic structure that is considered fixed or sacred; and/or states that do not have the capacity to directly rule their population – that is, failed states.

These scope conditions render the Balkans states following World War I an ideal set of cases to study. The area at the time was ethnically heterogeneous, with many unassimilated ethnic groups; the ruling elites of these states had a clear national type in their minds; and all of these states had the capacity to pursue nation-building policies.[40] Moreover, we can control for important factors. All states were primarily agricultural societies with low urbanization levels, they faced the same international system of minority rights protection, they had experienced similar forms of past rule – as parts of the Ottoman Empire – and they had a similar understanding of nationhood. Importantly, there is significant variation in nation-building policies across and within these states. Finally, studying cases from the interwar period is less difficult than studying recent cases where the historiography has not matured and archival materials have not been declassified.

One might argue that the interwar Balkans experience belongs to the distant past, that the era of nation-building and assimilation has reached its limits, and that the time when citizenship is no longer connected to ethnicity is – or ought to be – near.[41] Indeed, there might be a threshold of economic development beyond which the citizens of a state become immune to nationalist ideology. And yet political realities around the world challenge the euphoria of the early 1990s regarding the prospects of multiculturalism and cosmopolitanism. Issues of ethnicity, nationhood, and citizenship remain complexly bound up with one another throughout

---

[37] Within multiethnic empires, that by definition are not driven by a homogenizing imperative, accommodation rather than assimilation is the default option. In such situations, external support by an ally is definitely not required for a group to be accommodated. I borrow the expression "age of nationalism" from Hobsbawm's work (1990 and 1991).

[38] In such cases assimilation is by definition impossible, see Weber 1978. These systems involve an "ideology of inferiority for the subordinate groups" and thus an almost fixed ethnic structure that is perceived as natural. For more on hierarchical systems, see Horowitz 1985: 21–32.

[39] For the distinction between direct and indirect rule, see Hechter 2000.

[40] To be sure, there was plenty of instability in Albania and Turkey during the first years after World War I but calling them failed states would be wrong.

[41] Benhabib 2004; Joppke 2005; Kymlicka 1995; Young 1993.

the globe – even in developed countries, as evidenced by the recent policy debates in France, Germany, the United Kingdom, Belgium, Slovakia, and Switzerland.[42]

While it is true that exclusion seems inconceivable in contemporary consolidated democracies, even liberal states are likely to deviate from their multiculturalist arrangements under certain geopolitical and economic conditions. I argue that consolidated democracies can afford to accommodate non-core groups because of their participation in powerful alliances such as NATO or the EU, which significantly reduce threat perceptions and provide security protection. In other words, in the absence of these alliances or if faced with imminent security threats even consolidated democracies will pursue exclusionary policies when confronted with enemy-backed non-core groups, as the internment of Japanese-Americans during World War II illustrates.[43]

Moreover, the increased security measures that states pursued following the terrorist attacks on 11 September 2001 and the intensifying efforts to control illegal immigration have further strengthened border controls. Thus we are faced with a paradox: "people are at the same time both more closely united [because of globalization] and more carefully divided through increased physical and legal barriers."[44] All in all, the forces of globalization far from supersede the role of the nation-state both within and beyond its territorial limits.

In a world where territory is important and border changes are possible, we must consider external support for non-core groups. Despite the well-known arguments that territory is becoming increasingly less important in our globalized world, that border changes are – or will be – rare events in our international system, and that borders are increasingly obsolete,[45] territorial disputes, border changes, and strict border controls are with us and will be with us in the future.[46] For territorial disputes, one just needs to ask people in Cyprus, Mali, India, Israel, China, Armenia, and Azerbaijan, to name just a few countries with ongoing disputes. For border changes one needs to look in the former USSR, former Yugoslavia, Eritrea, East Timor, South Ossetia, Georgia, and Sudan, to name just a few recent cases. When we add to the list above the scores of "nations without a state"[47] or "stateless nations"[48] then we get a sense of the potential for territorial conflicts in the near future.

Returning to the initial puzzle, my theory suggests that in order to understand the shift of Ottoman policies toward Armenians from accommodation to exclusion, we need to pay attention to the patterns of external involvement and

---

[42] Akturk 2011; Caldwell 2009; Howard 2009.
[43] Harth 2001; Robinson 2009.
[44] Ganster and Lorey 2005: xi.
[45] Camilleri 1990; Friedman 2000 and 2007; Sassen 1996, 1998, and 2002; Schaeffer 2003; Strange 2000.
[46] Buchanan and Moore 2003; Doremus et al. 1998; Fearon and Laitin 2011; Vasquez and Henehan 2001; Wilson and Donnan 1998.
[47] Guibernau 1999.
[48] For example, Minahan (2002) documents 300 developed or emerging national groups without their own state worldwide. For Europe alone, see Bodlore-Penlaez 2010.

interstate relations. The Armenian genocide was neither destined to happen due to a long-standing ideological conviction by the Young Turks to eliminate the Armenians nor strategically provoked by Armenian armed groups in order to force the Great Powers of the time to intervene on their behalf.[49] It was the increasing Russian, and later French, military and diplomatic support of the Armenians – rather than merely the cultural or religious difference between Armenians and Turks per se – that transformed the perception of this group in the eyes of the Ottoman ruling elites and set the stage for the persecution of the Armenians. And this transformation was happening in parallel with the transformation of the Ottoman Empire itself from a multiethnic to a homogenizing empire.[50] Once the international conditions for exclusionary policies were there, and the Ottoman Empire under the Young Turks was no longer driven by the multiethnic precepts of the past, then ethnic differences and local conditions became operative. Variables such as cultural or religious differences take a long time to change, but nation-building policies can – and often do – shift at a faster pace. In order to account for the variation in nation-building policies across space and over time, we need a theory that incorporates variables that change at a pace similar to these policies. In this book I present such a theory.

WHY STUDY NATION-BUILDING POLICIES?

The primary reason to study and understand the logic of nation-building policies toward non-core groups is that inter- and intra-state wars often result from conflict over such policies.[51] For example, Imperial Russia used the pretense of protecting the rights of the Orthodox Christian *millet* to intervene in the affairs of the Ottoman Empire. The politics between the Kingdom of Serbia and Austria-Hungary surrounding the Serb minority in Bosnia and Herzegovina spurred World War I.[52] Similarly, Hitler referred to the political unification of the German *Volk* residing outside Germany's borders as the driving principle behind his military moves that led to World War II.[53] The Turkish government justified its 1974 military intervention in Cyprus based on the principle of the protection of its co-ethnics.[54] More

---

[49] Suny et al. 2011.

[50] Findley 2010; Reynolds 2011; Üngör 2011.

[51] There is an extensive empirical and theoretical literature establishing this connection. For more on this, see Ambrosio 2001; Brown 1996; Byman and Van Evera 1998; Carment et al. 2006; Connor 1972; Davis and Moore 1997; Goertz and Dichl 1997; Heraclides 1990 and 1991; Horowitz 1985; Lake and Rothchild 1998; Saideman 1997 and 2002; Saideman and Ayres 2000; Sambanis 2001; Snyder and Walter 1999; Taras and Ganguly 2002; Woodwell 2004.

[52] Another theory is that Franz Ferdinand's assassins wanted to prevent the reorganization of the Habsburg Empire on a trialist basis (a plan to include the Slavs in the Dual Monarchy in order to check the Hungarians), which would have severely undermined Serbian aspirations in Bosnia and Croatia (Sowards 1996).

[53] Weinberg 1995: 95–146.

[54] Stern 1975: 38, 78; Coufoudakis 1976: 469–471.

recently, Russia used similar justifications in its military intervention in Georgia in support of South Ossetia and Abkhazia.[55]

This trend is not unique to the Balkans or post-communist Europe. In the Middle East a potential Kurdistan threatens four sovereign states: Iraq, Turkey, Syria, and Iran. In Kashmir, a nuclear confrontation between India and Pakistan is a real possibility. In Asia, Tibetans and Uyghurs are becoming more assertive toward the Chinese government. In Africa, hundreds of ethnic groups straddle existing state borders. The fates of these peoples and many others with similar statuses depend very much on the international politics of nation-building. Ironically, so do the fates of their host states.

Beyond anecdotal evidence, scholars studying the onset of civil wars statistically have found that political competition among ethnic groups is central to our understanding of armed conflict. Cederman, Min, and Wimmer show that specific ethnic power configurations at the state's center are more likely to lead to conflict than others. In particular ethnic groups that are excluded from state power, have a mobilizational capacity and have experienced conflict in the past are much more likely to rebel.[56] Studying how the abovementioned configurations emerge in the first place is thus crucial.

Understanding the logic of state-planned nation-building policies can help decisionmakers at the United Nations (UN) or in regional organizations such as the European Union (EU), the African Union (AU), or the Association of Southeast Asian Nations (ASEAN) anticipate political developments and devise incentives to prevent ethnic cleansing, encourage accommodation, or foster national integration. Granted, this understanding is not enough on its own; it has to be coupled with effective monitoring and enforcement mechanisms by international organizations. But the latter can be better calibrated if based on a deeper understanding of the logic of nation-building policies.

At least three policy implications flow from my argument. First, one way to prevent exclusionary policies is by upholding the principle of state sovereignty. Second, ethnic cleansing and exclusionary policies may be prevented – along with a whole host of unintended consequences such as spill over of conflict, refugee flows, and humanitarian crises –[57] if governments are particularly judicious when they venture to assist non-core groups in enemy host states. In such cases they either need to commit as many resources as needed to help the non-core group or not interfere at all. Finally, for the probability of accommodation to increase, we need to increase interstate alliances through regional integration initiatives and international and regional institutions such as the EU and ASEAN.

BOOK PLAN

The book comprises eight chapters and a methodological appendix. In Chapter 2, I present the building block concepts and the basic logic of my theory. I also situate

---

[55] King 2008.
[56] Cederman et al. 2010.
[57] Kuperman 2008; Salehyan and Gleditsch 2006; Weiner 1996.

my argument in the existing literature. The first empirical chapter, Chapter 3, introduces the Balkan region and the six states under study to the reader. Besides the methodological justifications for studying the Balkans after World War I, which I briefly discussed above, and the parallels one can draw with the wars and extreme nation-building policies pursued in the same region during the 1990s, I hold that many of today's developing countries are experiencing challenges analogous to those faced by the Balkan states in the interwar years, including incomplete nation- and state-building; weak political institutions unable to accommodate increasing political participation; unconsolidated democracy; religiously, linguistically, and culturally heterogeneous populations; people accustomed to a world of corporate privileges; external involvement; and economic "backwardness."

Chapter 4 tests the theory using a cross-national dataset I compiled on all non-core groups residing within the recognized boundaries of Balkan states immediately after World War I. Results from the statistical analysis corroborate the success of my argument in predicting nation-building policies in the Balkan region. Overall, my argument correctly predicts 81 percent of the cases. Holding alternative explanations to their mean value and varying my main variables of interest produces thought-provoking results.

Consistent with my theory, assimilation is most likely for non-core groups supported by enemy powers and residing in status quo host states. Accommodation has the highest mean probability for non-core groups that are supported by allied powers – or do not have any external support – and reside in states that favor the international status quo. In contrast, non-core groups that are supported by an enemy power and live in revisionist host states face a zero mean probability of being accommodated. Finally, exclusion is most likely for enemy-supported non-core groups in host states dominated by revisionist politics. Again, a non-core group that is not supported by an enemy power has a practically zero mean probability of being targeted with exclusionary policies. These findings confirm my intuitions and nicely illustrate the substantive effects of the variables of interest while controlling – both by design and statistically – for a multitude of variables.

Beyond the support for my argument, significant patterns emerged from the statistical analysis. In the special case when a host state and an enemy external power are contiguous and both have each other's co-ethnics with whom they cultivate links, exclusionary policies become more likely than assimilationist policies toward these non-core groups. However, this variable is not as helpful when we are looking at the choice between accommodation and assimilation. Whether a non-core group had an external homeland or previously dominated the current core group does not appear to have an impact in deciding between policies – at least not in the post–World War I period. Turning to demographic characteristics we observe that group size does not help us distinguish amongst nation-building policies either. Cultural characteristics do matter but in ways that undermine the ethnic antipathy arguments. A difference in religion *and* language between the core and the non-core group makes accommodation more likely than assimilation. This statistically significant finding goes against the prediction of exclusion that cultural distance arguments would make.

In Chapter 5, I take a close look at cases from post-World War I Balkans that do not conform to the predictions of my theory and identify some interesting dynamics that illuminate counterintuitive aspects of nation-building and set up a new research agenda. Looking at the outliers of my statistical analysis, four methodological issues emerge: (a) determining the appropriate time horizon for analysis, (b) dealing with mixed policies followed by governments, (c) distinguishing terminal from transitional policies, and (d) considering the role of external powers' foreign policy priorities and the degree of symmetry in alliances in the decision making process of host states. Finally, I identify a "divide and rule" strategy that Balkan governments pursued both to fragment large non-core groups and to prevent the subnational assimilation of smaller non-core groups to larger ones.

The findings from the cross-national study support my argument. However, to get a better picture of the mechanisms at work and test the microfoundations of my argument I rely on case studies using archival evidence and extensive secondary sources. In Chapter 6, I conduct a subnational study of Western Greek Macedonia using archival material I collected on nation-building policies pursued toward eight non-core groups for a four-year period (1916–1920). This chapter is based on archival research conducted in Greece in 2005 and 2006 at the Museum of the Macedonian Struggle, the Gennadius Library, the General State Archives of Macedonia, ELIA (The Hellenic Literary and Historical Archive), and the Diplomatic and Historical Archives of the Hellenic Ministry of Foreign Affairs.

To reconstruct the nation-building policies followed by the Greek administration at the time, I rely mostly on confidential reports written by the General Governor of Western Macedonia, Ioannis Eliakis. To be sure, this individual had his own agenda in mind when writing these reports. Nevertheless, the confidential nature of these reports and the richness of the material, coupled with the historical context within which I place it, add texture to our understanding of the phenomenon. Eliakis's reports provide us with a unique opportunity to access the reasoning behind the planning of nation-building policies.

More importantly, this region is particularly fruitful for study because of the extremely heterogeneous population that was incorporated into a state with a clear national character, in the midst of many competing national programs from neighboring countries. In this small region we observe all types of nation-building policies (including mixed ones), as well as significant variation in my main variables of interest – interstate relations between external powers and the host state, foreign policy goals, homeland politics, cultural distance, and status reversal. Crucially, my access to various types of archival material as well as local newspapers allowed me to trace elite decision-making in this region.

In Chapter 7, I move north and test the argument in Serbia and later on the Kingdom of Serbs, Croats and Slovenes (KSCS) over several decades. I use newspapers, memoirs, and archival material, as well as an extensive secondary literature, to trace the logic underlying the policies followed by the Serbian ruling political elites toward Albanians from 1878 to 1941. Studying nation-building policies over time allows me to keep important regional, state- and group-level factors constant and isolate the effect of my main variables of interest, external power involvement and host state foreign policy goals.

The findings from the subnational studies in Greek Macedonia and in Kosovo support my theory. In both chapters, variation in external support for non-core groups and foreign policy goals of the host state help us explain nation-building policy shifts. Existing arguments alone cannot account for the variation, with most of their predictions remaining constant over time.

In Chapter 8, I conduct an out-of-sample test relaxing some of the assumptions described in Chapter 2. The cases I discuss in this section, ranging from China to Estonia, explore whether the argument still applies – or how it needs to be modified in order to apply – in situations where the states involved are Great Powers, Communist regimes, or consolidated democracies, as well as in different international systems and norm standards.

I conclude, in Chapter 9, with a discussion of main findings and methodological lessons. I lay out a research agenda on nation-building and recapitulate the caveats I experienced including: (a) the politics of "counting people"; (b) the conflation of intentions, policy choices, policy implementation, and policy outcomes; and (c) the principal-agent problems involved in the implementation of nation-building policies. Finally, I discuss the policy implications that flow from my argument and conclude with some thoughts on the impact of the international system structure on the future of nation-building policies.

PART I

THEORY

2

The International Politics of Assimilation, Accommodation, and Exclusion

Three hundred years ago, the existence of a state did not necessarily presuppose any national sentiments among the population.[1] Other forms for legitimizing authority – cultivating the belief that the governing institutions have the right to rule[2] – were prevalent around the world. States existed long before the age of nationalism, but only during the past two hundred years has the cultivation of nationalistic sentiments become an important part of an increasing number of political leaders' repertoire for establishing order and securing sovereignty within their borders.[3] Since the rise of nationalism as an organizing principle of political communities,[4] national sentiments have countered dissent (including the evasion of conscription), enhanced the taxing abilities of states, fostered compliance with the laws, and prevented separatist movements. However, these same nationalist sentiments have also led to inter- and intrastate conflict, the deaths of many civilians, population displacements, and even genocide.[5]

Legitimate authority in modern national states is connected to popular rule, to majorities. Nation-building is the process through which these majorities are constructed. In this context, foreign powers that want to destabilize a state attempt to undermine its legitimacy by encouraging and nurturing linguistic, ethnic, or religious differences and regional identities within its borders. Thus, governing elites see benefit in harmonizing the political and the national units through the construction and propagation of a common national identity among

---

[1] Following Weber, I define a state as a political organization whose "administrative staff successfully upholds the claim to the monopoly of the legitimate use of physical force in the enforcement of its order" (1978: 54).

[2] Weber 1978.

[3] Spruyt 1994; Tilly 1975, 1992, 1994.

[4] For more on this transformation, see Anderson 1983; Deutsch 1965; Emerson 1960; Gellner 1983; Hroch 2000; Kohn 1945; Snyder 2003 and 2008; and Wimmer 2012.

[5] According to Wimmer (2012, chapter 1) "over three quarters of all full-scale wars – those conflicts costing more than 1,000 battle deaths – were fought, at the end of the twentieth century, either by nationalists who seek to establish a separate nation-state or over the ethnic balance of power within an existing state."

	Explanations	Predictions
Domestic	**H1. Primordialism/ Cultural Distance**	Populations that do not share the same pre-modern ethnic community with the core-group are more likely to be excluded or accommodated than targeted with assimilationist policies.
	H2. Status Reversal/ Ethnic Antipathy	Once a previously disadvantaged group takes control of the state its ruling political elites are likely to target the previously advantaged group(s) with exclusionary policies.
	H3. Reputation	Governments faced with few secessionist non-core groups are more likely to pursue exclusionary (or assimilationist) policies than governments with fewer non-core groups in order to signal resolve and discourage future challengers.
International	**H4. "The Dark side of Democracy"**	The international diffusion of the ideal of popular rule during democratization puts pressure to convert *demos* into *ethnos*, this in turn generates *organic nationalism,* and it ultimately encourages ethnic cleansing of those that do not fit the definition of the *ethnos*.
	H5. National Homeland	Non-core groups with an external homeland are more likely to be targeted for exclusion than assimilation because of the security threat they pose and the high cost of assimilation.

FIGURE 2.1. Predictions of existing explanations.

the population of their state.[6] Now, how do ruling political elites decide who to assimilate, who to accommodate, and who does not belong in their state?

There are two broad categories of arguments in the social science literature that speak to this question: theories that account for nation-building policies based on national-level characteristics of the host state or the attributes of the non-core groups (domestic); and theories that account for nation-building policies based on international structural conditions (international). Figure 2.1 summarizes the existing explanations.

According to advocates of primordialism, people's identities do not change; ethnicity is fixed, predetermined.[7] Nation-state formation would not be possible without some ethnic origins, or what Geertz calls "primordial sentiments," that are transformed into national ones.[8] This intellectual group includes "the new ethnicists" such as Daniel Moynihan, Nathan Glazer, Walker Connor, and Wendell Bell. The pith of their argument is that people who do not want to lose their ethnic identities and core communities do not want to contaminate the purity of their groups.[9] Thus, according to this group of scholars, core groups

[6] Gellner 1983.
[7] Van de Berghe 1981. With respect to primordialist theory I am in agreement with Darden's work, which argues that identities are malleable but under certain conditions operate as if they are fixed; see Darden forthcoming.
[8] Geertz 1963.
[9] Birch 1978.

are more likely to exclude or accommodate populations that do not share the same pre-modern ethnic identity with the core group than target them with assimilationist policies.

Many accounts in the literature focus on the ethnic character of politics. They posit a direct link between ascriptive characteristics and ethnic identities. The latter produce ethnic politics and ultimately lead to ethnic conflict.[10] In this context, an ongoing "struggle for relative group worth" is the driving mechanism that leads to conflict.[11] Backward groups are likely to be hostile toward advantaged groups in an effort to restore their self-esteem and reduce their own anxiety. Horowitz argues that the backward population *also* has the impression that the advantaged group thinks of it as inferior. The masses follow their leaders against the advantaged group, in order to "retrieve their self-esteem."[12] Research in social psychology provides a mechanism supporting this hypothesis – namely, that individuals seek to maximize their self-esteem, and that creating a positive social identity (usually at the expense of some "other") is one way of reaching the desired goal.[13] In sum, according to this type of explanation, in cases where the dominant group was previously dominated by the non-core group, the relations will be conflict-ridden and we should observe no assimilation or accommodation attempts; on the contrary, exclusion is more likely.[14]

The third important line of argument in the "domestic" camp highlights the importance of opportunities for the non-core group. Prominent political scientists and sociologists have argued that ethnic group size, territorial concentration, grievances, rootedness, and past experiences of accommodation are all crucial characteristics that determine the propensity of a group to challenge the host state.[15] This argument of course presupposes the political salience of cultural differences between core and non-core groups. The logic is that large, territorially concentrated, indigenous groups are more likely to demand autonomy or even fight for self-determination than small, dispersed, and/or recently settled groups. In sum, groups with such characteristics are more threatening and thus more likely to be repressed.[16] Governments focus on such characteristics when they plan their nation-building policies.

[10] Gurr 1993; Horowitz 1985: 17–18, 53; Kaufman 2001.
[11] Horowitz's work is the most cited in support of the *ethnic antipathy* theory (1985: 143). David Laitin (2001) tests Horowitz's theory and demonstrates that explanations based on "cultural antipathies" in several post-Soviet territories did not allow us to make correct predictions about which republics would experience rebellion, and also failed to predict the timing of those rebellions which did occur.
[12] 1985: 181. Horowitz acknowledges that the leaders of these backward groups are thinking of the resources that they will obtain if they are successful.
[13] Hechter 2000: 99.
[14] Petersen 2001 and 2002.
[15] Brubaker 1993; Fearon and Laitin 2003; Toft 2003; Treisman 1997.
[16] Fein 1993; Harff 1987 and 2003.

Walter builds on this line of research and argues that governments facing many large and territorially concentrated groups are more likely to be bellicose than governments that face fewer such groups. The logic is that they have to crack down heavily in order to build reputation, discourage, and signal resolve to other potential challengers.[17] Treisman's findings from his study of post-Soviet Russia are in line with Walter's logic; indeed Treisman suggests that when non-core group elites observe benefits from separatist activities of other groups, they are likely to follow their example.[18] Thus, states with few large, mobilized, and territorially concentrated and potentially secessionist groups are more likely to pursue exclusionary or assimilationist policies than states with one or none such groups.

I now turn to theories that account for nation-building policies based on international factors. According to several scholars, systemic transformations such as the emergence of the modern state, industrialization, modernization, and democratization have provided motives and rationalizations for the pursuit of violent policies toward specific ethnic groups.[19] Mann in particular argues that exclusionary policies are the product of the spread of democratic norms, which equate *demos* with *ethnos*. Similarly, Straus argues that the Rwanda genocide was the result of the Hutu leadership's strategy to remain in power in a post-Cold War environment of liberalization and democratization.[20] Thus, the international diffusion of the ideal of popular rule during a period of democratization puts pressure to convert *demos* into *ethnos*, generates organic nationalism, and ultimately encourages ethnic cleansing of those who do not fit the definition of the *ethnos*.

Weiner has underlined the importance of the triangular relationship among a nationalizing state, a national minority, and the national homeland (i.e., a state whose core group is considered to be of the same ethnic background as the ethnic group abroad).[21] Building on Weiner, Brubaker has argued that if a national minority does not have a national homeland it is more likely to be targeted for assimilation.[22] To be sure, Brubaker suggests that he is not interested in prediction but from his work we can deduce that a nationalizing state is not likely to target for assimilation a national minority with a homeland, because the costs are high and the likelihood of success low. Deportation, population exchange, or mass killings are more likely in such cases.

Pieter van Houten, inspired by this line of research and Fearon's work,[23] has proposed a different version of the homeland argument.[24] Elites in a national homeland make credible commitments to co-ethnics abroad, and these

---

[17] Walter 2009; Van Evera 1994.
[18] Treisman 1997: 246.
[19] Bartov 1996; Mann 2005; Snyder 2000.
[20] 2006.
[21] 1971.
[22] Brubaker 1996: 66–67.
[23] Fearon 1998.
[24] 1998.

commitments in turn make the ethnic group assertive. At the same time, the core group does not offer a credible commitment to accommodating the non-core group's demands. This situation can lead to a secessionist war.[25] The implicit prediction with respect to nation-building policies is that ethnic groups with national homelands are likely to be mobilized along ethnic lines against the host state, and thus will be targeted with exclusionary policies. Thus, non-core groups with an external homeland are more likely to be targeted for exclusion than assimilation.

The above arguments capture important elements of the process but make inconclusive predictions with respect to the full range of nation-building policies. This is not surprising given the fact that none of them directly addresses the variation I have set out to explain. Overall both theories that emphasize domestic factors and theories that emphasize international factors conceptualize policy variation narrowly (e.g., exclusion versus inclusion), while in some cases are only interested in explaining the occurrence of just one policy (e.g., assimilation or not, violence or not). Thus, they do not provide a comprehensive account of nation-building policies. I attempt to complement these accounts and explain dynamics they have neglected.

In what follows, I describe my dependent variable and the relevant actors. Next, I discuss the motivations and consequences of different types of external involvement (clandestine, covert, and overt). In the third section, I present my theory of nation-building. Finally, I conclude with a discussion of various causal paths that can lead to observationally equivalent nation-building policy choices; some paths that are compatible with my argument and some that are not.

NATION-BUILDING POLICIES: ASSIMILATION, ACCOMMODATION, AND EXCLUSION

There are multiple ways that one can conceptualize nation-building policies. The dichotomy of inclusion versus exclusion is a common way of categorizing policies. I hold that this categorization does not capture the full range of the observed variation. On the other hand, McGarry and O'Leary's important contribution[26] goes too far disaggregating policies. In order to better capture the options available to nation-builders, I conceptualize nation-building policies by constructing a categorical variable that can take the following possible values: assimilation, accommodation, and exclusion.

"*Assimilationist policies*" refer to educational, cultural, occupational, matrimonial, demographic, political, and other state policies aimed at the adoption of the core group culture and way of life by the targeted non-core group. These policies usually directly target a specific group (or part of a specific group), but

---

[25] For more on this, see Grigoryan 2010; Jenne 2004; Thyne 2009.

[26] For a useful taxonomy of eight macro-methods of conflict regulation, see McGarry and O'Leary 1994; for other conceptualizations, see also Heraclides 1991; Koppa 1997; Mavrogordatos 1983 and 2003.

might be presented under the guise of an impartial law. I also include under this category "nation-wide assimilation" policies that aim at the acquisition of certain traits such as language, dress, or behavioral patterns by the whole population; the ultimate goal of such policies is national integration. "Nation-wide" policies differ from group-specific ones because they do not target any group in particular, though in reality they often end up disproportionately affecting a specific group (or part of a specific group).

Assimilation can also take more violent forms. I identify two such types: Colonization of the territories inhabited by a non-core group – often coupled with internal displacement of its members; and/or exclusion of the elites of a non-core group and assimilation of the rest of the members.[27]

All in all, the goal of assimilationist policies is to secure the loyalty of an individual or a community by "conquering" their belief system and ensuring their obedience to the national state. An implicit normative assumption of such policies is that the core group's culture is superior to the non-core group's culture. States use assimilationist policies to create co-nationals.

"Accommodation" refers to situations where the "differences" of a non-core group are more or less respected and institutions that regulate and perpetuate these differences are put in place. The host state grants the status of "minority" to that non-core group. The latter is allowed to have certain separate institutions such as schools, churches, cultural associations, and so forth. This "minority" status does not mean that the host state is indifferent toward the loyalty of the non-core group's members. The state requires political loyalty to central state institutions and obedience to general laws. Finally, the fact that "difference" is accepted and perpetuated does not necessarily mean that the non-core group does not still face discrimination both by state institutions and by individual members of the core group. Accommodation produces national minorities.

"Exclusionary policies" refer to policies that aim at the physical removal of a non-core group from the host state (or specific areas of it). Policies under this category include population exchange, deportation, internal displacement, pogroms, or even mass killing. Exclusion can also take the form of segregation, which does not involve the physical removal of the non-core group as the experiences of apartheid in South Africa and Jim Crow in the United States indicate.[28] Although such policies constitute instances of exclusion they do not physically remove the population from the state's territory but they might involve internal displacement. Exclusionary policies produce refugees and victims of state violence.

---

[27] One may wonder, where do affirmative action policies fit in my typology? We can only answer this question empirically and on a case-by-case basis. If the ruling elites' policies aim at preserving the difference between the non-core and the core group then affirmative action policies fall under the accommodation category. If the ruling elites' policies aim at eroding that difference then they fall under the assimilation category.

[28] Marx 1999.

There are many ways in which we can rank these three policy choices. An important dimension is whether the state uses physical violence or not. Exclusionary policies are the most violent. Assimilationist policies are usually non-violent (based on a definition of violence that focuses on physical violence),[29] but they often are coercive. Accommodation refers almost exclusively to non-violent policies.[30] In order to best understand and distinguish between these policies, however, we must consider the different governmental goals that lie behind each in specific instances, and not merely whether they involve the use of violence or not.

Another dimension is the cost involved in implementing each policy. In general, it is hard to produce an abstract ranking of the three policies, since the strategic nature of these decisions often overrides the mere monetary cost of implementing them. The ranking of policy choices in terms of monetary cost has to be contextual. The cost of assimilation, for example, depends on the particular attributes of the non-core group that differentiate it from the core group. The cost of accommodation depends on the type of institutions that will be used by the state, and the cost of exclusion depends on the methods used.

The cost-benefit analysis of a nation-builder has to take into account the strategic and security costs of failing to pursue the appropriate policy toward a non-core group as well. For example, if the security threat posed by a certain non-core group can put in jeopardy a host state's survival in the future, then I would expect the government to pursue assimilationist policies – assuming it is in favor of the international status quo – despite the fact that the monetary cost of such policies may be higher than accommodating the same non-core group. Ruling political elites always consider the strategic trade-offs between the elimination of a security threat posed by a non-core group, and the amount and availability of resources needed for the host state to eliminate the threat.

ACTORS: HOST STATE, NON-CORE GROUP, EXTERNAL POWER

Host State: The Core Group and Its Ruling Political Elites

Let's now turn to the actor that pursues these nation-building policies, the "host state." When I refer to a host state, I mean the elites governing the national state in the name of the "core group" – the members of the ruling political organization that has the military and administrative capacity to enforce its decisions within the borders of a state. But what is the core group?

Naturally, in order to speak of non-core groups we first have to define the core group.[31] For example, in the case of Germany, the core group can be identified as

---

[29] For different definitions of violence, see Žižek 2008.
[30] To be sure, terrible instances of warfare, ethnic cleansing, and scapegoating were preceded by accommodationist arrangements. In other words, the purpose of this discussion is not to suggest that accommodation is morally superior to assimilation or vice versa.
[31] Hollingshead 1952: 685.

white people of German ancestry whose native language is German. Similarly, in Greece the core group can be identified as white Orthodox Christians of Greek origin and/or national consciousness who speak Modern Greek. Thus, my argument applies in cases where the core group has a clear "national type" and the latter is being actively propagated within the territorial borders of the state.[32] Indicators of a well-defined national type include one or more of the following: an official language, a national historiography that attains a high degree of consensus among the core group members, an official (or state-favored) religion, common cultural customs and practices or some form of phenotypic stereotype (a combination of physical attributes). There is no restriction in terms of which markers are the most important ones (e.g., race, religion, language, shared culture).[33]

The term "core group" refers to all the inhabitants of a country who share a common national type in one or more of the ways just outlined. Often the core group forms a demographic majority. Whether the core group is a majority or not, it is represented by the ruling political elites of the state.[34]

The ruling political elites of the host state do not necessarily coincide with the economically dominant class or with the intellectuals of the state.[35] The ruling political elites aim at the survival of the state and the preservation of their own position in it. They may be – and often are – supported or controlled by external powers.[36]

Moreover, I use the term "ruling political elites" rather than "nationalizing state"[37] because the latter term suggests a specific set of policies – nationalizing – and operates as a characterization of the state as a whole. The term "ruling political elites," on the other hand, does not imply a specific policy. The ruling political elites can exclude, assimilate, or accommodate a non-core group and can pursue different policies toward disparate non-core groups in the country. As I mentioned in my introduction, to these elites nation-building is not considered complete until there are no threatening non-core groups within their state. They are driven by a homogenizing imperative.

Finally, there may be – and often is – disagreement within the ruling political elites of a host state with respect to the definition of the core group as well as the nation-building policies pursued toward non-core groups.[38] In such instances I give primacy to the views and policies of the dominant section of the ruling elites.

---

[32] Deutsch 1965. The national type may change over time. In fact it often does.

[33] An interesting research question is if some kinds of markers are more powerful in achieving national integration than others and why? In my cases there is no important variation along these lines.

[34] We can assume that the ruling political elites of the core group at any given point try to determine the constitutive story of the "nation" in such a way that it ensures the legitimacy of their hegemony over any competitors.

[35] For a distinction between ruling and political classes, see Aron (1966: 204) and Weber (1978: I, 56).

[36] This is especially true for small powers in a bipolar or unipolar international system.

[37] Brubaker 1996: 63–66.

[38] For an elaborate discussion on this, see Shevel 2011.

State Capacity

One of the scope conditions of my argument in Chapter 1 referred to the capacity of a state to directly rule the population. However, this is a requirement that deserves further discussion. There are at least two ways in which state capacity (captured by measures of administrative, policing, and military capabilities of a state) influences nation-building policies choices: *relative* and *absolute*.[39] The first one has to do with the power balance between the external power(s) supporting the non-core group and the host state and its external patrons.[40] The second one has to do with state capacity in absolute terms, that is, whether a government has the capacity to implement its ideal set of nation-building policies or not.

Taking a closer look at state capacity in a relative sense, we find at the one extreme a situation where the power balance is clearly in favor of the external power(s) supporting the non-core group. In this case, a successful secessionist movement or the capture of the host state is likely. My argument predicts that the host state is likely to respond with exclusionary policies if the external power is an enemy, but predictions are almost trivial in this situation since the host state is likely to be defeated quickly. A relevant example is that of the Sudeten Germans in Czechoslovakia during 1938. The Czechoslovak government did impose martial law in the area and persecute the German nationalist elites but Hitler's Germany annexed the Sudetenland and five months later occupied the rest of Czechoslovakia.

Turning now to the cases where the power balance is clearly in favor of the host state, enemy external powers will hesitate to support non-core groups within such a state for two reasons: the prospect of a destructive interstate war will operate as a deterrent,[41] and the likelihood of such mobilization succeeding is extremely small. In the event that an external power attempts to mobilize a non-core group within a powerful state, its effort is likely to fail, as the non-core group members will probably choose to side with the powerful host state. Non-core groups in hegemonic states such as the United States are such examples.

Finally, state capacity in absolute terms is very important. A host state may want to target a specific non-core group with assimilationist policies but because of a weak state apparatus it might pursue accommodationist policies first and wait until it can pursue more ambitious policies.[42]

---

[39] For more on military power balance and nationalism, see Van Evera 1994.

[40] For brevity, when I refer to the host state in the text I will not explicitly mention the possibility of an external patron backing it. Such instances are very common. I consider this backing as part of the host state's capacity.

[41] This consideration is only enhanced if the host state has powerful backers of its own.

[42] A number of outliers from my statistical analysis in Chapter 4 are partially explained in this manner in Chapter 5.

Non-Core Group

The mere existence of a culturally distinct group within a national state does not necessarily entail a competing claim to the political allegiance of this population. Cultural distinctiveness per se is politically irrelevant unless there is a group-formation process, which would increase the salience of the difference with the core group, cultivate group solidarity among the non-core group's members, and turn it into a social identity.[43] As Hechter puts it, "one can only identify with a given group when such a group actually exists."[44]

This begs the question, when is a non-core group unlikely to have a politically salient social identity? Nomadic groups, groups that are territorially dispersed, or small isolated communities are not likely to have any political identity linked to their cultural, linguistic, religious, or other type of distinctiveness. Moreover, research findings in social psychology indicate that individuals from such non-core groups are likely to quickly assimilate into a "higher status" group in order to maximize their self-esteem.[45] As a result, over time many of these groups have been absorbed by neighboring larger groups; they have been "selected out" by the structure of the system. In contrast, groups that are large, sedentary, and territorially concentrated (e.g., the Kurds in Iraq) are more likely to build local institutions and link their cultural, linguistic, religious or other distinctiveness to a political identity. Non-core groups of the latter kind are also more likely to be selected by external powers trying to destabilize or weaken the host state.

A Statist Perspective

I follow a statist perspective for the identification of non-core groups. By the term "non-core group," I mean any aggregation of individuals that is perceived as an unassimilated ethnic group (the relevant marker can be linguistic, religious, physical, or cultural) by the ruling political elites of a country at the beginning of a period analyzed. The non-core group members may or may not be citizens of the state, but are certainly not considered members of the nation before they are targeted with assimilationist policies.

Importantly, prevailing perceptions with respect to the loyalties of a non-core group do not always reflect the reality and are often formed by considerations that are independent of the actual preferences/attitudes of non-core group members. For example, a non-core group could be perceived as posing a security threat because its homeland (or aspiring homeland) has engaged in an act of aggression against the host state. The Serbs in Croatia in the early 1990s are such a case. A great percentage of them did not share – then – Serbian President Milošević's views; however, they were equally likely to be targeted by Croatian anti-Serbian policies.

---

[43] For more on how ethnic markers do not always correlate with salient ethnic identities, see Chandra 2001; Giuliano 2011; Posner 2003 and 2004. For more on the concept, see Barth 1998.
[44] 2000: 97.
[45] Hechter 2000: 99.

But why not use the term "minority"? Do we really need a new term? In the literature the term minority is commonly used to refer to:

[A] group numerically inferior to the rest of the population of a state, in a non-dominant position, whose members – being nationals of the State – possess ethnic, religious or linguistic characteristics differing from the rest of the population and show, if only implicitly, a sense of solidarity, directed toward preserving their culture, traditions, religion or language.[46]

I refrain from using the term "minority" for a variety of reasons. First, the non-core group category is broader than that of a minority, since it includes aggregations of people who are conscious of their difference from the dominant national type without necessarily being mobilized around this difference. Second, the term "minority" usually refers to "numerically inferior" groups, while the term non-core group does not imply anything about size. Third, the term "non-core group" allows us to view even stereotypical members of the demographic core group as targets of assimilationist policies by the ruling political elites and not necessarily assume their national loyalty. In the initial stages of nation-building even people who fit the criteria of inclusion in the core group are often not conscious of their national identity and in that sense have to be assimilated. Finally, and most importantly, terming a non-core group a minority often implies either a legal status, recognition from the host state, or the existence of a claim by the non-core group. Thus, referring to "non-core groups" as "minorities" carries a wide range of assumptions that are often unwarranted. In sum, a minority is a non-core group that has been targeted with accommodationist policies or at the very least aspires to get minority status.

Organization

There is wide variation in the types of non-core groups across space and time. This variation is a function of the content of the national constitutive myth[47] of each country and the relevant attributes of the groups that reside within it. A non-core group could be an ethnic or tribal group, or a religious, linguistic, racial, or even cultural group.

The organization of non-core groups can take various forms. They can have formal institutions such as cultural associations and political parties, or simply informal institutions such as family and/or clan networks. They can be more or less hierarchical and more or less cohesive.[48]

In the period I am studying, the formality and complexity of the organizational structure of the various non-core groups can be approximated by considering whether a group was nomadic, rural, or urban. Nomadic groups were less likely to have formal institutions than urban and rural groups.[49] Moreover,

---

[46] Capotorti's definition of a minority quoted in Clogg 2002: xii.
[47] For more on this, see Smith 2001 and 2003.
[48] Hechter 1987.
[49] For more on nomadic groups, see Khazanov and Wink 2001.

while churches, mosques, and synagogues existed in both urban and rural settings, cultural associations and societies existed mostly in cities. Over time, the organizational structure of non-core groups has become more formal: today, the proliferation of nongovernmental organizations has led to the formal organization of many previously informal groups. Prominent examples are the aboriginals in Australia and New Zealand and the indigenous people in various Latin American countries. In my framework, variation in non-core group organization might account for the variation in the type of measures a host state pursues once a policy choice has been made, but not for the choice of the policy per se.

Political Demands

The host state's nation-building policy is directly linked to the non-core group's political demands. Non-core group demands can be either territorial or nonterritorial. Nonterritorial demands range from legal recognition of the non-core group by the host state, to institutionalized political representation at the national level. Territorial demands range from claims for local autonomy to calls for independence.[50]

What is the origin of the non-core group's political demands? Non-core group demands are often theorized as endogenous to size and geographic distribution of a group, to history of past autonomy, or to host state policies.[51] In accordance with my general thesis I proceed from the axiom that non-core group demands are also influenced by the geopolitical situation and the preferences of external powers. Non-core groups supported by allies of the host state or with no external links may demand recognition and/or accommodation of their differences but not much more. Non-core groups supported by external enemies are more likely to demand autonomy or self-determination than those without external support.[52]

To be sure, as I have mentioned above, large populations that differ from the core group and are concentrated close to border areas may be more likely to make territorial claims *and* be supported by external enemies. By contrast, non-core groups that are small and dispersed are less likely to be supported by external powers and more likely to make nonterritorial demands, such as ask for minority rights and equal treatment. Similarly, non-core group demands can change based on the host state policies. For instance, violent state policies might lead to an escalation of non-core group demands, unless the state manages to completely suppress the group.

Whether the demand for self-determination or minority rights is the outcome of external involvement or not is an empirical question. In my model, I endogenize non-core group demands to the external power's preferences in cases where a non-core group wants to attract the interest of an external power. The external

---

[50] See Kliot 1989; Mikesel and Murphy 1991.

[51] Gurr 1993; Toft 2003.

[52] It is understood that a non-core group that seeks self-determination is also demanding recognition.

power preferences are in turn endogenous to interstate relations with the host state and the broader geopolitical situation. But what is of paramount importantance is the decision on behalf of the external power to get involved.[53] We do not know what percentage of external interference is a product of "dragging in" effects. Moreover, there are many cases where the external power acts without any prior agency from the non-core group. An interesting empirical question is the extent to which non-core group variation in homegrown mobilization impacts external powers' decisions to get involved.[54]

Ideally, I would have data on the actual demands of the non-core groups. In the absence of such data, tracing the origin of non-core group demands and identifying whether they were genuinely developed by non-core group members, or were superimposed by an external actor (or were the outcome of some combination of the two) would greatly enhance our understanding of the process of nation-building. Non-core group demands are not always reducible to the machinations of external powers.

External Power

The third actor in my framework is the "external power" – a neighboring state, a great power, a diaspora group, or a combination[55] – that is involved with the political fate of a non-core group in the host state. The external power does not need to be territorially contiguous to the host state. Having said that, contiguous countries are more likely to interfere in each other's internal politics than countries that are continents apart.[56] Great Powers and increasingly non-state actors are the main exception to this rule. The external power can provide financial, military, political, or other support to the non-core group.[57] Moreover, the support can be covert or overt and the intensity varies greatly from case to case. What is important from the perspective of my argument is the perception of external support by the ruling political elites of the host state. At different points in time, the external power can be an enemy or an ally of the host

---

[53] For more on the "marketing of rebellion," see Bob 2005.

[54] For a more elaborate discussion, see the sections on motivations and effects of external involvement below.

[55] Today, non-state actors are becoming increasingly important in this process. Diasporas, large refugee groups, terrorist organizations, nongovernmental organizations, religious networks, and even powerful corporations can substitute for the role of states in this configuration. In the rest of the book I discuss states as the main actor that provides external support; however, my argument still applies in cases of non-state actors. The main difficulty lies in discerning whether the external non-state actor is actually an "ally" or an "enemy" of the host state. For more on transnational dynamics, see Salehyan 2009.

[56] Miller 2007: 9.

[57] As I mentioned above, host states can also be – and often are – supported by external powers that are usually allies of the country. This was especially the case during the Cold War, where there would be a government supported by one side and a non-core group supported by the other side. I discuss such examples in Chapter 5.

state, depending on changing international alliance blocs and shifts in foreign policy choices between successive governments.[58]

Support by an enemy power is different from support by an ally. although both involve maintaining ties with the non-core group that sustain and/or nurture the difference between the core and the non-core group. Support by an ally, however, by definition is not aiming at provoking secessionist goals or providing an alternative to the host state. Some – but definitely not all – instances of enemy support definitely have the latter goal in mind. I assume that the host state elites are going to err on the safe side and prepare for the worst. Thus, in this book I do not attempt to quantify the type or the actual level of support but just identify whether the ruling elites of the host state perceive a non-core group as externally supported or not and the status of the interstate relations between the external power and the host state.

How should my theory be modified when there are competing external powers? For example, during the Cold War the United States and the USSR – as well as regional allies of the two – each backed several movements and non-core groups in their efforts to enlarge their respective blocs by establishing friendly regimes around the world.[59] There are cases where there are multiple external supporters. The Tibetan case mentioned above is such an example, where the United States, United Kingdom, India, and Nepal all acted as external supporters for the Tibetans.

Things get complicated if a non-core group is backed both by an ally and an enemy. In such situations my theory would have to be modified in a different manner depending on the empirics of the case. If the ally external power supports a different faction than the one that the external enemy is supporting then I treat these subgroups as "separate" non-core groups. In the rare event of the ally and the enemy external powers both supporting the same non-core group, my argument is inconclusive; however, the host state's response will most likely depend on which relationship is most valuable and the relative state capacity of these external powers. The host state is likely to accommodate the non-core group if the ally is strong and the alliance is asymmetrical or exclude and/or assimilate the non-core group if the ally is weaker and the alliance is symmetrical.

But what accounts for the variation in external support across non-core groups? Do external powers choose to support specific non-core groups based on the geopolitical importance of the territory they reside in; their ethnic identity; their size; their location?

Motivations for External Involvement

External support and sponsorship of movements in foreign states is a very old practice in the international system. In the modern era, the Napoleonic Wars stand out as the first concerted effort to use non-core groups in enemy states

---

[58] Alliances can take many forms ranging from informal alliances all the way to confederations, see Weber 1997.

[59] Barnet 1968; Chomsky 1985 and 1993/1994; Weiner 2007.

to enhance the chances of conquering these states as the case of Poland exemplifies.[60] The Russian Empire had pursued this policy even earlier against the Ottoman Empire. During one of the many Russo-Turkish Wars of the eighteenth century (1768–1774), Russian Empress Catherine II (Catherine the Great) attempted to use the Greeks in the Peloponnese as a fifth column in order to distract the forces under the command of Sultan Mustafa III and to create a pro-Russian state in the Mediterranean.[61] It was during the war, in 1770, that count Orlov[62] successfully mobilized some Greeks in the Peloponnese. To be sure, this did not happen overnight. Tensions between Greeks and the Ottoman administration in the Peloponnese pre-existed. Importantly, emissaries from the Russian Empire operated in the region as early as the 1760s recruiting support for a potential movement against the Ottomans. By the time Count Orlov's warships arrived in Mani things were ready for the revolt.

Indeed, external involvement in ethnic minority politics is not a phenomenon that belongs to the past by any means. During both the Cold War and the post–Cold War eras, states never ceased to interfere with "minority politics" in other states. We have ample evidence that the Soviet Union promoted the accommodation of various non-core groups within the communist bloc during the Cold War. Various non-core groups were supported by the USSR and were thus targeted with assimilationist or exclusionary policies by United States-friendly host states and vice versa.

But even in the post–Cold War era the same practices take place. The list of examples from around the world is long. Seymour Hersh publicized the Bush administration's secret moves against Iran;[63] the Russian Federation actively supported South Ossetia in its secessionist efforts against Georgia during the 1990s and interfered on behalf of Ossetians in 2008 ultimately fighting a Russo-Georgian War;[64] and Bahrain's King recently suggested that Iran may have been covertly fomenting the Shi'a protests in Bahrain.[65] However, the post–Cold War cases of nation-building are more difficult to study since the necessary archival material has not been declassified.

There are many different motivations behind a state's adoption of a policy that sponsors a movement in a distant land that falls short of annexing the land

---

[60] For more on the role of the Polish legions, see Biskupski 2000: 23–24.

[61] Comstock 1828, Rotzokos 2007.

[62] Count Aleksey Grigoryevich Orlov (1737–1808) was a Russian military officer and statesman, who served in the Russian Army. He defeated the Ottoman fleet at the battle of Çeşme.

[63] Hersh wrote in 2008: "Late last year, Congress agreed to a request from President Bush to fund a major escalation of secret operations against Iran, according to current and former military, intelligence, and congressional sources. These operations, for which the President sought up to four hundred million dollars, were described in a Presidential Finding signed by Bush, and are designed to destabilize the country's religious leadership. The clandestine activities involve support of the minority Ahwazi Arab and Baluchi groups and other dissident organizations. They also include gathering intelligence about Iran's suspected nuclear-weapons program" (*The New Yorker*, July 7, 2008).

[64] King 2008.

[65] "Bahrain Hints at Iranian Role over Country's Shia Uprising," 2011.

in question. The motivations of an external power to support a non-core group in another state range from destabilizing the host state to securing resources or precipitating a regime change. An important distinction should be made between external interference, which refers mainly to covert or clandestine operations during peacetime, and external intervention, which refers to overt operations that take place once there is a conflict between a host state and a non-core group. In this book I highlight the importance of the former type of external involvement, although I recognize that it is often hard to distinguish between the two empirically. Often – how often is an empirical question – the external power that clandestinely supports a non-core group ends up intervening overtly once a conflict escalates.

Most scholars of international conflict focus on the motivation for external involvement once a conflict is under way – in other words, they focus on external intervention. Understandably, very little work exists on the early clandestine actions taken by external powers, since the documentation of such cases is very difficult.[66] In this section, I will provide an overview of the various motivations for external involvement that have been advanced by scholars to date, and discuss the hypothesized effects external intervention has on political outcomes.

How can we best explain what motivates a state to adopt a policy of external involvement? Many scholars of international relations posit that external involvement is an outcome of ethnic ties between the non-core group and the external power.[67] According to Hale,[68] based on the psychology of groups, ethnicity connotes a sense of common/shared fate. This may be a reason for supporting co-ethnics abroad. For example, Saideman argues that ethnic ties influence the decision of an external power to support a non-core group more than the threat a non-core group poses for the host state's sovereignty or the relative power dynamic between the external power and the host state.[69]

Several non-realist scholars argue that the motivation behind external involvement in another state's minority politics might be democratization or humanitarian considerations.[70] Some scholars argue that external powers intervene once conflicts have erupted, in order to stop the fighting;[71] but more recent work suggests that intervention could be motivated by a desire to promote the external power's preferred outcome, above and beyond the goal of increasing the likelihood of a settlement.[72]

Realist thinkers emphasize security and geopolitical considerations. For example, Byman et al. write: "when ethnic kin or religious brethren do receive support, it is often done to further *realpolitik* ambitions as opposed to being

[66] For a discussion of this problem, see Gullather 2006.
[67] Davis and Moore 1997; Gartzke and Gleditsch 2006; Saideman 1997; Saideman and Ayres 2000, 2008.
[68] 2008.
[69] Saideman 2002; see also Miller 2007.
[70] Heraclides 1990: 371. For a history of humanitarianism, see Barnett 2011.
[71] Regan 2000: 2; De Maio 2005: 57.
[72] Gleditsch 2007: 295.

an end in itself. Ethnic and religious justifications are often mere window dressing."[73] Heraclides, focusing on support for secessionist groups, suggests as causes for external intervention "the existing constellation of states for and against the secessionists, strategic gains, the positions of allies, great and middle powers and friends, and relations with the state (government) threatened by secession."[74]

My reading of the historical record is closest to the realist worldview. Great Powers and states around the world strategically select which non-core groups to support. Non-core groups in geopolitically important areas – that is, economically or militarily important regions and regions with valuable resources – have a higher probability of receiving external support from interested powers. External powers – operating in the age of nationalism – attempt to find populations in such areas that share a common marker (such as language, religious affiliation, race) with their own core group, or organize propaganda teams across the border with the aim of forging a common national consciousness. Examples are many; in Chapter 6, I discuss the policies of Bulgaria, Greece, and Serbia in geographic Macedonia during the early twentieth century.

To be sure, non-core groups that can be presented as co-ethnics abroad are more likely to be supported since such an endeavor is easier to legitimize in the domestic arena under the banner of nationalism. Nevertheless, non-core groups that reside in geopolitically unimportant areas are unlikely to enjoy external support, regardless of their ethnic ties with neighboring states or the level of human rights abuses against them. For example, in Chapter 5 I describe the relative neglect of the Greek community of Monastir (today's Bitola) by the Greek government following World War I compared to the resources devoted to the Asia Minor campaign at the same time.

I argue that external support for non-core groups is an inherent feature of the international system. External support itself does not disappear although its shape and form, as well as its intensity, varies over time and is shaped by technological change, the configuration of the international system, and the norms of intervention.[75] Accordingly, during the Cold War, the United States and the USSR were the most prominent external supporters of non-core groups, and in the post-Cold War period, the number of regional powers using this tactic has increased.[76] All in all, cultural affinity is neither a necessary nor a sufficient condition for external support – though together with other events it can become a sufficient but unnecessary condition.[77]

---

[73] Byman et al. 2001: 23.

[74] Heraclides 1991: 207.

[75] For more on the changing norms of intervention, see Finnemore 2004.

[76] Byman et al. (2001: xvi) highlight another important trend in outside support for insurgent movements, the rise of non-state actors such as diasporas, "refugees, foreign guerilla movements, religious organizations, wealthy individuals, and even human rights groups."

[77] For more on causality, see Mackie 1988.

Effects of External Involvement

Having discussed the various motivations for external involvement, I turn now to its effects. I divide these effects into two sets, "early" and "late." The former refer to instances of overt, covert, and cladestine external involvement that include the politicization of the non-core group's identity and the initial mobilization of its members. This process is crucial in the development of many movements and has not been given the appropriate attention even in seminal works on the topic such as Hroch's *Social Preconditions of National Revival in Europe*.[78] The "late" effects refer to instances of overt external intervention and its impact on the outcome of state/non-core group conflicts.

In his work on proto-insurgencies, Byman summarizes the "early" effects of external involvement. He emphasizes the importance of external power support across a wide range of issues – from offering a safe haven, money, training, and help with political mobilization, to fostering political legitimacy and international recognition.[79] In my own work I have demonstrated that external involvement is an important path to national mobilization and the politicization of ethnic differences in the Balkans.[80] Recently, Jenne has argued that "external actors – and particularly regional players – influence minority behavior at the substate level."[81] Jenne argues that if an external power is supportive of the claims of a minority, then the minority will radicalize its demands against the host state. In turn, the host state can be repressive or nonrepressive. The combination of these two dimensions accounts for the different outcomes of state–minority relations: interethnic cooperation, repression, concessions, and conflict. The important lesson to draw from Jenne's work for our purposes is the central role that outside support plays in non-core groups' decisions to radicalize their demands.[82]

The "late" effects refer to the impact of overt external intervention on the accomplishment of a non-core group's stated goals. External support is a significant predictor of the onset of civil war and may actually determine which side wins.[83] A survey of insurgent movements around the world conducted by RAND's National Security Research Division in 2001 concludes that many rebel movements have received external support for their insurgencies since the end of the Cold War. Various external powers have supported insurgencies in Asia, Africa, Europe, and the Middle East. In particular, external support played an important role in initiating and sustaining insurgencies, as well as bringing victory to the rebels in 44 out of 74 post-Cold War insurgencies surveyed.[84]

---

[78] Hroch 2000.

[79] Byman 2007: viii; Salehyan 2009.

[80] Mylonas 2010.

[81] Jenne 2007: 5. See also Grigoryan 2010; Thyne 2009; van Houten 1998.

[82] Ibid., pp. 38–53.

[83] Gleditsch 2007; Horowitz 1985: 230.

[84] Byman et al. 2001: xiv; Regan (2002: 55) finds that third-party interventions to end intrastate conflicts tend to extend expected durations rather than shorten them, unless they are biased in

The abovementioned figures depict the situation with respect to external support and violent rebel movements with more than 1,000 battle deaths per conflict. If the researchers used a lower threshold of battle deaths, then the number of cases of external support included in Byman et al.'s work would definitely increase since many cases do not reach that threshold. Salehyan, following a much more inclusive definition of civil war, suggests that 55 percent of all active rebel groups since 1945 "had undertaken extraterritorial operations in countries beyond their target state."[85]

Salehyan focuses on transnational rebel groups, which by definition require at minimum sanctuary by neighboring states – unless the neighbor is a failed state. In his framework "safe haven" is the main *good* that foreign states can provide to rebel groups. This is what "critically affect[s] the bargain between states and challengers by altering the apparent internal symmetry of force."[86] This external mobilization and support makes bargaining failure and the outbreak of violent conflict more likely.[87]

Furthermore, if one considers the extent of external support for non-violent movements across the world, it becomes clear that external involvement for non-core groups around the world is actually a much more prevalent and consequential practice than the above statistics indicate.

The purpose of this discussion is not to claim that national movements are the *ex nihilo* product of external powers' machinations. Homegrown movements are equally a reality. However, an unanswered empirical question is how most national movements in the past two centuries came into being. The purpose is to demonstrate that external involvement is an important path to national mobilization and the politicization of ethnic differences. Host states, non-core groups, and external powers interact in a dynamic process forming multiple configurations that give rise to different nation-building policies.

A GEOSTRATEGIC ARGUMENT: ALLIANCES AND FOREIGN POLICY GOALS

Nation-building entails a parallel process whereby the ruling political elites maintain and often reinforce differences with "nations" in surrounding states and either accommodate or eliminate differences within their own boundaries. Although people have been conscious of national or ethnic differences for many centuries, in modern times this consciousness became intertwined with what has been broadly labeled the political program of self-determination.[88]

favor of either the government or the rebels. For more on third-party interventions and the duration of intrastate conflicts, see Elbadawi and Sambanis 2000.

[85] 2009: 5.

[86] Ibid., p. 7.

[87] Ibid., p. 24.

[88] Banac's (1984: 27) definition captures this well: "nationalism should only indicate an ideology, a comprehensive, modern world view, distinguished by its all-inclusive penetration of national consciousness into every going pursuit.... The old national consciousness was not necessarily concerned with specific cultural or political goals."

My argument is based on the interaction between host states and external powers on the one hand, and host states and non-core groups on the other. I link international geopolitical dynamics to subnational state policies through the mechanism of interstate alliance. To account for the conditions under which ruling political elites of a host state assimilate, accommodate, or exclude different non-core groups, I rely on six assumptions about beliefs held by the host state's ruling political elites:[89] First, assimilating non-core groups makes future interference by external powers less likely.[90] Second, a non-core group supported by an ally is less of a security threat than a group supported by a state that is part of an enemy alliance bloc.[91] Third, the strategic benefits coming from the alliance with an external power are greater than the cost of accommodating the non-core group supported by that power.[92] Fourth, exclusionary policies are more likely than either accommodation or assimilation to lead to a new interstate war that can jeopardize the status quo.[93] Fifth, accommodating a non-core group that is mobilized by an enemy state could threaten the host state's territorial integrity in the future; some form of ethnic engineering is required and internal colonization with core group members is a common policy.[94] Sixth, an externally supported movement working against the state may only constitute a fraction of the non-core group population, but host state leaders are likely to assign threat to the whole non-core group community since they treat the group as a category, exaggerating homogeneity within it and differences between it and the core group.[95]

Given these assumptions, I present four configurations that lead to different policy choices, and have so far been neglected in the literature. First, a policy of assimilation toward the non-core group is likely if the group has no external support. Second, a host state is likely to accommodate a non-core group if an ally is supporting that group. Third, a host state is likely to exclude a non-core group when the state has revisionist aims and an enemy is supporting the non-core

[89] These assumptions about beliefs should be considered together with the assumptions discussed in the Introduction and within the scope conditions of my overall argument.

[90] This assumption is consistent with Darden's argument that the initial round of assimilation of a population into a national identity through Western-style mass schooling leads to extremely fixed identities (forthcoming). For the benefits coming from state homogeneity, see also Alesina and Spolaore 2003.

[91] The host state worries that harsh treatment of the non-core group could embitter its alliance with the patron and harm its external security position.

[92] An auxiliary assumption is that the alliance is symmetrical. However, if the alliance is asymmetrical in favor of the host state then assimilationist policies may ensue. In Chapter 5, I relax this assumption.

[93] For more on how war can erupt from the oppression of minorities, see Van Evera 1994: 14.

[94] Accommodation in such cases can only be a transitional policy before assimilationist pressures or exclusion follows. For more on transitional policies, see Chapter 5.

[95] This assumption is consistent with Hale's work on ethnicity (2008).

External Power Support

	Yes		No
	Interstate Relations		
	Ally	Enemy	
Revisionist *(Lost Territory and/or Rose in Power Relative to Competitors)*	Accommodation	Exclusion	Assimilation[1]
Status Quo *(Gained Territory and/or Declined in Power Relative to Competitors)*	Accommodation	Assimilation[2]	

Host State's Foreign Policy Goals

FIGURE 2.2. Theory predictions.
[1] Sometimes takes the form of assimilation through accommodation.
[2] Takes the form of internal colonization or displacement.

group.[96] Finally, a host state is likely to pursue assimilation through internal colonization if the state favors the status quo and an enemy is supporting the non-core group (see Figure 2.2).

I have built my argument following the work of many scholars whose work emphasizes the importance of looking at international dynamics in order to understand minority policies.[97] In my framework, however, the external actor does not have to be a national homeland, ethnic kinship does not have to be the motivation or even the excuse for external involvement, and the distinctiveness of the non-core group does not have to be politically relevant or salient before the external actor interferes. In fact, I argue that external involvement often drives the politicization of the targeted non-core group's identity and, more importantly, the host state's perception of the non-core group and the group's demands. This process is key to the understanding of nation-building policies.

In what follows, I illustrate the hypotheses discussed above through various configurations that result in different nation-building policies toward non-core groups. The real world is more complex and factors such as the military

[96] Below, I also discuss a special case where both the host state and the external power have co-ethnics within their boundaries.
[97] Bob 2005; Brubaker 1996; Byman et al. 2001; Heraclides 1991; Jenne 2007; Koppa 1997; Kuperman 2001; Rosenaue 1964; Saideman 2002; Salehyan 2009; Van Evera 1994; Van Houten 1998; Weiner 1971.

capabilities of states, the nature and/or intensity of external support, non-core group characteristics, and the quality of political leadership can in special cases become the most important determinants of the actual policy decisions of the ruling political elites of host states. Nevertheless, my argument captures a great deal of the action of nation-building, despite the fact that some of its assumptions may need to be relaxed in individual cases.[98]

Configuration I: Immunization Through Assimilation

All non-core groups are potential targets for mobilization and support by external powers. Thus, in the "age of nationalism," the ruling political elites of the host state have incentives to target non-core groups that are not mobilized by any external power with assimilationist policies rather than accommodate or exclude them.[99] The absence of external interference in some cases may be the outcome of group-level characteristics, but in many cases it results from a long-term regional status quo that allows the host state to complete its national integration (see Figure 2.3). The majority of non-core groups fit this configuration and this explains why we have not heard much about them.

The assumption here is that the non-core group is weak relative to the core group,[100] does not have ethnic organizations, and thus is an easy target for assimilation. Moreover, assimilationist policies produce co-nationals and with that more and deeper bonds among the population of the state.[101] Assimilationist policies function as an "immunization" of the population from future agitation projects of external powers.[102]

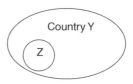

FIGURE 2.3. Non-core group residing in area "Z" is not supported by any external power.

---

[98] I relax some of these assumptions in Chapters 5 and 8.

[99] Exceptions do exist. The ruling political elites might accommodate a non-core group even when it does not enjoy external support when the non-core group's economic skills are linked to its "difference." Such cases include nomadic trading groups, groups with specific linguistic expertise, or peripheral groups that perform a specific function in the internal division of labor (Hechter 1975; Laitin 1995).

[100] The fact that the non-core group may be weak does not necessarily mean that it is numerically inferior. Similarly, the size of area "Z" in the figures of this chapter does not suggest a specific group size.

[101] In some of today's developed states, a policy of assimilation may appear as a policy of accommodation since the pluralist assimilation model does not require acculturation. For a discussion of assimilation in the United States, see Alba and Nee 1997 and 2003.

[102] Darden forthcoming.

Following the above logic, we should not observe a strategy of instigating nationalist propaganda by either Great Powers or neighboring states toward nationally integrated states that are comprised of literate, nationally conscious citizens. In such cases Great Powers or neighboring states are more likely to pursue alternative strategies such as ideological penetration (e.g., communism, fascism, etc.) or direct interstate war.

Configuration II: Accommodation of Non-Core Groups Supported by Allies

Non-core groups that are mobilized by external powers are more likely to develop a distinct political identity than the ones that are not. I have argued above that external powers around the world do not randomly select which non-core groups to mobilize and support. Non-core groups in geopolitically important areas have a higher probability of being mobilized. Overall, states are more likely to target non-core groups that are in the periphery of the host state, since they are usually harder to control, making for easier targets. This implies, conversely, that a non-core group is less likely to be mobilized by an external power if it is residing in a geopolitically unimportant area, is far from the borders, and/or has already been assimilated by the host state and is thus a "former non-core group." The degree to which this political identity will be perceived as threatening by the host state, however, will depend on interstate relations.

I already discussed the different justifications that an external power can use to interfere – ranging from a common marker (e.g., the Russian empire claimed that it was assisting its co-religionists in the Balkans) to an international norm, such as claims to be protecting a non-core group's human rights, or just naked material interest. But, under what conditions is a non-core group likely to be considered an internal threat by the host state? I single out challenges to a state's sovereignty as most important. Challenges to a government's claim to authority and secessionist movements can be the result of external involvement by an external power that wants to weaken, or obtain concessions from, a specific host state. For example, Israel supported the Maronites against the Palestinians in Lebanon during the Lebanese civil war. One rationale for this support was that the Maronites were an under-siege minority, like the Israelis. However, it is hard to imagine that alliance forming without the Palestinian-Israeli conflict and the utility of this support within this broader context. Finally, challenges can and do result from independent or homegrown national movements.[103] A non-core group can be perceived as disloyal and constitute a security threat independently of receiving support by an external power – although external support might follow in due time.

---

[103] There is a large set of cases comprised of all "potential" non-core groups; within this set there are two smaller sets: non-core groups mobilized by external powers and non-core groups mobilized independently, they are "homegrown." A movement is homegrown when it has developed without external support or direct instigation from abroad. For a discussion of the factors that may account for the emergence of such movements, see Connor 1973; Horowitz 1985; Hroch 2000; Sambanis and Milanovic 2009; and Treisman 1997.

Not all nationally conscious communities, however, are perceived as threats to the host state. As my hypothesis above suggests, homegrown non-core groups are likely to be targeted with assimilationist policies.[104] The question remains for the ones supported by an external power – irrespective of whether they are homegrown or not. I argue that in such cases the policy choice will depend on the interstate relationship – alliance or rivalry – between the host state and the external power supporting the group.

The host state government perceives non-core groups either as challengers to the government's claims to authority, or as loyal groups, based on its interstate relations with the external power supporting the non-core group. If external support for the non-core group comes from an allied power, then the group is not perceived as a threat. The assumption is that allied powers are not likely to push a non-core group to challenge the host state. At the same time, the host state is not likely to assimilate or exclude a non-core group that is supported by an allied state, since this would jeopardize the alliance.

Why would an allied power support a non-core group? Often states cultivate relations with non-core groups abroad for economic reasons. For example, following World War I, Romania kept ties with Vlachs living in Greece – an ally at the time. In an article published in a Romanian newspaper, *Renasterea Romana*, by one of its chief editors we find out that Romania is cultivating these ties "not just because of feelings toward Romanians beyond the Danube River but also because of economic considerations, since these Romanians are very bright, hard working, and phenomenal merchants."[105] Alliances do change and the links that have developed between a non-core group and an external power are sometimes hard to sever. Moreover, two states might end up in the same international alliance bloc for reasons unrelated to their bilateral relations (e.g., Bulgaria and Romania during the Cold War).

All in all, non-core groups supported by an ally are likely to be accommodated by the host state (see Figure 2.4). This prediction refers to the first round of interaction between the non-core group and the host state. In the long run, having accommodated a non-core group may operate as a precedent that decisively impacts

FIGURE 2.4. Non-core group residing in area "Z" is supported by an allied power.

---

[104] In such cases, accommodation could be a transitional policy with assimilation being the terminal one. This might be the result of state capacity constraints, domestic politics, or a strategic choice dictated by special geopolitical circumstances. For a discussion of specific cases, see Chapters 5 to 8.

[105] Quoted in AYE, 1921, 32/6, Report by the Greek delegation in Bucharest to the Greek Ministry of Foreign Affairs, Bucharest, 5 January 1921.

the future interaction between the host state and the non-core group. Having now acquired the legal status of a "minority" the non-core group becomes an easier target for external powers but also homegrown demands may develop more easily. The situation changes drastically when the host state faces a group with outside support from an enemy power. Things may turn even more explosive if the minority has been given some form of territorial autonomy.[106]

Configuration III: Exclusion of Enemy-Supported Groups in Revisionist States

Nation-building is not considered complete until there are no disloyal groups in a nation-state. In particular, when a host state is threatened by an enemy-supported group, the ruling political elites will definitely not accommodate it, because they will anticipate a future fifth column situation. Whether a host state will pursue assimilation or exclusion toward a non-core group supported by an external enemy power will depend on the foreign policy goals of the government, as well as the immediacy of the threat to its rule by that group. These factors in turn are influenced by the broader geopolitical situation and the readiness of host state resources.[107] For example, in a situation where there are two non-core groups supported by enemy powers, then we may get differential responses reflecting gradations of threat by each group and the need to conserve resources.

But what determines the government's foreign policy orientation? The ruling political elites of a state are likely to be motivated by revisionist foreign policy goals if they have lost territories in war and have received a large number of refugees or have a significant number of co-ethnics in nearby states as a result. The loss of territory radicalizes domestic politics in a rather direct manner through the collective disappointment experienced by all core group members and the resulting feelings of revenge and anger.[108] However, there is a more indirect way for radicalization to occur. Lost territories usually create refugee flows, and these refugees in turn are likely to demand more revisionist policies from the ruling political elites. This was the case for example in Bulgaria following the Balkan Wars. When this domestic pressure is coupled with the imperative for defending the state against an external power that is linking up with an internal "fifth column," we get exclusionary policies.

A few clarifications are necessary at this point. Irredentism is a variant of revisionism, and becomes the foreign policy goal when a state has recently lost territory in war and/or has "unredeemed co-ethnics."[109] Revisionism in my

---

[106] Brubaker 1996; Roeder 1991 and 2007; Triesman 1997.

[107] In this decisionmaking process, the core group members who are not part of the ruling political elites only indirectly influence decisions, even in democratic settings. Decisions with respect to the non-core groups are usually made behind closed doors, on behalf of the "nation" but without its direct approval. Nevertheless, there is an important way that core group members matter in the process. Their prejudices, discriminatory views, and desire for revenge may derail the policy pursued by the ruling political elites. Such developments are particularly hard for nation-builders to anticipate.

[108] Petersen 2002.

[109] For different varieties of irredentism, see Van Evera 1994: 12–13.

framework refers to a state's *ex ante* stated foreign policy goals, not necessarily its behavior.[110] Nazi Germany, for example, was a revisionist state because it harbored revisionist aims, not because it attacked allied powers. Analogously, I argue that Serbia was a limited-aims revisionist state before 1918 because its aim was to enlarge its borders, not because it fought Bulgaria and Austria-Hungary.

Additionally, revisionism can be the result of a pure expansionist desire, which may be instigated either by population growth or military strength and technological innovations. The motivations behind expansionism could be strategic ones, such as access to sea, expropriation of resources, or more defensible borders.[111] Moreover, a host state can become more assertive in its revisionist claims when it obtains the approval and support of one or more of the Great Powers. Finally, the pressure from the external enemy state could be so great that it might actually lead to the transformation of a status quo state into a revisionist state (i.e., a radical party wins the elections). Regardless of the origins of such foreign policy goals, revisionist elites want to alter the international status quo.

From the considerations I have just now outlined, I derive the following hypothesis: when the host state has revisionist foreign policy goals, its ruling political elites are likely to pursue exclusionary policies toward non-core groups that are supported by an enemy power (see Figure 2.5). This is to prevent a "fifth column" situation and to discourage elites of other non-core groups from pursuing such schemes.[112] Importantly, exclusionary policies involve extreme measures that might jeopardize the international status quo and lead to a war. A revisionist host state is more likely to undertake such policies than a status quo one – despite the fact that this state's foreign policy may not "track objective material power trends closely or continuously."[113] Within this subset of cases, ethnic cleansing becomes more likely in wartime when the stakes are high, the time horizon is short, and international monitoring is absent.

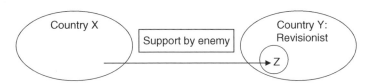

FIGURE 2.5. Non-core group residing in area "Z" is supported by an enemy power, host state revisionist.

---

[110] Davidson 2002. See the relevant discussion in the Introduction and earlier in this chapter
[111] There is an important distinction to be made between revisionist and irredentist policies. Both aim at territorial expansion; however, the latter usually involve contiguous territories and a willingness to nationally integrate the desired territories into the core nation–state. Imperialist policies, by contrast, need not involve contiguous territories, and are premised on an hierarchical exploitative relationship with their dominions.
[112] This auxiliary hypothesis is consistent with Walter's argument that I discussed above (2009).
[113] Rose 1998: 147.

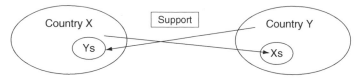

FIGURE 2.6. Host state and external power are contiguous and have each other's co-ethnics.

Given this prediction, we should observe few non-core groups willing to accept support from enemy powers. Indeed, most non-core groups do not seek enemy support and when they do they try to cover it as much as possible (e.g., the CIA involvement in Tibet after 1956 was not advertised by the Tibetan movement).[114] Other times, only a small part of the non-core group collaborates with an enemy power but the host state – incapable of distinguishing between the various factions – ends up perceiving the whole non-core group as disloyal. Why would an enemy external power pursue such a policy? First of all, external powers usually try to keep these operations secret. Alternatively they may try to justify it based on an international norm.[115] However, often the goal of the external enemy is to provoke the most destabilizing situation possible for the host state. The external power does not worry as much about the fate of the non-core group.

Irredentism (a special form of revisionism) could be provoking tit-for-tat retaliation on the part of the neighbor state. This is more likely for contiguous states that both have co-ethnics within their boundaries, which is a plausible scenario but also a special case where mutual deterrence is likely and where tit-for-tat pushback could play out. Thus, the prediction based on the configuration shown in Figure 2.6 is mutual deterrence, and a lower likelihood of exclusionary policies.

However, the option of population exchange is also available in such a configuration, as the cases of Bulgaria and Greece in 1919 or Greece and Turkey in 1923 suggest. Thus it is difficult to make a clear prediction just based on this setup.[116]

Configuration IV: Assimilation of Enemy-Supported Groups in Status Quo States

Status quo host states, in contrast, do not seek border changes. Status quo foreign policy goals may be the result of the host state declining in power relative to its competitors, or because it has recently expanded its territory and needs to

[114] Knaus 1999; McGranahan 2010.
[115] Kuperman and Crawford 2006.
[116] In order to test this argument in my statistical analysis I add a dichotomous variable coding for all of these cases in my dataset; see Chapter 4.

FIGURE 2.7. Non-core group residing in area "Z" is supported by an enemy power, host state is status quo.

consolidate. The logic here is that such developments will have either significantly decreased the number of "unredeemed" co-ethnics, or moderated the core group's aspirations and thus decreased the salience of irredentist politics. At the same time, however, a territorial expansion usually brings with it additional non-core groups that already are considered – or could potentially become – internal threats. An example is Romania after World War I.

When the host state wants to preserve the status quo in newly-acquired regions, it is likely to pursue assimilationist and internal colonization policies toward the members and political exclusion toward the elites of a non-core group supported by an enemy power, rather than exclusionary policies for all that could easily trigger a new round of hostilities and a breakdown of the status quo (see Figure 2.7).[117] To be sure, assimilation is more likely than exclusion if there is enough time for it, but otherwise more brutal, decisive measures may be taken. For instance, in wartime a status quo host state may pursue exclusionary policies if it faces a non-core group supported by an enemy simply because it has no time for assimilationist policies. Finally, under such circumstances, accommodating the non-core group is not an option since it would allow for future manipulation of the "minority issue" by the external enemy power in an opportune moment.[118] Internal colonization also dilutes the territorial concentration of the non-core group thus making the group a less appealing target for external powers to support.

What happens when external support of a non-core group ceases? The effects of external power support for a group are hardly reversible precisely because they operate in the realm of ruling political elite's perceptions. In other words, there are lingering effects of supporting a non-core group that do not simply go away when the actual support ceases. The main development that can alter this dynamic has to do with a change in the alliance structure that renders the external power and the host state allies from enemies. If an ex-supporter ceases to be an enemy and becomes an ally, we are likely to observe a move from assimilation or exclusion – depending on the host state's foreign policy goals – to accommodation.

---

[117] This is consistent with Van Evera's hypothesis 1.4. "The more severely nationalities oppress minorities living in their states, the greater the risk of war" (1994).
[118] Weiner 1971.

In all the predictions above, I assume that there is enough time to pursue the government's favorite policy. Time limitations – including the variation in governments' time horizons – do exist, however, and impact the decisionmaking process. As we will see in Chapters 5 to 8, such pressures are present primarily during wartime and may account for the higher frequency and/or intensity of exclusionary policies in certain cases.

Possible Causal Paths

The causal path discussed above assumes that a host state takes the initiative and chooses its policies toward a non-core group based on whether an external power is actively engaged in mobilizing it or not, as well as in light of its relations with the external power in question. However, one could think of many other causal paths that would be consistent with my argument. For example, a non-core group might be the first to act, asking for more local autonomy. An external actor may have secretly instigated this demand. The host state might then implement harsh policies against the group, an escalation that leads to a conflict. The elites of the non-core group might then turn to outside powers and ask for their support against the host state. In this case, the external power(s) would have to decide whether to overtly intervene or not. In this scenario my argument would still explain the variation in nation-building policies.

What if there is mobilization in the absence of clandestine or overt support from external powers? Many studies of international relations posit that outside support is the outcome of violent nation-building policies pursued by nationalizing host states, rather than something causally prior to such policies.[119] According to this view, external intervention is the outcome of a security dilemma that non-core groups face at the domestic level that motivates them to request external support: they seek help only after they have reason to feel insecure. In this scenario non-core groups choose their allies based on the existing alliance structure following the logic: "the enemy of my enemy is my friend."[120]

According to my argument, non-core groups that have no external support are more likely to be targeted with assimilationist policies by the host state. It is possible, however, that the assimilationist campaign escalates into conflict and the non-core group elite seeks external intervention.[121] In reaction, the host state may then resort to preemptive exclusionary measures (e.g., the case of Serbia in the 1990s). This causal path is different from, though not inconsistent with, my general argument. My argument would be fundamentally undermined only if host states more often than not accommodate or pursue exclusionary policies[122] toward non-core groups that are not supported by any external power.

---

[119] Lake and Rothchild 1998; Posen 1993b; Snyder 1991.

[120] For more on negative association, see Evrigenis 2008.

[121] For an argument of how direct rule leads to peripheral nationalism, see Hechter 2000.

[122] A possible causal path involves power-hungry leaders who may engage in scapegoating of specific non-core groups when they believe this is a popular strategy; see Brass 1991; Gagnon

To be sure, there are prominent cases of homegrown movements that have not been targeted with assimilationist policies by their governments but I would argue that they are the exceptions that prove the rule. The majority of non-core groups that had no external support have been targeted with assimilationist policies and, more often than not, have been successfully assimilated.

Another possible causal path is one in which the host state's policies are merely reactions to observed past behavior of the various non-core groups. For instance, many scholars argue that a history of past violence makes exclusionary policies more likely. If this past behavior is influenced by external power involvement, then my framework still applies. If, however, the non-core groups' past (and current) behavior is unrelated to external support or instigation, then my argument predicts assimilation rather than exclusionary policies.

The actual causal mechanism at work in each situation is an empirical question; nevertheless, the empirical record of "unsolicited" external involvement is vast and renders my main causal path a plausible – yet neglected – one. One of the difficulties related to adjudicating this empirical question is that much external involvement occurs secretly, thus shielding the myriad relevant facts from inspection by social scientists; often the declassified archival material that is available does little to remedy this problem. Thus, scholars need to rely on the few cases where enough useful archival material has been made available as to permit them to unravel the complete causal story. For example, after the end of the Cold War, both the United States and Russia released a series of confidential documents that unveiled many "secret histories" of such clandestine action around the globe. A couple of decades ago we would categorize many cases of ethnic conflict differently than we do nowadays, after this new wave of evidence has come to light.[123]

But maybe alliances are endogenous to nation-building policies. One might argue that the pattern of alliances between the external power and the host state is caused by the nation-building policies of the host state rather than being causally prior to them. In this way, there could be an endogeneity problem. Whether a country is an enemy or an ally might be endogenous to nation-building policies in the first place – especially if these policies target a non-core group that can be construed as an "ethnic kin." This is questionable both theoretically and empirically.

Theoretically speaking, this consideration does not even come up in the literature on alliances – except perhaps as part of the arguments highlighting ideological or cultural affinities between states.[124] The primary considerations

1994/1995 and 2004; Harff 1987; and Snyder 2000. It is an empirical question how common such a strategy is. For a more extensive discussion of scapegoating, see Chapter 8.

[123] Gaddis 1997.

[124] An exception is Steven David's work and his concept of "omnibalancing" (1991). David suggests that state elites often have to balance internal and external threats. In fact, he goes further to argue that in Third World contexts external alignment is often a function of internal threats to the regime ruling a state and intergroup relations. I am positing that causality, more often than not, runs in the other direction.

behind the formation of alliances explored in the literature are either balancing a threatening state (or bloc of states) by siding with its enemies, or else siding with a strong threatening state (or bloc of states) – a practice known as bandwagoning.[125]

Empirically, Walt has shown that states form alliances principally to balance external threats.[126] One might argue that states try to side with the likely winner; however, this cannot always be easily discerned and even when it is alliances do not automatically shift. For instance, Walt reminds us that during World War I the alliance of Great Britain, France, and Russia controlled around 28 percent of world industrial production, while Germany and Austria-Hungary controlled 19 percent. In 1917, with Russia facing the October revolution and the United States joining Britain and France, the percentage opposing the Central Powers went above 50 percent but the international alliance structure during World War I did not change significantly during the war.[127]

Moreover, external powers rarely intervene solely to protect national minorities from nation-building policies pursued by host states. Empirically we know that the motivations behind external involvement (covert or overt) vary significantly from case to case. Some external powers support non-core groups solely in order to destabilize a neighbor or to precipitate a regime change; others claim to do so in order to support the separatist goals of their co-ethnics or co-religionists (often a cover up for expansionist intentions); while others aim to secure resources and regional influence. King and Melvin, focusing on the post-Soviet states, conclude that:

[I]n the realm of ethnicity and international relations, identity politics is often more about politics than about identity. Disputes over the allocation of scarce resources, competing visions of foreign policy directions, domestic political contests, and other prosaic features of political life frequently trump any putative duty that political elites might feel toward individuals who share their language or culture beyond their own frontiers.[128]

Furthermore, in a recent survey of insurgent movements in the post-Cold War era, Byman et al. find that "states are primarily motivated by geopolitics rather than ideology, ethnic affinity, or religious sentiment" when they support non-core groups in other states.[129] Such findings provide additional support to my theoretical framework. I maintain that more often than not, "vertical escalation"[130] of ethnic conflict is an outcome of prior covert external involvement that has occurred for reasons unrelated to the treatment of the relevant non-core group by the relevant host state.

---

[125] Snyder 1991.
[126] Walt 1985, 1987, and 1988.
[127] Walt 1985: 9.
[128] 1999: 109.
[129] 2001:23.
[130] Vertical escalation refers to increases in the intensity or level of violence within a conflict; see Lake and Rothchild 1998: 24.

CONCLUSION

In this chapter I developed a theory that accounts for the variation in nation-building policies resulting primarily from the interaction of host states and external powers, rather than non-core groups and host states. I argued that a host state's foreign policy goals, as well as its interstate relations with external powers that may be supporting its non-core groups, drive nation-building choices. The presence of external support for a non-core group and the interstate relations between the external power and the host state determine whether the group will be perceived as threatening or not. A non-core group supported by an enemy external power and residing in a revisionist host state is more likely to be excluded than targeted with assimilation or accommodation; if a similar group were to reside in a status quo state, it would most likely be targeted with assimilationist policies; taking the form of colonization by core group members and internal displacement of non-core group members. Finally, non-core groups supported by allied states are more likely to be accommodated than be assimilated or excluded.

From the discussion above, it becomes clear that the attributes of non-core groups are secondary in the process I am describing. "Ethnicity" matters, but only when it is activated in the international arena. Similarly, the existence of a "homeland" is also endogenous to interstate relations with the host state, since an external power chooses when to *act* as a homeland based on these very relations and its strategic interests.

Unlike Gellner or Anderson, who emphasize the importance of industrialization and print capitalism for the spread of nationalism, or Kedourie and Kohn, who highlight the causal priority of willful idealism in the process, I hold that the emergence of nationalism is the result of an interaction between strategic choices made under the structural conditions of international competition for territory and resources within the Westphalian system of states, on the one hand, and the technological innovations[131] and intellectual currents that emerged during the Enlightenment, on the other.[132] One of the strategies that external powers used to weaken their rivals has been to support ethnically homogeneous populations, residing in geopolitically important locations, preferably at the periphery of their competitor state. The process I described above has contributed to the spread of nationalism and has even had an ethnogenetic role in many cases. My argument helps us understand the host state's motivation to adopt assimilationist policies[133] – to fend off future external involvement – and likewise helps us understand many cases of

---

[131] Posen 1993a; Hobsbawm 1990 and 1991.
[132] Fichte 1968; Herder 2004; Kedourie 1993; Kitromilides 1994; Kohn 1945; Renan 1996; Rousseau 1985.
[133] Hechter 2000.

ethnogenesis where external agitation and support turned non-core groups into "awakened nations."[134]

In the following chapters (Chapters 3 through 7), I focus on the politics of nation-building in those states that emerged from the gradual dissolution of the Ottoman Empire in Europe. These cases provide an excellent context in which to study nation-building policies for a number of reasons: protracted intermingling of peoples, common experiences of past rule, similar modernization trajectories, a great deal of external involvement, and variation in the timing of their state-building experiences. I test my theory next to various prominent arguments such as cultural distance, status reversal, and homeland at multiple levels of analysis and using a variety of data sources. In Chapter 8, I move out of the southeast corner of Europe in order to test the generalizability of my argument.

[134] Hroch 2000.

PART II

EMPIRICAL EVIDENCE

3

Why the Balkans?

This book focuses on the Balkans,[1] that is, those areas of Southeastern Europe that were part of the Ottoman Empire.[2] Studying one region during a specific period of time allows me to make some credible assumptions about actors' preferences, increase my analytical leverage, and control for several macro-historical and geopolitical factors that affect the planning of nation-building policies. Moreover, choosing a region and studying all non-core groups inhabiting it allows me to avoid the most common form of selection bias, namely focusing on the most prominent and well-studied cases.

Overall, the Balkan states provide an excellent laboratory in which to study nation-building policies because of the protracted intermingling of heterogeneous populations and the variation in the timing of their state-building experiences. This set of cases is also a crucial test for some of the most prominent explanations in the literature.[3] The Balkan states have been considered as stereotypical cases of deep-rooted "ethnic hatreds"[4] or symbolic politics.[5] "Balkanization" is still used by journalists and academics as a pejorative term describing a range of processes from political fragmentation to irrational ethnic violence and chaos.[6] All in all, the Balkan Peninsula is typically considered as the most turbulent and nationalistic part of Europe;[7] thus it should be harder to

---

[1] For historical surveys of the region, see Janković 1988; Jelavich and Jelavich 1965 and 1977; Mazower 2001; Pavlowitch 1999; Quataert 2005; Roudometof 1996 and 2001; Stavrianos 1957; Sugar 1977.

[2] Southeastern Europe is the neutral term that many scholars use today as an alternative to politically/culturally loaded and anachronistic terms such as "the Balkans" and "Turkey-in-Europe," respectively. Specifically, I include in the analysis any country of Southeastern Europe following World War I that was a part of the Ottoman Empire for more than two centuries. In particular: Greece, The Kingdom of Serbs, Croats, and Slovenes, Romania, Bulgaria, Albania, and Turkey.

[3] Gerring 2007: 86–150.

[4] Kaplan 1993.

[5] Kaufman 2001.

[6] Glenny 2001: xxi–xxvi; Mazower 2001; Todorova 1997.

[7] Pavlowitch 2000.

discern a geostrategic logic in nation-building policies here than anywhere else. Finding a pattern would question the validity of analyses that treat the Balkans as an exception, an aberration of sorts, and improve our understanding of the process of nation-building.

In what follows I critically discuss the Ottoman legacy in the Balkans, introduce the reader to the geopolitics of the Balkan Peninsula, and conclude with a brief introduction of the six states under study in Chapter 4.

OTTOMAN LEGACY IN THE BALKANS

Broadly speaking, the Ottoman system was comprised of nonterritorial religious communities (*millets*) that had varying degrees of autonomy in terms of the administration of justice and local affairs. Thus, certain things were common across the whole of the Ottoman Empire but, then again, not throughout the entire period of Ottoman rule.[8] This realization complicates things. After initial conquest, the local ruling classes of the Balkan peoples were crushed or incorporated into the Ottoman system (depending on whether they resisted or not, respectively).[9] As a result, the local population was "left leaderless, anonymous, and silent."[10] These were all predominantly agricultural societies that lived in a world of corporate privileges for religious groups rather than individual rights. The merchants were very few. Stavrianos summarizes this well: "The typical Ottoman subject thought of himself primarily as a member of a guild if he lived in a city or as a member of a village community if he lived in the countryside. If he had any feeling of a broader allegiance, it was likely to be of a religious rather than of a political character."[11]

The *Millet* System

An institution that many scholars highlight as an important Ottoman legacy across the Balkans is the *millet* system. This system of managing difference has been identified as the main reason behind the salience of religious identities in the minds of ruling political elites in the new Balkan states.[12] While it is true that the *millet* system did have an impact on identity formation across the Balkans, both its implementation and its effects varied.

For example, the Ottoman Empire did not engage in assimilation or religious conversion campaigns on a systematic or massive scale. But there is significant variation since the Ottoman state did pursue religious conversion in "Albania, Bosnia, Herzegovina, parts of Bulgaria, and the island of Crete."[13] Thus, when

---

[8] For more on the Ottoman Legacy, see Hajdarpašić 2008; Hartmuth 2008; Mylonas 2011 and 2012; Philliou 2008; Sabatos 2008; Yilmaz and Yosmaoğlu 2008.
[9] Mazower 2004.
[10] Stavrianos 1957: 96.
[11] 1957: 338.
[12] Katsikas 2009; Roudometof 2001; Tsitselikis 2007.
[13] Stavrianos 1957: 335; Todorov 1983.

the "Age of Nationalism" came at its door there was a myriad of differences that had survived Ottoman rule and could be politicized. Religion was one of them.

Allowing for an important degree of local communal autonomy (especially in everyday matters), keeping urban centers religiously segregated, and eliminating local aristocracies (instead of using them to control the local peasants) facilitated the perpetuation of most communities and their cultures.[14] Moreover, as Göçek notes, although legally speaking everybody in the Ottoman Empire had the same inheritance and land-use rights these rights were only applicable within each *millet* and not across.[15] This social barrier between Muslims and non-Muslims structured many of the independence movements and patterns of alliance at the local level during the nineteenth century.

National categories such as "Greek," "Bulgarian," or "Turkish" did not signify the same thing to everybody. It was common to refer to Orthodox Christians as "Rum (or Romioi)" – a term that has been used interchangeably with the term "Greek" – regardless of their native languages or ethnic backgrounds. Christians would use the term "Turk" to refer to Muslims of all types of ethnic and linguistic background; thus they could mean an Albanian, a Bosnian Muslim, a Pomak, a Donmeh, or a Muslim Vlach. The majority of the population still identified themselves in religious terms. When somebody was called "Bulgarian" in geographic Macedonia, it basically meant that the person had joined the Bulgarian Exarchate, a church organization established with Russian backing as recently as 1870.[16] Until the early twentieth century, most people collapsed religious and national categories in very counterintuitive ways, from a modern point of view. As Mazower put it, "[t]he illiterate Slav-speaking peasants tilling the fields outside the cities rarely felt strongly about either Greece or Bulgaria and when asked which they were, many insisted on being known simply, as they had been for centuries, as 'Christians.'"[17] This is not to say that there were no national identities in the Balkans, but just to highlight the fluid character of these identities in the minds of many inhabitants of the Balkan Peninsula.[18]

The Emergence of New Nation-States

Another thing that is usually referred to as common among Balkan states is that they all got their independence through secession from the Ottoman Empire during the age of nationalism.[19] As a result, they all emulated the homogeneous European nation-state model (which was obviously just a programmatic goal rather than a reality even in Western Europe).[20] Nationalism largely based on an

---

[14] Stavrianos (1957: 339) illustrates this point through a comparison between the Venetian and Ottoman rules over Crete and other parts of the Balkans.

[15] 1993: 515.

[16] Meininger 1970.

[17] 2004: 257.

[18] Friedman 1999 and 2001.

[19] Hobsbawm 1991; Mylonas 2006.

[20] Todorova 1997.

ethnocultural understanding of nationhood – with strong religious undertones – was the face of modernity in the Balkans.[21] To be sure, the understanding of nationhood in the various Balkan states has been contested. Most Balkan states had – and most still have – a predominantly ethnocultural understanding of nationhood. However, all of them have been flexible with their definition when their foreign policy goals and domestic expediency required them to do so.

New states emerged in Southeastern Europe in the nineteenth century:[22] Serbia between 1815 and 1830, Greece in 1830, Romania in 1862, and Montenegro and Bulgaria in 1878. Serbia, Greece, and Bulgaria fought secessionist wars against the Ottomans to carve out their lands from the pre-existing *vilayets* (territorial administrative units) of the Empire. Romania (Moldavia and Wallachia) and Montenegro developed into independent states after being vassal-states of the Ottoman Empire for centuries. Albania and Turkey were the last two states to be established in the European territories of the Ottoman Empire in 1913 and 1923, respectively. This marked the end of the Ottoman Empire.

The state-building experience of each of these states has been different. The path each state took in order to achieve its independence and the events that took place during that period have a lasting impact on the constitutive story of each nation and shape the actual effect and perception of the Ottoman legacy itself. All of these nation-states had unredeemed co-ethnics outside their borders.[23] Some states were left with a significant number of co-ethnics abroad while others were not. Some had constitutive myths that urged the re-establishment of medieval or ancient borders regardless of ethnic demography. As I theorized in Chapter 2 and as we will see in the empirical chapters that follow, these "facts" in turn influenced the foreign policy goals of the ruling political elite of the country and were often codified in some type of a revisionist ideology or a "Great Idea." Until the goals stated in this ideology were satisfied these states were under the spell of these nationalist programs.[24] But what did nation-building look like in the nineteenth century?

The Antecedents of Nation-Building in the Balkans

Studying nation-building policies in the nineteenth century reveals that the newly established states more or less ignored the national consciousness of

---

[21] Banac 1995.

[22] Jelavich and Jelavich 1977; Koppa 2002.

[23] Mazower captures this reality well: "All states could point to 'unredeemed' brethren or historic lands which lay outside the boundaries apportioned them by the Powers: Romanians in Hungarian Transylvania, Serbs in Habsburg Croatia and Ottoman lands; Bulgarians in the lands of the San Stefano state they had been cheated of; Greeks – in thrall to the 'Great Idea' of a new Byzantine Empire – redeeming Hellenism across the Ottoman Empire from Crete to the Black Sea. Popular irredentism mobilized public opinion, financed cross-border incursions by bands of irregulars, and often forced unwilling Balkan monarchs into rash adventures against the advice or wishes of the Powers" (2000: 101–102).

[24] For more on the variation in the scope of the desired state borders by nationalist movements, see Mylonas and Shelef 2012.

their rural populations regardless of its ethnic, religious, linguistic, or cultural background. Nation-building policies were linked to the processes of state central-ization and modernization. Wherever these latter processes occurred in the Balkans, national integration policies also took root. Group-specific nation-building policies were largely linked with the creation of the new Balkan states and the Ottoman reactions to these movements. The pattern involved exclusionary policies followed by the rebels toward Muslims and Ottoman reprisals toward the co-ethnics of each secessionist group within the Empire.[25] Consistent with modernization theories, assimilation was mainly an unintended consequence of migration to the urban centers as well as church-run schooling. In this manner, people of "low cultures" assimilated into "high cultures" and enjoyed upward social mobility.[26]

In the case of Ottoman Europe, the choice between different high cultures was more or less determined by religious affiliation, which was institutionalized by the *millet* system. For example, a Vlach from the Pindos mountains or a Slavophone from the plains of Macedonia – both members of the Rum *millet* by virtue of their Christian Orthodox faith – would assimilate into Greek "high culture." This Ottoman form of accommodation was based solely on religious, not national, grounds. Toward the end of the nineteenth century – and especially after the 1878 Russo-Turkish war – competing national programs collided and the stage was set for the enactment of a series of nation-building campaigns throughout the peninsula.

Especially during the late nineteenth century, amidst an intense Great Power competition, assimilationist policies intensified but were primarily focused on contested borderland areas rather than inside the borders of Balkan states. These cases constitute special cases of nation-building policies taking place within the Ottoman Empire.[27] The most common strategies were the establishment of schools,[28] the control of churches, and the organization of armed bands, which would ultimately imprint the "correct" national consciousness in the hearts and minds of the local population.[29] Urban centers and groups of the dominant Muslim faith were largely left out of this competition but were exposed to Ottomanization and later on Turkification campaigns. Moreover, exclusionary policies pursued by the aspiring Balkan nationalist movements could be used only selectively on individuals since the Ottomans still controlled these territories.

GREAT POWERS, BALKAN STATES, AND THE "EASTERN QUESTION"

The six states I focus on were all engaged in the "Eastern Question," namely Great Power competition for spheres of influence,[30] instigated by the gradual

---

[25] Ilicak 2011.
[26] Gellner 1983.
[27] Akhund 2009.
[28] Vouri 1992.
[29] Aarbakke 2003; Dakin 1966; Gounaris 1996; Livanios 1999; Perry 1988. For more, see my discussion of these policies in geographic Macedonia in Chapter 5.
[30] The Powers involved include Britain, France, Austria-Hungary, Russia, and later Imperial Germany and Italy.

disintegration of the Ottoman Empire. During the nineteenth century, the Ottoman Empire was relatively weak and the Great Powers of Europe were directly trying to achieve a settlement of the Eastern Question; at the same time, they were pre-occupied with their colonial scramble for land and political influence elsewhere. Initially, Great Power competition for spheres of influence in the Ottoman Empire took the form of the establishment of "friendly," and preferably Christian, states. Russia was the first to move in the process of national agitation of peoples inhabiting neighboring Empires (both Ottoman and Austro-Hungarian) just as France had played that role since Napoleonic times in the West (see Illustration 3.1).[31] As a response to these pressures from abroad the Ottoman Empire undertook the *Tanzimat* reforms (1839–1876), an

ILLUSTRATION 3.1. "At present he works Bulgaria." *Source*: Library of Congress Prints and Photographs Division, Washington, D.C.

[31] Driault 1921.

attempt to modernize the administration and the army that resulted in the apogee of direct rule in the Balkans.[32]

Pavlowitch describes well the international context within which the Balkan states emerged. He highlights the importance of great powers in the foreign policies of Balkan states. "They were encouraged and manipulated. Their size, shape, stage of growth, even their existence in final analysis was regulated by the Powers in the hope of gaining influence."[33] Pavlowitch, however, reminds us that the small Balkan states were not without agency; they also exploited the mutual jealousies of the Powers.

The joint production, by the Great Powers and the local Balkan elites, of both the Balkan states and the main policy initiatives of these states is an undisputed fact in Balkan historiography. According to Janković, the Eastern Question was the product of conflict between the Great Powers over their interests in these areas. It was these plans that "caused problems everywhere or kept them simmering to serve as pretexts for intervention or bargaining for compromises and divisions of spheres of interest."[34]

During the late nineteenth and early twentieth centuries, competition between Bulgaria and Serbia, and later between Bulgaria and Greece,[35] aimed at linguistic assimilation, religious conversion (when necessary), and the instillation of "correct" national feelings in the people inhabiting the Ottoman *vilayets* of Selanik, Monastir, and Kosova.[36] Linguistic differences were present, but were not as entrenched and politicized as religious institutions. The *millet* system was ever-present in daily lives and peoples' imagination, yet national identities and ideas were not broadly held. For the new Balkan national movements to succeed, the Orthodox *millet* had to be fragmented into "national churches."[37]

In this regard, the establishment of the Bulgarian Exarchate in 1870 was very significant for developments in the region.[38] The Sultan issued a *firman*[39] in 1870 that recognized a separate *millet* status for the Bulgarian-speaking Orthodox Christians – the Bulgarian Orthodox Exarchate. The Sultan's goal was to appease the Bulgarians, who were supported by the Russians, and to check Greek aspirations.[40] The Bulgarization of the massive Slavic-speaking peasant population in geographic Macedonia, which until then was grouped under the Orthodox Christian *millet*, began around 1835 with the

---

[32] Shaw 1974: 73; Hechter 2000.

[33] 2000: 144.

[34] 1988: 7.

[35] Romania and Italy were involved as well, but to a lesser extent; they primarily claimed the loyalty of the Vlach-speaking populations in the region.

[36] Koliopoulos 1987; Perry 1988; Yosmaoğlu-Turner 2005. Catholic and protestant missions operated in the region in the nineteenth century, but with limited success; see Vouri 1994: 54–56.

[37] Kitromilides 1994.

[38] For the role of Russian diplomacy in this affair and the politics surrounding the event, see Meininger 1970.

[39] *Firmans* were decrees, edicts, or special licenses issued by the Sultan.

[40] Meininger 1970.

introduction of Bulgarian-speaking schools. That was in large part a response to the growing assimilation of these people and many of their elites into Rum or Romioi, the Orthodox Christian *millet* loyal to the Patriarch in Istanbul.[41] Although this was originally presented as a struggle over the language used in church within the Rum *millet*, in the end it became a struggle for jurisdiction over territories. Article ten of the *firman* stated that "the Exarch shall be allowed to send a Bishop to any district where at least two-thirds of the Christian inhabitants shall have been proved to be Bulgarians." This article immediately spurred competition among the Greeks, Serbs, and Bulgarians over disputed territories.

After the promulgation of the *firman*, Bulgarian bishops were appointed by the Exarch to various dioceses and were sanctioned by the Porte. As a result: "In these newly-constituted dioceses nearly all the churches, schools, cemeteries, and other ecclesiastical property with their revenues, although virtually belonging to the Greeks,[42] were seized and appropriated by the Bulgarians; and consequently, the Greek bishops, finding themselves deserted by the Christian population, had to remove their residences elsewhere."[43] It was clear from the beginning that this state of affairs would ultimately lead to some form of autonomous Bulgarian self-rule, or even an independent state.

The competition over the Christian population of these territories intensified after the Russo-Turkish War and the San Stefano and Berlin Conferences (1878) – both of which were clear signals that the Ottoman territories in Europe would be up for grabs in the near future.[44] It is no coincidence that a few years later, in 1886, the Society of St. Sava was established to "spread Serbian national propaganda among the Slav-speaking Macedonians."[45] Propaganda and political killings by state-sponsored guerrillas of the competing states were common (especially between Bulgarians and Greeks).[46] These proxy armies also staged a handful of local revolts against the Ottomans. At the same time, efforts to gain the loyalty of the peasants through schooling and church catechism, as well as by explicit threats by armed bands, were systematically pursued.[47]

Up until the Russo-Turkish War of 1877–1878 (fought to establish a kind of a Russian protectorate in the heart of the Balkan Peninsula and gain access

---

[41] The term was often used interchangeably with the term "Greek" at the time, especially by outsiders to the region. For more on this Hellenization process, see Aarbakke 2012.

[42] Technically they belonged to the Orthodox Ecumenical Patriarchate in Istanbul. Consul-General Blunt, however, equates the "Rum" *millet* with the term "Greeks" in this document.

[43] Enclosure 1 in No. 54, Consul-General Blunt to Sir W. White, 8 December 1888 [FO 287/13].

[44] Karavas 2010.

[45] Kontogiorgi 2006: 27.

[46] For more on the use of propaganda in the Balkans, see Ilchev 1996.

[47] For the competition over Macedonia, see Aarbakke 2003; Brailsford 1906; Dakin 1966; Danforth 1995; Gerolymatos 2002; Gounaris 1996; Karakasidou 1997; Kofos 1964; Koliopoulos 2003; Livanios 1999; Michailidis 2003; Panaiotov 1946; Perry 1988; Wilkinson 1951. Specifically for educational issues, see Vouri 1992, 1994, and 2005.

to the Aegean Sea) Austria-Hungary and Russia were the main Powers directly caught up in the Balkans.[48] At that juncture, Great Britain viewed the preservation of the Ottoman Empire as the best way to ensure unmitigated access to India and Egypt and thus strived for its independence and territorial integrity.[49]

After the Russo-Turkish War and the Treaty of San Stefano (1878), all of the Great Powers got directly involved in the "solution" to the Eastern Question. The Berlin Conference convened by Bismarck ensured that the new Bulgarian Principality would be much smaller than the one described in the San Stefano Treaty and that it would have no access to the Aegean Sea (see Map 3.1).

Following the Berlin Treaty (1878), Bulgaria became an autonomous principality. Austria-Hungary occupied Bosnia and Herzegovina and put guards at the Sanjak of Novi Pazar (then part of the Kosova *vilayet*). Three years later, Greece peacefully annexed Thessaly, and the same year Romania, Serbia, and Montenegro formally achieved their independence (1881). Seven years later the Bulgarian principality caught the Ottoman Empire by surprise and annexed Eastern Rumelia (1885).

These boundary changes left the Ottoman Empire with a relatively small but geopolitically important area in the Balkan Peninsula. Broadly speaking, this region coincided with the geographic regions of Epirus, Macedonia, and Thrace.[50] Epirus was important for Italy in its quest to control the Adriatic. Geographic Macedonia was a passageway of important trade routes, had the "largest and most protected harbor of the northern Aegean Sea [Thessaloniki]," and large fertile plains.[51] Thrace was vital for the protection of Istanbul and control of the Straits. More importantly, access to the Aegean for both Serbia and Bulgaria, and indirectly Russia, would require the annexation of parts of southern Macedonia or Thrace.

With some Christian Balkan states already established, the Great Powers had to negotiate and form alliances in order to pursue their respective agendas. The old argument of helping the local Christians in their struggle against the Muslims was no longer as convincing. The Russians wanted access to the Aegean, but Britain wanted to prevent such access. Austria-Hungary and Italy wanted to create an as-large-as-possible Albanian state in order to check Serbian and Greek expansion in the region. The Greek Ottoman War of 1897, which ended with the defeat of Greece and a certain boost for the Ottoman Empire, was yet another instance of Greek irredentism in action, a failed effort to emulate the successful Bulgarian annexation of Eastern Rumelia a decade earlier.[52]

---

[48] Jelavich 1991.
[49] For perceptive analyses of the Eastern Question by Marx and Engels, see Kondylis 1985.
[50] The *vilayets* of Shkodër, Kosova, Janina, Monastır, Selanik, and Edirne.
[51] Kostanick 1948: 6.
[52] Giannoulopoulos 1999.

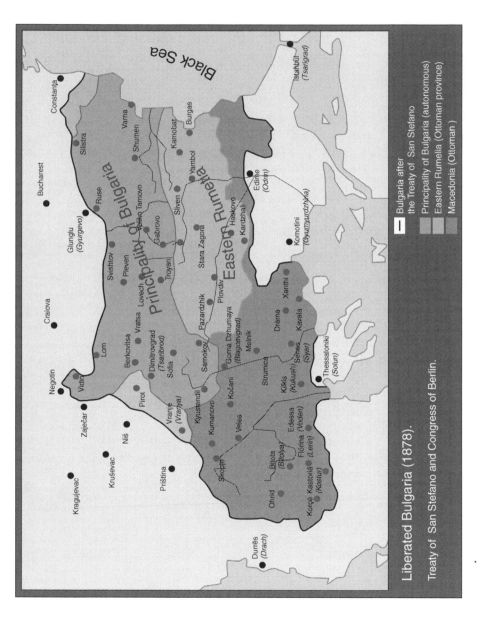

Liberated Bulgaria (1878).

Treaty of San Stefano and Congress of Berlin.

MAP 3.1. Origins of Bulgarian revisionism. Available at: http://en.wikipedia.org/wiki/Treaty_of_San_Stefano.

ILLUSTRATION 3.2. Eight members of the Ottoman cavalry on horseback with flags. *Source*: Library of Congress Prints and Photographs Division, Washington, D.C.

The Ottoman Empire was in the midst of the Young Turk Revolution when Bulgaria declared its independence (1908);[53] subsequently, Austria-Hungary annexed Bosnia, and Crete was on the threshold of unifying with the Greek Kingdom. But the Ottoman Empire was almost completely pushed out of the Balkan Peninsula with the Balkan Wars.[54] After a war with the Ottoman Empire in 1911, the Italians claimed and occupied the Ottoman provinces of Tripolitania and Cyrenaica as well as the Dodecanese (see Illustration 3.2). That same year the Russian Empire advised Serbia and Bulgaria – its two quasi-protectorates in the region – to reach an agreement on their respective claims in Macedonia and attack the Ottoman Empire.[55] Once this was accomplished, Russia managed to convince Greece to enter the conflict on their side. With the Tripolitania War in the background, a successful Albanian revolt followed by Ottoman atrocities in the spring of 1912 provided an opportunity for Montenegro to declare war on the Ottoman Empire and then Serbia,

[53] For more on the Young Turks, see Hanioğlu 2001.
[54] The First Balkan War involved Serbia, Bulgaria, Greece, and Montenegro against the Ottoman Empire, 1912–1913. The Second Balkan War involved Bulgaria against (mainly) Greece and Serbia, 1913.
[55] Mijatovich 1917: 235.

Bulgaria, and Greece to follow suit.[56] The first Balkan War was an attempt by these states to solve the last phase of the Eastern Question by military conquest. Bulgaria hoped to achieve the borders described in the Treaty of St. Stefano; Serbia was dissatisfied by the incorporation of Slav-majority territories by Austria-Hungary[57] and claimed parts of geographic Macedonia;[58] Greece, for its part, was pursuing the *Megali Idea* (Great Idea) of turning the Aegean Sea into a "Greek lake" (see Map 3.2).

The Ottoman Empire lost the war and was forced to sign a peace treaty on 30 May 1913, with the four Christian states. This marked the end of more than four centuries of Ottoman rule over these territories. The Greek Army entered Thessaloniki on 26 October/8 November 1912,[59] just a few hours before the Bulgarian troops did (see Illustration 3.3). This military success, which took place within the context of the first Balkan War, was the culmination of the prolonged and multifaceted competition between Greece and Bulgaria (and to a lesser extent Serbia) over the European parts of the Ottoman Empire.

Bulgaria, however, was not content with the proposed terms in the peace negotiations held in London after the First Balkan War, and fought the Second Balkan War against Greece and Serbia.[60] It was eventually defeated. With the Treaty of Bucharest (July 1913), Greece incorporated Crete, a part of Epirus, southern Macedonia, and the eastern Aegean islands – though not yet finally; Bulgaria incorporated Western Thrace and northeastern Macedonia but had to cede Eastern Thrace back to the Ottoman Empire; Serbia incorporated Kosovo and northwestern Macedonia.[61] However, this delimitation of frontiers never satisfied all sides equally.

In the early twentieth century, and especially during the Balkan Wars, we observe a drastic intensification of nation-building policies in the newly annexed territories by five belligerent peoples: Serbs, Greeks, Bulgarians, Montenegrins, and Ottomans. Serbs pursued exclusionary policies against Albanians in Kosovo, Bulgarians against Greeks in Eastern Macedonia, and Greeks against Bulgarians in Central Macedonia.[62] During the Balkan Wars, all Christian Balkan nations pursued exclusionary policies to a certain extent

---

[56] According to a memorandum written by the Central Department of the Foreign Office, "the actual pretext [for the first Balkan War] was the demand of the Balkan League for the enforcement of article 23 of the Treaty of Berlin, which ... had remained a dead letter." BNA, FO 371/14317 [C5316,/82/7] "The Origins of the Macedonian Revolutionary Organization and its History since the Great War," 1 July 1930, p. 7.

[57] The annexation of these territories to Serbia would entail access to the Adriatic Sea.

[58] This would guarantee Serbian access to the Aegean Sea.

[59] Julian and Gregorian calendar date respectively.

[60] The Serbs did not respect the secret agreement with respect to the claims on Macedonia and Austria-Hungary encouraged the Bulgarians to antagonize Russian interests and fight Serbia and Greece. For a vivid description of this period, see Mijatovich 1917: 236–241.

[61] For a detailed history of the diplomatic affairs, see Helmreich 1938, Psomiades 1968; for the military events of the period, see Gerolymatos 2002, General Staff of the Army 1940; finally, for the relationship between external dependence and internal politics, see Leon 1974.

[62] Kennan 1993.

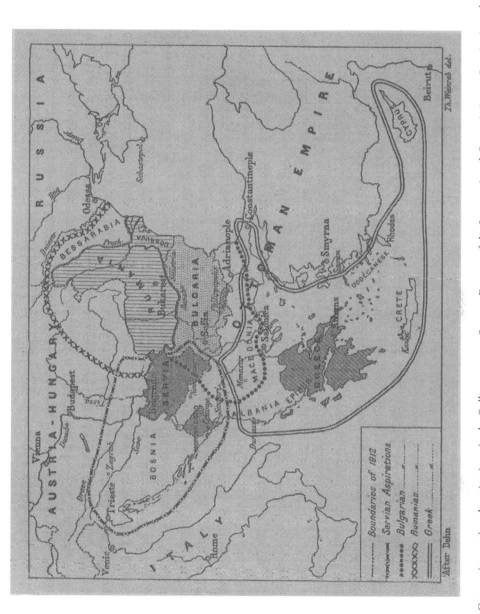

MAP 3.2. Competing national aspirations in the Balkans, 1912. *Source*: Report of the International Commission to Inquire into the Causes and Conduct of the Balkan Wars, Carnegie Endowment for International Peace, 1914. www.CarnegieEndowment.org.

ILLUSTRATION 3.3. Greek infantry officers. *Source*: Library of Congress Prints and Photographs Division, Washington, D.C.

against Muslims. According to estimates, somewhere between 15,000 to 41,000 Muslims (noncombatants) either fled or lost their lives in Greek Macedonia alone.[63]

During the early twentieth century, Bulgaria received refugees from various parts of geographic Macedonia, Thrace, and Dobrudja.[64] Following World War I, Greece received refugees from Asia Minor, the Black Sea, the Caucasus, South Russia, Bulgaria, and various parts of geographic Macedonia. Turkey received refugees from all over the Balkans.[65] Albania received refugees from Kosovo and Greece. Romania and the Kingdom of Serbs, Croats and Slovenes both expanded to include most of their ethnic kin and thus received a much smaller numbers of refugees.

By the time of the Balkan Wars, the various national programs had already crystallized and internal nation-building intensified.[66] The alliance pattern of the Second Balkan War was preserved during World War I. This fact – which could have been otherwise – solidified these cleavages. Before we turn to the cross-national analysis of nation-building policies in Chapter 4, it is important to

---

[63] Glavinas 2008: 13.

[64] According to the secretary of the Macedonian National Committee of Sofia, in 1934, there were in Bulgaria 480,000 refugees. FO 371/18370, R6757, 24/11/1934. Cited in Livanios 2008: 35.

[65] See Pallis 1925; McCarthy 1995. In my estimates I am not including the refugees from Bulgaria following the 1878 war or the refugees from 1881.

[66] Carabott 1997; Gounaris 2005; Karakasidou 1997; Michailidis 1998 and 2003.

provide the reader with a brief sketch of the situation in all of the countries under study.

THE BALKAN STATES FOLLOWING WORLD WAR I

The "Defeated"

The "Sick Man of Europe,"[67] the Ottoman Empire, had sided with the Central Powers[68] and collapsed after the end of World War I. The Empire had been gradually transforming into the modern Turkish republic during this time.[69] A revisionist Turkish National Movement emerged from the ashes of the Ottoman Empire with Mustafa Kemal as its leader.[70] On 23 April 1920, an assembly gathered and made Mustafa Kemal its first president and Ismet Inönü Chief of General Staff. Kemal assumed full governmental powers and established the Turkish Parliament (Grand National Assembly) in Ankara in May of the same year. He was the national hero and leader of the Turks during the interwar period. Mustafa Kemal secularized and westernized Turkey.

The other defeated power in the Balkans was Bulgaria, which entered World War I on the side of the Central Powers in an effort to undo the unfavorable outcome of the Second Balkan War. By the end of the Great War it had lost yet another war. In the postwar environment, however, it needed a leader who had opposed the Central Powers. It found such a leader in Aleksander Stamboliiski, a man who was arrested for his anti-German stance during World War I. The same motivation lay behind King Ferdinand's abdication in favor of his son Boris. In the summer of 1919, Stamboliiski emerged from hiding and won the national election by a small margin. His Peasant Party was devoted to advancing peasant interests. He was in power for four years. During his rule, he enacted extensive land reform, reformed the legal system, signed the Treaty of Neuilly, and tried to form an alliance with the Kingdom of Serbs, Croats, and Slovenes, though to no avail. Stamboliiski's diplomatic efforts turned the Internal Macedonian Revolutionary Organization (IMRO)[71]

---

[67] This term, referring to the state of the Ottoman Empire during the mid-nineteenth century, first appeared in print in an 1860 *New York Times* article and was attributed to Czar Nicholas I of Russia; see "Austria in Extremis," *New York Times*, 12 May 1860, p. 4.

[68] The Central Powers in World War I consisted of the German, Austrian-Hungarian, and Ottoman Empires and Bulgaria.

[69] For more on this transformation in Turkey, see Findley 2010; Kasaba 2008; Zürcher 2004.

[70] Mustafa Kemal Atatürk (1881–1938) was an Ottoman army officer and the founder of the Republic of Turkey. For more on Kemal, see Mango 1999.

[71] The Macedonian Revolutionary Organization, as it was initially named, was founded in 1893 by Slav Macedonians in Thessaloniki initially claiming autonomy for the *vilayets* of Kosova, Selanik, and Monastir. A few years after its establishment the organization was captured by Bulgarian nationalists and was renamed IMRO following World War I; see Kofos 1964; Mylonas and Shelef 2012; Perry 1988.

and the Slav Macedonian refugees from Serbia and Greece against him. IMRO supporters ultimately assassinated him.

The "Victors"

Romania entered the war on the side of the Allies late. Marghiloman's pro-German government gave way to Brătianu's pro-Entente Liberals toward the end of World War I.[72] Bratianu resigned and Aleksandar Vaida-Voevod took over when the former was dissatisfied with the post-War settlement that Romania was getting. King Ferdinand of Romania dismissed Vaida because he was planning to collaborate with the Peasant Party. The King chose Marshal Averescu as a successor. Averescu, a war hero, won elections and subsequently pushed for an extensive land reform, particularly in Bessarabia. In 1922, the Liberals, who dominated Romanian politics until 1928, succeeded Averescu. Having incorporated Transylvania, Bukovina, and Bessarabia the Kingdom of Romania was now in favor of the international status quo.

Another victor was Greece. Greece was literally divided over whom to side with in World War I.[73] Finally, Greece – reunified – was on the side of the Allies after 1917. Venizelos's Liberal Party was in power until the end of 1920. There was an interim of Anti-Venizelist rule by the Popular Party, which collapsed after the Asia Minor Catastrophe in 1922. A Venizelist coup replaced the previous government and executed those held responsible for the military defeat.[74]

The creation of the Kingdom of the Serbs, Croats, and Slovenes resulted from the victory of the Allies in World War I and the consequent collapse of Austria-Hungary and the Ottoman Empire. The kingdom's unification took place under the Serbian Karadjordjević dynasty in 1918 and was recognized by the Paris Peace Conference in May 1919. The new state, on the side of the winners in World War I, was in favor of the international status quo. The Serbian elites, especially Pašić and his Radical Party, dominated the political scene. This was a radical party that was based on the Serbian middle class and the peasantry. As Protić put it, "[the party's] commitment to constitutionalism, the middle-class background of its leadership and a class alliance affirmed in its programme made it a party of the centre. Its emphasis on democracy, its struggle for social justice and its socialist roots made it a party of the left."[75]

---

[72] The Entente powers in World War I consisted (mainly) of Great Britain, France, Italy, and the United States. The Russian Empire, Belgium, Serbia, Canada, Australia, Italy, Romania, and Greece also fought on this side.

[73] Mavrogordatos 1983.

[74] See discussion in Chapter 6. For more on this, see Leon 1974; Mavrogordatos 1982.

[75] For a more detailed account, see Protić 2007: 189. For more on the politics in the KSCS, see the relevant section in Chapter 7.

A Bystander

Prince William of Wied[76] was nominally at the helm of the Principality of Albania at the outbreak of World War I[77] and fought as an individual on the side of the Central Powers. Albania, however, was neutral in World War I. Albania remained a geographical concept during World War I that both sides of the conflict occupied. Early in World War I, Greece, Italy, Serbia, and Montenegro occupied most of Albania, which according to the secret Treaty of London (May 1915) was to be dismembered after the war with only a small autonomous state surviving in central Albania. Early in 1916 the Central Powers prevailed in the region, with Austria-Hungary and Bulgaria taking control over Albania. Toward the end of 1916, Entente powers, especially the Italians, occupied significant parts of southern Albania. By the end of the war Italian, Greek, French, and Serbian troops were on Albanian soil. These powers wanted to partition Albania, but the American president Woodrow Wilson successfully opposed their plans. As a result of the peculiar situation Albania was in – with a prince who had fought on the side of the Central Powers and a territory under occupation during most of the War – the Albanians were not officially represented in the Paris Peace Conference in 1919.[78] In 1920, Albanians drove out the Italian troops and received international recognition. However, their border concerns were not resolved until 1923.[79]

The Albanian system of government following World War I was based on a council of regents and a bicameral parliament. The actual power lay with powerful individuals (heads of various Albanian tribes).[80] As Fischer put it, "the system, as it worked out in practice, was a combination of the principality constructed by the Great Powers in 1912 and traditional tribal autocracy."[81] As expected, such a system was vulnerable to manipulation by neighboring states. A liberal government gave way to a populist one.

The state was in disarray until Ahmed Zogolli[82] gained power in the mid-1920s with Yugoslav support.[83] For most of the interwar period, Albania's elites

---

[76] Prince William of Wied (1876–1945), whose actual name was Wilhelm Friedrich Heinrich, was a Lutheran Prince born in Neuwied, Germany.

[77] The Prince ruled from 7 March 1914 to 3 September 1914. His reign officially ended on 31 January 1925, when Albania was declared a Republic. However, he never really exercised power since the Entente powers would not allow someone who fought against them in the war to rule over Albania. For more, see Heaton-Armstrong 2005.

[78] Kola 2003: 18–19.

[79] For more information on this period, see Chapter 5.

[80] Zickel and Iwaskiw 1994.

[81] 2007: 25.

[82] Ahmet Zogolli (1895–1961) was the most influential political figure in interwar Albania. Before becoming Prime Minister in 1924 he held various influential positions including that of Minister of Interior (1921–1924). He was Prime Minister (1922–1924) and President of Albania (1925–1928). He was also King of the Albanians from 1928 to 1939, when Mussolini ousted him. For more on King Zog, as he was later called, and this period, see Fischer 2007: 19–49.

[83] For more on this period, see Chapter 7.

were driven by revisionist foreign policy goals. The main focus of their energies was the mobilization of Kosovo Albanians more so than those living in Tetovo. As we will see in Chapter 7, Zog rather quickly forgot about the Yugoslav support and turned Albania into a vassal state of Italy.

All in all, the Balkan states following World War I meet my scope conditions. Their ruling political elites represented well-defined core groups, part of the population in each country was not assimilated, and all of the states had the capacity to impose direct rule over their territory – with Albania being the weakest in this respect. Up to this point I have introduced the region and justified the case selection; let me now turn to the empirical test of my theory.

4

Cross-National Variation

Nation-Building in Post–World War I Balkans

Analyzing nation-building policies toward non-core groups across Balkan states following World War I reveals strong support for my argument. Non-core groups supported by enemy powers and residing in states that favored the international status quo were most likely to be targeted with assimilationist policies. Exclusion was most likely for the non-core groups supported by external enemies, but which resided in states dominated by revisionist politics. Finally, non-core groups supported by allied powers were most likely to be accommodated.

Group size and the presence of a homeland did not significantly affect states' nation-building strategies in the post–World War I Balkans. A difference in language and world religion between the non-core and core groups in a state made accommodation of the non-core group more likely than assimilation, but such differences do not help predict policy choices between exclusion and assimilation. The latter finding is rather surprising considering the well-established *millet* system and national historiographies that emphasize the role of religion in the nation-building process. Finally, whether a non-core group had been previously dominant does not seem to be a good predictor of nation-building policies. For instance, this finding implies that Christian states in the Balkans were not more likely to target Muslims, the previously dominant group of the Ottoman Empire, with exclusionary policies after World War I – when controlling for my argument.[1] These findings qualify both status reversal and cultural distance arguments.

This chapter should not be read in isolation from the rest of the book. It summarizes multiple individual cases in a systematic manner but is no substitute for the archival detail of Chapter 6 or the dynamic narrative in Chapter 7. In what follows, first, I describe my research design, the data, and the operationalization of the variables. In the next section, I present the results from my

---

[1] To be sure, exclusionary policies against the Muslim population were pursued during the nineteenth century Balkan rebellions as well as during the Balkan Wars but even after World War I a large number of Muslims lived in the Balkan Peninsula (Glavinas 2008; McCarthy 1995).

analysis and consider the explanatory power of domestic and international level factors I could not test statistically.

RESEARCH DESIGN: OPERATIONALIZATION AND MEASUREMENT

I test my theory of nation-building against alternative explanations on a dataset I have compiled on ninety non-core groups in post–World War I Balkans. My universe of cases includes all ethnic groups, which were perceived as unassimilated by the ruling political elites, that resided within the recognized boundaries of national Balkan states and satisfy my scope conditions. Indeed, elites aiming at securing the national loyalty of the population of their country ruled in all nation-states under study. Importantly, there were plenty of non-assimilated non-core groups in every country and ruling elites had a clear definition of the core group in their minds.

The combination of secondary sources, archival material, and exchanges with experts allowed me to identify and document ninety non-core groups in the six Balkan states after World War I.[2] All my independent variables presented below were coded for 1918 or earlier in order to guarantee exogeneity to the nation-building policies pursued by governments after the war.[3]

The Dependent Variable: Nation-Building Policies

For each country under study, I identify all groups perceived as non-core groups by the various governing elites in the Balkans at the end of World War I (T_o). When ruling political elites accommodate a non-core group, I assign the value "0"; when they pursue assimilationist policies I assign the value "1"; finally, when they adopt exclusionary measures, I assign the value "2." For this cross-national test I assume that the policies pursued toward non-core groups are a reliable indicator for coding state intentions. In the rest of the empirical chapters, I rely on archival material, confidential reports of governmental officials, and relevant legislation in order to identify and analytically distinguish between state intentions and pursued policies.

A problem I faced while coding these cases was the presence of mixed policies where, for example, part of a group was targeted with assimilationist policies while the majority was excluded (or vice versa). To address this problem in the statistical analysis, I necessarily simplified the picture and focused on the

---

[2] For a discussion of this difficult task and the caveats involved in this process, see Appendix A: The Politics of "Counting People."

[3] For more, see the Codebook in the Methodological Appendix. The coding of these variables is based on archival material as well as extensive secondary sources listed in a special section of my bibliography. I also conducted a coding reliability test with regional experts in Southeastern Europe. I describe this process and the problems associated with it in the Methodological Appendix.

"dominant" policy. I call a policy dominant when it is employed with respect to at least 80 percent of the non-core group. Thus, if a country targets 81 percent of a non-core group with assimilationist policies and 19 percent with exclusionary policies, I infer that the "dominant" policy of the government toward that group was assimilation. I hold that this threshold is sufficiently high to capture the state's intentions. The difficulty lies in distinguishing between cases where the mixed policy is either the result of principal-agent and local implementation problems or the result of a state intentionally pursuing a "mixed policy."[4]

Independent Variables

Most of my explanatory factors (language, religion, urban/rural location, group size) were relatively easy to code. The terms "Revisionist host state" and non-core group "supported by external enemy" as well as "homeland" deserve further attention. I code a non-core group as "externally supported" when the host state has proof or is otherwise convinced that the group's leaders are logistically and/or diplomatically supported by an external power and as "not externally supported" otherwise.[5] This coding is not capturing the non-core group member's subjective preferences; rather it is more attuned to the perceptions of the ruling political elites of each state with regard to the matter. This emphasis of my argument in the role of perceptions is the reason that I am not coding for the intensity or type of external support. Besides, with the exception of overt military intervention that is easy to code, most external involvement takes place secretly. Thus, this asymmetry of information forces governments to err on the safe side when they have reasons to doubt the loyalty of a group.

Similarly, I code a non-core group as "supported by ally" when the external power perceived as supporting a group is in the same international alliance bloc or the countries are in a bilateral alliance. I refer to a non-core group as "enemy supported" if the external power perceived as supporting that group is in competition with the host state (i.e., a power belonging to the enemy alliance bloc during World War I).

For the purposes of the statistical test conducted in this chapter, the relationship between the external power and the non-core group must have originated during World War I or immediately afterward. Similarly, within the post–World War I Balkan context I code a host state as "revisionist" if it lost territory in World War I, and as "status quo" otherwise. To test for the special case (depicted in Figure 2.6) where two contiguous states have non-core groups that are co-ethnics of the two countries, respectively, I construct a variable

---

[4] In Chapters 5 to 8, I consider genuine "mixed policies." In fact my argument predicts such cases. Although I decided to not include this category in my statistical analysis here, I am working on a paper conducting a statistical analysis where "mixed policy" is included as a separate category from assimilation, accommodation, and exclusion.

[5] For brevity I will use the term "external support" in the text to refer to the "perception of external support by the host state."

assigning the value "1" if a non-core group is supported by an external patron that has a non-core group of the host country within its territory, "0" otherwise.

I now turn to the operationalization of the variables derived from the existing literature that I can test for in the Balkan context. I code a non-core group as having a "homeland" if both the non-core group elites and the "kin state" recognize a relationship of ethnic kinship, "no homeland" otherwise. This is not always an easy task. This coding problem is related to a problem inherent in the logic of this argument. In particular, although it sounds unlikely that "the nationalizing state's preferences" over the treatment of a non-core group can produce a homeland, it is not impossible. For example, a country can sign a treaty or make a concession that allows another country to conduct nation-building (i.e., mobilize the non-core group and cultivate its national awareness) within the former's territory. As a result of this arrangement, we might get a non-core group that comes to identify with this country and thus comes to have an external homeland. For example, the treaty of Bucharest in 1913 provided Romania with such a nation-building opportunity across the Balkans.

The argument that governments may be harsh on secessionist groups for reputational reasons is operationalized in the following way. I assign the value "0" to a country if there is less than one large, territorially concentrated secessionist non-core group, and the value "1" if there are more.

To operationalize cultural distance one has to discern whether a group of people is different from the dominant definition of the nation, the "national type" (with respect to, e.g., language, religion, race), and study the statements of the ruling political elites of the state. Criteria for membership in a nation, however, do change in response to territorial or demographic changes. Very careful process tracing is the only way to make sure that the relevant definition of the nation has been in place before the incorporation of the new territory or non-core group, and that the definition did not shift as a consequence of this change.

The "status reversal" hypothesis is relatively easy to operationalize. I code a non-core group as having experienced a status reversal if they were included in the definition of the dominant group prior to the period of study, but are no longer included during the period under study.

I have also constructed three measures of non-core group size, the percentage of total population and two dummies, one capturing whether the group is above 1 percent and another for groups above 5 percent of the total population. Finally, I attempt to capture residential patterns and organizational characteristics with the variable "urban" coded as "1" if the non-core group was primarily urban, "0" otherwise.

ANALYSIS

Patterns: Descriptive Statistics

Despite the fact that World War I was fought based on the principles of nationalism, the region was still ethnically heterogeneous at the end of the

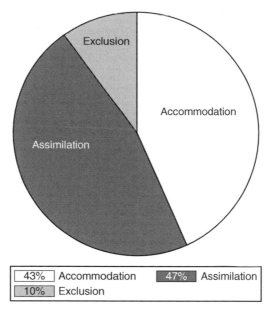

GRAPH 4.1. Nation-building policies in post–World War I Balkans, 1918–1923.

war. Looking at the distribution of nation-building policies, we see that contrary to present day perceptions about the Balkans, the most common strategy toward non-core groups in the immediate period following World War I was assimilation (see Graph 4.1). Forty-seven percent of the non-core groups were targeted with assimilationist policies, while only 10 percent were subject to exclusionary ones; the remaining percentage was accommodated. Most of the literature focuses on this 10 percent, and neglects the remaining 90 percent of the cases. However, a theory of nation-building has to be able to explain both violent and non-violent policies.

The above patterns characterize the post–World War I Balkans. The descriptive statistics of another period would look different. In particular, before the Balkan Wars, assimilation was much more prevalent whereas exclusionary policies were ubiquitous during the Balkan Wars and World War I. This pattern is consistent with my theory. In the nineteenth century, prior to the Balkan Wars, the various Balkan nation-states did not border each other, and external interference amongst them was less prominent. As a result, exclusionary policies within Balkan states were very infrequent.[6] Right before the Balkan Wars, during the Macedonian Struggle in 1903–1908,[7] states escalated their support for non-core groups residing in contested territories, resulting in

[6] Prominent exceptions involve the Ottoman reactions to the various secessionist movements that were externally supported. This dynamic is also consistent with my argument.
[7] For more, see Gounaris 2005; Livanios 1999; Perry 1988.

TABLE 4.1. *Descriptive Statistics*

Variable	Observations	Mean	Std. Dev.	Min	Max
Policy	90	0.66	0.65	0	2
Revisionist	90	0.43	0.49	0	1
External enemy	90	0.26	0.44	0	1
Status	90	0.15	0.36	0	1
Homeland	90	0.47	0.50	0	1
Urban	90	0.32	0.46	0	1
World religion	90	0.3	0.46	0	1
Religion	90	0.61	0.49	0	1
Language	90	0.74	0.43	0	1
Contiguous	90	0.28	0.45	0	1
Reputation	90	0.56	0.49	0	1
Primarily urban	90	0.67	0.46	0	1
Population in 1918	90	2.62	3.81	0.03	23.77

an increase in exclusionary policies. It was during the Balkan Wars, however, that we observe the most violent policies vividly described in the Carnegie Report.[8]

Turning to my main explanatory variables, 74 percent of the groups in my analysis spoke a different language and more than half, 61 percent, had a different religious denomination from the core group. The average size of a non-core group was around 2.6 percent of the total population, with the smallest group being 0.03 percent and the largest 23.77 percent. Only one third of the groups were primarily urban and around half had an external homeland. Finally, one quarter of the non-core groups in my analysis were supported by an enemy state while 43 percent lived in revisionist states (see Table 4.1).[9]

The different variables I have discussed are assumed to operate cumulatively, thus multivariate statistical analysis is the best way to capture the effects of these factors on nation-building policy choices. Yet since the number of non-core groups is small relatively to the number of variables, it is useful to examine the bivariate relationships through cross-tabulations first and then turn to the analysis of the multinomial logit regression results.

One third of the non-core groups that had a different language from the core group of their host state were targeted with assimilationist policies (see Table 4.2.i). Certainly, groups with a different language were more likely to be excluded or accommodated than groups sharing a principal language with the

[8] Carnegie Endowment for International Peace 1914.
[9] These are the non-core groups living in Bulgaria, Turkey, and Albania.

TABLE 4.2.I. *Language*

Policy	Same	Different	Total
Accommodation	3 (13%)	36 (54%)	39 (43%)
Assimilation	19 (83%)	23 (34%)	42 (47%)
Exclusion	1 (4%)	8 (12%)	9 (10%)
Total	23 (100%)	67 (100%)	90 (100%)

Pearson χ^2 (2) = 16.0809 Pr = 0.

TABLE 4.2.II. *Religious Denomination*

Policy	Same	Different	Total
Accommodation	8 (23%)	31 (56%)	39 (43%)
Assimilation	26 (74%)	16 (29%)	42 (47%)
Exclusion	1 (3%)	8 (14%)	9 (10%)
Total	35 (100%)	55 (100%)	90 (100%)

Pearson χ^2(2) = 17. 2538 Pr = 0.

core group, but the fact that one third of them were targeted with assimilationist policies contradicts cultural distance arguments. Not surprisingly – from the conventional point of view, non-core groups that shared a common language with the core group were more often targeted with assimilationist policies than with accommodation or exclusion.

As shown in Table 4.2.ii, non-core groups that had the same religion[10] as the core group were targeted more often with assimilationist policies than with accommodation or exclusion. Non-core groups of different religious denominations were more likely to be accommodated than targeted with assimilation or exclusion. However, contrary to the predictions of primordialist arguments, 16 non-core groups (29%) with a different religion were targeted with assimilationist policies. This pattern is surprising for the Balkans, where religion has traditionally been such a salient cleavage.

We do find some support for the cultural distance logic when we look at exclusionary policies. Non-core groups with a different religion were more likely to be excluded by the core group. Fifteen percent of the non-core groups with a different religion faced exclusion compared with 3 percent of the non-core groups with the same religion. Nevertheless, this effect is mitigated when we look at the breakdown by world religion.

[10] This variable captures differences within world religions as well. For example, Christian Orthodox loyal to the Ecumenical Patriarchate in Istanbul, Christian Orthodox loyal to the Bulgarian Exarchate, Christian Catholic, etc.

TABLE 4.2.III. *World Religion*

Policy	Same	Different	Total
Accommodation	24 (38%)	15 (56%)	39 (43%)
Assimilation	33 (53%)	9 (33%)	42 (47%)
Exclusion	6 (9%)	3 (11%)	9 (10%)
Total	63 (100%)	27 (100%)	90 (100%)

Pearson χ^2 (2) = 2.8467 Pr = 0.241.

TABLE 4.2.IV. *Non-Core Group Primarily Urban*

Policy	No	Yes	Total
Accommodation	20 (33%)	19 (65%)	39 (43%)
Assimilation	36 (59%)	6 (21%)	42 (47%)
Exclusion	5 (8%)	4 (14%)	9 (10%)
Total	61 (100%)	29 (100%)	90 (100%)

Pearson χ^2 (2) = 11.6618 Pr = 0.003.

Conducting a cross-tabulation with "world religion,"[11] rather than religious denomination, as the breakdown category we see in Table 4.2.iii that the relationship between religion and policy choice is statistically insignificant. Non-core groups were almost equally likely to be targeted with exclusionary policies whether or not they were members of the same world religion as the core group. This empirical record directly contradicts cultural distance arguments, implying that there must be some other process that accounts for the variation in nation-building policies. All in all, cultural distance theories overpredict exclusionary policies and preclude the possibility of accommodation. But both assimilation and accommodation are very common.

Looking at Table 4.2.iv, we see that primarily urban non-core groups were three times less likely to be targeted with assimilationist policies than others. In fact they were two times more likely to be accommodated. This empirical pattern is consistent with the logic of my argument about non-core groups that live in peripheries of a host state. The latter are more likely than other groups to be (or become) targets for national agitation and/or support by external powers, leading ruling political elites to – sometimes even preemptively – pursue assimilationist policies. Exclusionary policies were almost equally likely, but ruling political elites were more likely to accommodate primarily urban groups. Again this is consistent with my argument's logic that it is easier for external enforcers of minority rights to monitor the fate of urban non-core groups.

[11] Muslim, Christian, Jewish.

TABLE 4.2.V. *Nomadic Non-Core Group*

Policy	No	Yes	Total
Accommodation	33 (43%)	6 (46%)	39 (43%)
Assimilation	37 (48%)	5 (39%)	42 (47%)
Exclusion	7 (9%)	2 (15%)	9 (10%)
Total	77 (100%)	13 (100%)	90 (100%)

Pearson χ^2 (2) = 0.6877 Pr = 0.709.

TABLE 4.2.VI. *Rural Non-Core Group*

Policy	No	Yes	Total
Accommodation	32 (58%)	7 (20%)	39 (43%)
Assimilation	17 (31%)	25 (71%)	42 (47%)
Exclusion	6 (11%)	3 (9%)	9 (10%)
Total	55 (100%)	35 (100%)	90 (100%)

Pearson χ^2 (2) = 14.8377 Pr = 0.001.

In Table 4.2.v, we see that the relationship between nation-building policies and whether a non-core group is nomadic or not is not statistically significant. Nevertheless, looking at the descriptive statistics we see that almost half of the nomadic non-core groups were accommodated. This pattern might be capturing the difficulty involved with targeting nomadic groups with assimilationist policies or the fact that these groups were not threatening to states, as they were small, unconnected to any specific territory,[12] and as such less likely to be externally supported.

Rural non-core groups were more likely to be targeted with assimilationist policies than other types of non-core groups (see Table 4.2.vi). The logic here is that a group residing in rural areas is a better target for an external power since state control of rural areas is harder to maintain than control of urban centers.[13] Accommodation was more prevalent for non-core groups that were not rural, confirming the intuitions of my argument.

Looking at Table 4.2.vii, we see that non-core groups that used to be part of the once dominant group are two times more likely to be excluded by the host state than non-core groups that were not dominant in the past. This is consistent with the status reversal logic. However, we also see that previously dominant non-core groups were accommodated by the host state in 57 percent of the cases.

[12] Toft 2003.
[13] Kocher 2004.

TABLE 4.2.VII. *Non-Core Group Has Experienced Status Reversal*

Policy	No	Yes	Total
Accommodation	31 (41%)	8 (57%)	39 (43%)
Assimilation	39 (51%)	3 (21.5%)	42 (47%)
Exclusion	6 (8%)	3 (21.5%)	9 (10%)
Total	76 (100%)	14 (100%)	90 (100%)

Pearson χ^2 (2) = 5.1579 Pr = 0.076.

TABLE 4.2.VIII. *Non-Core Group Has a Homeland*

Policy	No	Yes	Total
Accommodation	15 (32%)	24 (56%)	39 (43%)
Assimilation	29 (62%)	13 (30%)	42 (47%)
Exclusion	3 (6%)	6 (14%)	9 (10%)
Total	47 (100%)	43 (100%)	90 (100%)

Pearson χ^2 (2) = 9.0122 Pr = 0.011.

For example, the Greek government's choice of accommodation as a policy toward Muslims after World War I contradicts the status reversal logic.

Looking at the tabulation in Table 4.2.viii, we see that non-core groups with a homeland were more likely to be accommodated than those who lacked one. Consistently with Brubaker's work, groups without a homeland were most likely to be targeted with assimilationist policies. These policy choices are also consistent with my argument: Groups with no external support are targeted for assimilation in order to immunize the population from future propaganda. Interestingly, 13 non-core groups that had a homeland (30%) were nevertheless targeted with assimilationist policies. The homeland argument circulating in the literature would be hard-pressed to explain this pattern since, according to this argument, non-core groups with a homeland are not expected to be targeted with assimilationist policies.

Turning to non-core group size, according to Table 4.2.ix, there is no difference in a host state's nation-building policies whether a non-core group is larger than 1 percent of the total population of the host state or not. Small groups were as likely to be accommodated as groups larger than 1 percent. Non-core groups larger than 1 percent were slightly more likely to be targeted with exclusionary policies than smaller groups. This pattern is consistent with the security logic that underlies my argument since a larger group is more likely to be mobilized by an external power and the host state is more likely to perceive it as threatening.

Using a higher percentage produces, again, a statistically insignificant relationship. According to Table 4.2.x, a non-core group being larger than 5 percent

TABLE. 4.2.IX. *Non-Core Group Larger Than 1% of the Total Population*

Policy	No	Yes	Total
Accommodation	17 (46%)	22 (42%)	39 (43%)
Assimilation	17 (46%)	25 (47%)	42 (47%)
Exclusion	3 (8%)	6 (11%)	9 (10%)
Total	37 (100%)	53 (100%)	90 (100%)

Pearson χ^2 (2) = 0.3308 Pr = 0.848.

TABLE. 4.2.X. *Non-Core Group Larger Than 5% of the Total Population*

Policy	No	Yes	Total
Accommodation	30 (40%)	9 (60%)	39 (43%)
Assimilation	38 (51%)	4 (27%)	42 (47%)
Exclusion	7 (9%)	2 (13%)	9 (10%)
Total	75 (100%)	15 (100%)	90 (100%)

Pearson χ^2 (2) = 2.8967 Pr = 0.235.

of the total population of the host state does not have a statistically significant impact on the choice of nation-building policies. Groups larger than 5 percent of the total population were a little more likely to be accommodated than groups smaller than 5 percent. Non-core groups larger than 5 percent were less likely to be targeted with assimilationist policies than smaller groups but were almost equally likely to be targeted with exclusionist policies.[14] Overall, these patterns contradict several demographic arguments and put into question the convention of the 1 percent threshold in data collection that currently dominates the quantitative research in political science.[15]

Turning to my main explanatory variables, in Table 4.2.xi, we see that non-core groups that had no external support were never targeted with exclusion. Non-core groups that had external support were targeted with exclusion in 19 percent of the cases; a high percentage, given how rare exclusionary policies are overall. Consistent with Configuration I, assimilation was more likely for non-core groups without external support – 77 percent compared with 19 percent for groups with external support. Nevertheless, the ten cases of accommodation for non-core groups that did not have external support require further research. Are these outliers due to the relative cost of assimilation compared to the cost of accommodation? Are they capturing a "marginality"

---

[14] In the regression analysis I use a continuous measure of group size instead of a dichotomous coding of groups as larger or smaller than 1 or 5% of the total population.

[15] For more, see the section "The Politics of 'Counting People'" in the Methodological Appendix.

TABLE 4.2.XI. *Configuration I: External Support*

Policy	No	Yes	Total
Accommodation	10 (23%)	29 (62%)	39 (43%)
Assimilation	33 (77%)	9 (19%)	42 (47%)
Exclusion	0 (0%)	9 (19%)	9 (10%)
Total	43 (100%)	47 (100%)	90 (100%)

Pearson χ^2 (2) = 31.8558 Pr = 0.

TABLE 4.2.XII. *Configuration II: External Support by Allied Power*

Policy	No	Yes	Total
Accommodation	18 (26%)	21 (95%)	39 (43%)
Assimilation	42 (62%)	0 (0%)	42 (47%)
Exclusion	8 (12%)	1 (5%)	9 (10%)
Total	68 (100%)	22 (100%)	90 (100%)

Pearson χ^2 (2) = 32.7088 Pr = 0.

dynamic,[16] according to which a group is accommodated because it has valuable economic skills that are linked to its cultural distinctiveness? Is this an Ottoman legacy? I pursue this inquiry in Chapter 5.

As expected, non-core groups supported by allies of the host state were almost always accommodated (see Table 4.2.xii). In particular, a non-core group supported by an ally was accommodated in 95 percent of the observations but one that was not supported but an ally was accommodated only in 26 percent of the cases. Importantly, a non-core group supported by an ally was never targeted with assimilationist policies. Also consistent with Configuration II, non-core groups not supported by allies were almost three times more likely to be targeted with exclusion than non-core groups that were supported by allied powers.[17]

Non-core groups supported by external enemies of the host state were 20 times more likely to be targeted with exclusionist policies than groups without enemy support (see Table 4.2.xiii). A non-core group supported by an enemy power was excluded in one third of the observations but one that was not supported by an enemy power was excluded only in one case (1.5%).[18] Consistent with my argument, non-core groups not supported by enemy states

---

[16] Laitin 1995.
[17] I should note here that all groups that have "no external support" are also included in the category of "no ally support" and this probably explains the high percentage assimilation in that column.
[18] I pursue this outlier – Greeks in the KSCS – in Chapter 5.

TABLE 4.2.XIII. *External Support by Enemy Power*

Policy	No	Yes	Total
Accommodation	32 (48.5%)	7 (29%)	39 (43%)
Assimilation	33 (50%)	9 (38%)	42 (47%)
Exclusion	1 (1.5%)	8 (33%)	9 (10%)
Total	66 (100%)	24 (100%)	90 (100%)

Pearson χ^2 (2) = 19.9232 Pr = 0.

TABLE 4.2.XIV. *Host State Foreign Policy Goals*

Policy	Status Quo	Revisionist	Total
Accommodation	27 (53%)	12 (31%)	39 (43%)
Assimilation	22 (43%)	20 (51%)	42 (42%)
Exclusion	2 (4%)	7 (18%)	9 (10%)
Total	51 (100%)	39 (100%)	90 (100%)

Pearson χ^2 (2) = 7.1697 Pr = 0.028.

were almost two times more likely to be targeted with accommodation than non-core groups that were supported by enemy powers.[19]

Turning to Table 4.2.xiv, we observe that non-core groups residing in revisionist host states were almost five times more likely to be excluded than groups living in status quo states. Moreover, we see that assimilation was slightly more likely in revisionist states than in status quo states. This may be partly due to the fact that revisionist states were more likely to have received refugees – which they definitely intended to assimilate – since they lost territories in World War I. Nevertheless, as my argument suggests, to understand this distribution more fully we need to focus on the nature of the external support that these non-core groups enjoyed together with the foreign policy goals of their host states.

Most of the non-core groups in my dataset were either residing in status quo states, supported by allied powers, or had no external support at all (80 out of 90 non-core groups; see Table 4.2.xv). However, 10 groups were supported by an enemy power and lived in revisionist host states. In such circumstances my theory predicts exclusion. Indeed, consistent with Configuration III, from Table 4.2.xv, we see that 70 percent of these groups were excluded.

---

[19] Again, I should note here that under the category of groups that have "no external support by enemy power" both cases of "no enemy support" and of "allied support" are included. This explains to a large extent the high number of cases of assimilation in that column.

TABLE 4.2.XV. *Configuration III: Exclusion of Enemy-Supported Group in Revisionist State*

Policy	No	Yes	Total
Accommodation	38 (47.5%)	1 (10%)	39 (43%)
Assimilation	40 (50%)	2 (20%)	42 (47%)
Exclusion	2 (2.5%)	7 (70%)	9 (10%)
Total	80 (100%)	10 (100%)	90 (100%)

Pearson $\chi^2(2)$ = 45.0989 Pr = 0.

TABLE 4.2.XVI. *Configuration IV: Group Supported by Enemy in Status Quo State*

Policy	No	Yes	Total
Accommodation	33 (44%)	6 (40%)	39 (43%)
Assimilation	34 (45%)	8 (53%)	42 (47%)
Exclusion	8 (11%)	1 (7%)	9 (10%)
Total	75 (100%)	15 (100%)	90 (100%)

Pearson $\chi^2(2)$ = 0.4176 Pr = 0.812.

Only fifteen out of the ninety non-core groups in my dataset were residing in status quo host states and were supported by enemy powers (see Table 4.2.xvi). Consistent with Configuration IV, more than half of these non-core groups were targeted with assimilationist policies. However, the relationship does not come up as statistically significant. Primarily this has to do with the six non-core groups that were supported by an enemy power and lived in status quo host states that were accommodated instead of being targeted with colonization or other intense assimilationist policies. I discuss these outliers in Chapter 5.

Turning to the special case where the host state and the external power are contiguous and have each other's co-ethnics we see that exclusion is nine times more likely than in other cases (Table 4.2.xvii). Thus there is important evidence in favor of this hypothesis. This is capturing the population exchange dynamic that occured in such instances.[20] Regardless, accommodation was the most common policy within this special category. This may be capturing a strategy of accommodating a non-core group in fear of retaliation on your co-ethnics abroad.[21]

In Table 4.2.xviii, there appears to be a relationship between states that face multiple secessionist non-core groups and nation-building policies. According to the cross-tabulation, governments that faced more than one secessionist group

[20] Eberhardt 2003.
[21] Divani 1995; Mavrogordatos 2003.

TABLE 4.2.XVII. *Host State and External Power Contiguous and Have Co-Ethnics*

Policy	No	Yes	Total
Accommodation	28 (44%)	11 (42%)	39 (45%)
Assimilation	34 (53%)	8 (31%)	42 (44%)
Exclusion	2 (3%)	7 (27%)	9 (10%)
Total	64 (100%)	26 (100%)	90 (100%)

Pearson $\chi^2(2)$ = 12.4601 Pr = 0.002.

TABLE 4.2.XVIII. *Host State Faces More Than One Secessionist Non-Core Group*

Policy	No	Yes	Total
Accommodation	12 (31%)	27 (53%)	39 (43%)
Assimilation	17 (51%)	22 (43%)	42 (47%)
Exclusion	7 (18%)	2 (4%)	9 (10%)
Total	39 (100%)	51 (100%)	90 (100%)

Pearson $\chi^2(2)$ = 7.1697 Pr = 0.028.

did not use exclusionary policies more than governments that faced just one or no such groups. In particular, governments that faced one or no such groups were four times more likely to use exclusionary policies. Given this operationalization, the pattern contradicts the logic of the reputation argument. To be fair, this may not be the best test for this argument. In order to test it correctly we would need more archival evidence mapping out the logic behind the various policies.

Before I turn to the regression results, it is useful to look at a simple cross-tabulation of my theory predictions and the actual policies pursued toward the non-core groups in my analysis (Table 4.2.xix). Overall, my argument correctly predicts 81 percent of the cases (73 out of 90 observations in the dataset). Assimilationist policies are correctly predicted in 41 out of 55 cases (75%). In most incorrectly predicted cases, my theory indicates assimilation but the non-core groups were granted minority rights instead. Exclusionary policies are also correctly predicted in seven out of the nine cases (78%). My theory fares even better with respect to accommodationist policies, correctly predicting 96 percent of the cases, all but one. I pursue an analysis of the incorrectly predicted cases in Chapter 5.

Explaining Variation in Nation-Building Policies

While the cross-tabulations and statistical significance tests are useful for identifying strong relationships between variables, they are not allowing us to isolate

TABLE 4.2.XIX. *Correctly Predicted*

	Predicted Policy			
Actual Policy	Accommodation	Assimilation	Exclusion	Total
Accommodation	25 (96%)	13 (23%)	1 (11%)	39 (43%)
Assimilation	0 (0%)	41 (75%)	1 (11%)	42 (47%)
Exclusion	1 (4%)	1 (2%)	7 (78%)	9 (10%)
Total	26 (100%)	55 (100%)	9 (100%)	90 (100%)

Pearson χ^2 (4) = 93.5632 Pr = 0.

the effect of each one of the variables of interest in a multivariate context. In this section I attempt to achieve this through a multinomial logit regression and a series of simulations.

Given the case selection and the regional character of the data, a few important existing explanations are controlled for.[22] For example, there is very little variation in the modernization levels, the geopolitical context, the norms surrounding the treatment of minorities, the level of political development, and the understandings of nationhood across the states included in my analysis. As described in Chapter 3, all nation-states in the Balkans were mostly agricultural societies whose ruling political elites were motivated by a homogenizing imperative. Moreover, Balkan states were at comparable levels of political development and shared the Ottoman legacy.

Beyond these commonalities there was a great deal of heterogeneity within the Balkans that the dataset I have compiled attempts to capture. Using this dataset we are able to test a few group-level hypotheses such as the impact of cultural distance (measuring differences in language and religion), the effect of having an external homeland or not, a version of the status reversal argument, the importance of being an urban group as opposed to a rural or a nomadic one, and the impact of group size on the choice of nation-building policies.[23] The model specification that I used is depicted in Figure 4.1.

The results from the multinomial logit regression confirm my intuitions.[24] Non-core groups that are supported by enemy external powers are less likely to

---

[22] Still, there is no doubt that my model specification has omitted variable bias. This bias is in the error term of my model specification. Some variables of importance that I was not able to code include the personalities of leaders, political ideologies, and the impact of public opinion. I discuss these explanations at the end of this chapter and in the other empirical chapters.

[23] A correlation table of the variables shows that none are correlated above 0.45.

[24] A fundamental assumption underlying the multinomial logit is the independence of irrelevant alternatives (Hausman and McFadden 1984; Ray 1973). In my case this means that I assume the following: If assimilationist policies are preferred to accommodation with respect to a non-core group, then introducing the alternative strategy of exclusion will not make accommodation preferred to assimilationist policies. Nevertheless, I also ran a multinomial probit regression, which does not rely on this assumption, and the results were practically the same.

Model 1

Nation-building policy | assimilation
accommodation =
exclusion

$\beta_0 + \beta_1$ [Host State Revisionist] + β_2 [Non-Core group Supported by Enemy] + β_3 [Status Reversal] + β_4 [External Homeland] + β_5 [Primarily Urban] + β_6 [World Religion] + β_7 [Language] + β_8 [Group Size] + ε

Model 2

Nation-building policy
assimilation
accommodation =
exclusion

$\beta_0 + \beta_1$ [Host State Revisionist] + β_2 [Non-Core group Supported by Enemy] + β_3 [Status Reversal] + β_4 [External Homeland] + β_5 [Primarily Urban] + β_6 [World Religion] + β_7 [Language] + β_8 [Contiguous] + β_9 [Group Size] + ε

FIGURE 4.1. Multinomial logit models.

be accommodated than targeted with assimilation (Model 1 in Table 4.3). Similar non-core groups are more likely to be excluded by ruling political elites of revisionist host states than targeted with assimilation. Whether a non-core group has an external homeland does not have any statistically significant impact on nation-building choices. Whether a non-core group was previously dominant does not appear to have an impact in deciding between policies – at least in the post–World War I period. Clearly strategic considerations that my argument highlights were important in this decisionmaking process.

Before I discuss the impact of demographic and cultural characteristics of non-core groups, let me discuss the special case where the host state and the external power are contiguous and have each other's co-ethnics. Contiguous states sharing co-ethnics are more likely to pursue exclusionary policies than assimilationist policies toward their non-core groups when at least one of them is perceived as actively supporting its co-ethnics in the near abroad (Model 2 in Table 4.3). However, this variable is not helping us account for variation when we are looking at the choice between accommodation and assimilation. The rest of the results hold up with one exception.[25]

---

[25] In particular, whether a non-core group resides in a revisionist host state or not ceases to be statistically significant when deciding between exclusion and assimilation. This is probably due to the fact that much of the explanatory power of the "revisionist" variable is absorbed by the "contiguous" variable.

Empirical Evidence

TABLE 4.3. *Multinomial Logit Estimates for Nation-Building Policies in Post–World War I Balkans*

Model 1	Accommodation	Exclusion
Variable		
Revisionist Host State	−1.11	2.25
Group Supported by Enemy	−2.04	3.85
Status Reversal	0.47	0.37
External Homeland	0.97	−0.4
Primarily Urban	*1.45*	1.37
World Religion	1.7	0.47
Language	2.42	0.74
Non-core Group %	0.08	−0.03
_constant	−2.6	−6
Comparison Group:	Assimilation	
Model 2		
Variable		
Revisionist Host State	*−1.13*	1.22
Group Supported by Enemy	−2.26	4.17
Status Reversal	.44	3.19
External Homeland	1.2	−1.01
Primarily Urban	*1.3*	3.04
World Religion	1.07	2.18
Language	2.48	−2.22
Contiguous	−.31	5.25
Non-core Group %	.1	−.5
_constant	−2.6	−6.41
Comparison Group:	Assimilation	

Results are log ratios. They signify the log ratio between the **Probability of Accommodation/ Probability of Assimilation** in the first column and the log ratio between the **Probability of Exclusion/ Probability of Assimilation** in the second column. For example, looking at whether a non-core group is supported by an enemy power we find that a one-unit change decreases the log ratio of the Pr(accommodation)/Pr(assimilation) by 2.04.
Bold signifies 10% significance level. Bold and italics signifies 5% significance level.
Number of Obs. = 90; LR Chi-Squared (16) = 63.38; Prob>Chi-Sq. = 0; Pseudo R-Sq. = .37.

Turning to demographic and cultural characteristics, we observe that group size, measured as percentage of the total population, does not help us distinguish amongst nation-building policies. Primarily urban non-core groups were more likely to be accommodated than targeted with assimilationist policies. I also ran a model including a "territorial concentration" variable that came up as statistically insignificant and thus do not present these results here. This finding may be due to measurement error since data on non-core groups' territorial concentrations were not easy to collect for that period.[26]

Having a different world religion than the core group increases the likelihood of accommodation compared with assimilation; however, quite surprisingly for the Balkans, it does not have an impact when comparing exclusionary to assimilationist policies.[27] Similarly, having a different language than the core group increases the likelihood of accommodation compared to assimilation, although it does not have any effect when comparing exclusion and assimilation. In the next chapter, I take a closer look at the outliers of this analysis including cases of culturally different groups that were accommodated, trying to discern whether they were accommodated for reasons that are consistent with my theory or with the cultural distance argument.

Simulations

To demonstrate my findings in a more straightforward way than the presentation of regression coefficients, I employ Clarify.[28] I run simulations changing just my two principal explanatory variables, interstate relations between the host state and the external power supporting a non-core group and a host state's foreign policy goals, holding all other variables to their mean values. In Tables 4.4, 4.5, and 4.6, I report the mean predicted probabilities for each nation-building policy as my two main explanatory factors vary.

Consistent with my theory, assimilation is most likely for non-core groups supported by enemy powers and residing in status quo host states (mean probability 0.60). Accommodation has the highest mean probability (0.66) for non-core groups that are supported by allied powers – or do not have any external support – and reside in states that favor the international status quo. In contrast, non-core groups that are supported by enemy powers and live in revisionist host states face a zero mean probability of being accommodated. Finally, exclusion is most likely for non-core groups supported by enemies in host states dominated by revisionist politics (mean probability 0.68). Again the mean probability of a non-core group that is not supported by an enemy external power to be targeted with exclusionary policies is practically zero. These findings confirm my intuitions and nicely illustrate the substantive effects of the variables of interest while controlling for a host of variables.

---

[26] The rest of the results remain the same with one exception. The homeland argument is now statistically significant, suggesting that a non-core group that has a homeland is more likely to be accommodated than assimilated. The variable "homeland" remains statistically insignificant in distinguishing between the policies of exclusion and assimilation.

[27] Running a model including "religious denomination" instead of "world religion" does not significantly change the results. The main difference is that "revisionist state" and "primarily urban" are not as statistically significant in distinguishing between accommodation and assimilation.

[28] Clarify is a program developed by King, Tomz, and Wittenberg (2000) that uses stochastic simulation techniques to help researchers interpret statistical results. See also Tomz et al. 2003.

TABLE 4.4. *Probability of Assimilation*

		Non-Core Group	
		External Support by Enemy Power	Not Supported by Enemy Power[a]
Host State	*Revisionist*	0.28 (0.07–59)	0.56 (0.32–78)
	Status quo	0.60 (0.28–87)	0.33 (0.17–54)

[a] Includes non-core groups with external support from ally as well as groups with no external support.

TABLE 4.5. *Probability of Accommodation*

		Non-Core Group	
		External Support by Enemy Power	Not Supported by Enemy Power
Host State	*Revisionist*	0.03 (0.0–11)	0.38 (0.17–63)
	Status quo	0.18 (0.4–42)	0.66 (45–82)

TABLE 4.6. *Probability of Exclusion*

		Non-Core Group	
		External Support by Enemy Power	Not Supported by Enemy Power
Host State	*Revisionist*	0.68 (0.35–92)	0.05 (0–21)
	Status quo	0.21 (0.3–60)	0 (0–03)

ISSUES OF CAUSAL INFERENCE

Direction of Causality

Despite my treatment of the problem of endogeneity from a theoretical stand-point in Chapter 2, there may still be concerns with respect to the direction of causality. One might argue that the pattern of alliances in the Balkans during World War I was actually caused by the nation-building policies of neighboring states rather than causally preceding them. Host states may have chosen which side to take in the Great War based on concerns related to the treatment of non-core groups in neighboring countries. However, this is not the case. Mijatovich, for instance, informs us that the British believed up to the last moment "that Bulgaria could be won."[29] But, Bulgaria fought on the side of the Central powers in the end mainly because it was still bitter from the outcome of the Balkan Wars, not because of the policies that Greece or Serbia pursued toward Bulgarians in these places. In a confidential memorandum on the "macedonian question" written long after the war was over, in 1930, the Central Department of the British Foreign Office clearly states that "[n]or is it surprising that the Bulgarians should sympathize with and perhaps greatly exaggerate the sufferings of, the Bulgarophone population of Macedonia" and goes on to highlight the geostrategic considerations of the various Balkan states as the primary source of animosity and mistrust between these states.[30] According to the memorandum, the Bulgarian government was disgruntled and blamed particularly Great Britain for not supporting her against the Turks in the second Balkan War; "this made her [Bulgaria] ready to turn to Germany and influenced her in 1915 when she seized the chance to revenge herself on Serbia, hoping to regain Macedonia, of which she considered she had been unjustly defrauded."[31]

Based on the historical record, in the case of the Balkan states under study here, the choice of allies was an outcome of a combination of calculations about who is going to win and strategic considerations concerning which side will provide more territory (after the war) and support (during the war) in return for the alliance, not of nation-building policies of neighboring states. For example, during the late nineteenth century Russia supported Bulgaria's claims in Macedonia to the detriment of Serbia and for that period Austrian influence in Serbia prevailed. However, as we will see in Chapter 6, by 1913 this picture had been completely reversed. Now Serbia was supported by Russia and Bulgaria was closer to Austria-Hungary.[32]

---

[29] 1917: 243.
[30] BNA, FO 371/14317 [C5316,/82/7] "The Origins of the Macedonian Revolutionary Organization and its History since the Great War," 1 July 1930, p. 12.
[31] Ibid., 8.
[32] Mijatovich 1917: 244–245.

Regime Type, Ideologies, Core Group Size, and the League of Nations

But what was the effect of the political system and the ideological predispositions of the various governments in question? Such factors were difficult to incorporate into the quantitative analysis, but nonetheless bear on the present discussion. For instance, it could be the case that variation in nation-building policies is explained by the ideological differences of the ruling political elites across the six states under study rather than by the strategic logic I am proposing.

The foreign policy orientation variable in my model specification is certainly country-specific, taking a value based on whether a given state was on the side of the "victors" in World War I or not. Although this variable is, as we have seen, an important country-specific determinant of the nation-building intentions of ruling elites, it may be capturing other factors such as the content of political ideologies of the ruling elites or the effect of regime type. Below I take a closer look at regime type, political deologies, core group size, and the role of the League of Nations following World War II in all the six states under study in an attempt to evaluate whether any of these factors can account for the variation in nation-building policies across non-core groups.

Regime Type and Political Ideologies

Could the political ideologies of each state and the differences in regime type account for the variation in nation-building policies? Looking at Table 4.7 we see that, consistent with my argument, states that were on the losing side in World War I were much more likely to use exclusionary policies, whereas states that were on the winning side were more likely to follow accommodationist policies. The occurrence of assimilationist policies was more or less equal for both groups of countries.

Most of the Balkan states had some form of representative government. Turkey and Albania were still engaged in fighting for their territorial borders the first years after World War I, but Greece – a winner in World War I – was also engaged in the territorial conflicts. Moreover, neither Albania nor Turkey had a king following World War I. But Greece only nominally had a king until 1920, when Venizelos lost the elections. All of the states under study had a Western orientation and pursued modernization policies albeit with different degrees of success. Most governing parties were motivated by either liberal or popular political ideologies. But there does not seem to be a systematic state level pattern linking political ideology with nation-building policies within the post–World War I Balkans.[33] Most

---

[33] It is of course possible that arguments focusing on political ideologies may account for variation across regions or over time. For an argument focusing on domestic political processes – with an emphasis on ideologies – and a different conceptualization of "Regimes of Ethnicity" ranging from "mono-ethnic, to multi-ethnic, to non/anti-ethnic regimes," see Akturk 2007 and 2011. For an argument linking Liberalism to a specific type of treatment of non-core groups, see Joppke 2005.

TABLE 4.7. *Domestic Politics and Nation-Building Policies, c. 1918–1924*

Country	Population	Core Group % of Total Pop.[a]	Ruling Party	# of Groups	Assimilation	Accommodation	Exclusion
Albania	825,000	86	Liberal/Popular	7	4 (9.5%)	3 (8%)	0 (0%)
Bulgaria	4,500,000	70	Agrarian	16	5 (12%)	7 (18%)	4 (44%)
Greece	5,500,000	65	Liberal/Popular	16	7 (17%)	8 (20.5%)	1 (11%)
KSCS	14,798,000	38	Radical	19	10 (24%)	9 (20.5%)	1 (11%)
Romania	16,250,000	56	Peasant/Liberal	16	5 (12%)	11 (28%)	0
Turkey	13,000,000	50	Republican	16	11 (26%)	2 (5%)	3 (33%)

[a] Not including the refugees from the Balkan Wars and World War I.

likely security and national interest considerations trumped any impact that the various political ideologies may have had on the treatment of non-core groups. All in all, a pattern does not appear to emerge from these country level differences.

Core Group Size

What if the size of the core group in each of these Balkan states is causally related to the nation-building policies pursued in each case? Kaufmann and Haklai, for example, suggest that dominant minorities are having a hard time legitimizing their rule.[34] Following this logic, the Kingdom of Serbs, Croats and Slovenes (KSCS) could be viewed as such a case since the Serbs – the largest group – in 1918 did not form more than 38 percent of the total population. If one takes the regime's declarations at face value, then Serbo-Croats – a linguistic category – constituted an absolute majority with 63 percent of the total population.[35] In the statistical analysis, I treat the Serbs as the core group and include the Croats and the Slovenes as non-core groups. Given such a small core group size accommodation may have been an overdetermined outcome. For instance, one of my outliers, the Slovenes in the KSCS, had both a different language and religion from the Serbs, were territorially concentrated, and resided in the periphery of the KSCS. These factors together with the small percentage of the core group in the KSCS may have precluded assimilationist policies in this case. However, we see that the KSCS did not pursue accommodationist policies more often than Bulgaria and Greece did, both countries with demographically large core groups.

Albania also stands out since its core group was comprised of Albanian speakers of Muslim, Christian Orthodox and Catholic faiths. Nevertheless, most scholars studying the Albanian case use language as the most important marker and suggest that the core group was approximately 86 percent of the total population.[36] Ironically, the very construction of the core group in Albania in a way that overcomes religious cleavages serves as a counterargument to several versions of the cultural distance argument.

All in all, core group size does not appear to explain the cross-national variation in nation-building policies any better than regime type or political ideology, although it definitely matters in multiple other ways.

International Norms, the League of Nations, and Minority Treaties

Before concluding this chapter, it is important to note that the system that resulted from World War I was obliging small nations and only the defeated Great Powers to respect the rights of national minorities – or racial, linguistic, and religious minorities as the treaties called them to avoid defining the term

---

[34] 2008.
[35] Banac 1984:58.
[36] Clayer 2008: 128–129; Great Britain, Foreign Office 1920; Marmullaku 1975; Skendi 1967.

"nationality."[37] Moreover, the establishment of the League of Nations influenced the incentive structure for both non-core groups and nation-states. For example, revisionist states tried to use the League of Nations to avoid the assimilation of their co-ethnics abroad and destabilize enemy states.[38] States that were satisfied with the status quo tried to preserve it by assimilating most non-core groups – except the ones supported by allied powers – within their territory before revisionist powers undermined this process or attempted to alter the borders. These dynamics are consistent with the general logic of my argument.

Finney writes, "[T]hese states were weak and insecure, and feared that toleration would perpetuate the existence of distinct, aloof and alienated groups whose allegiances were deeply suspect; hence they were reluctant to treat the minorities generously."[39] According to Finney, the principle of self-determination had explosive consequences and was the main flaw of the World War I peace settlement. The emphasis that the Allies put on this principle – at least rhetorically – led most states to either deny the existence of minorities within their borders or to resort to repressive measures in order to prevent the development of secessionist movements.

The consensus in the literature is that the League of Nations despite its initial optimism and limited success could not and did not enforce the World War I treaties.[40] The victors of the war believed that the system of minority protection put in place by the League of Nations would initially accommodate the differences of certain non-core groups so that they could in the near future assimilate into their core societies. However, the minority protection regime constituted a perverse incentive structure undermining this – primarily British – expectation of assimilation. Overall, this system did not significantly impact the policy intentions of Balkan states but it may have influenced the form many policies took.

CONCLUSION

From the study of post–World War I Balkans certain patterns emerge. Outside support for non-core groups had an effect on the nation-building policies that host states pursued. Whether a non-core group is perceived to be externally supported or not and the interstate competition between the host state and the external power are important variables when we try to account for nation-building policies. Contiguous states that share co-ethnics were more likely to pursue exclusionary policies than non-contiguous states or states without each other's co-ethnics. Urban non-core groups with a different language and/or

[37] Azcárate 1945: 3; Mazower 1997 and 2009.
[38] Divani 1995: 36.
[39] 1995: 536.
[40] Azcárate 1945; Barros 1970; Divani 1995; Mazower 2009.

religion from the core group were more likely to be accommodated than assimilated.

Admittedly, my theory does not perfectly predict all of the Balkan cases. There are some incorrect predictions (19% of the cases).[41] In Chapter 5 I discuss the outliers of my statistical analysis. Chapters 6 and 7 provide a subnational and a temporal test of my theory in different regions of the Balkans. However, even though my argument does very well in explaining variation in the early twentieth-century Balkans, such success does not necessarily imply that it can travel across space or time. In Chapter 8, I focus on the generalizability of the argument and look at cases beyond the interwar Balkans including Cold War Asia and post–Cold War Estonia in order to address these challenges.

---

[41] See Table 5.1.

5

Odd Cases

Analysis of Outliers

Why did the Turkish state initially accommodate the Jews of Istanbul only to target them with assimilationist policies in the late 1920s? Why did the Greek state accommodate the Muslims in Northen Greece following World War I only to oblige them to move to Turkey after 1923? How come the Romanian state accommodated the enemy-backed Hungarian minority rather than follow intense assimilationist policies as my argument predicts? Why did revisionist Albanian elites not target the Greek-backed communities in the south of their country with exclusionary policies but rather accommodated them? What accounts for the accommodation of most Eastern European Jewish communities immediately after World War I? Why were they not targeted with assimilationist policies as my theory predicts? Why were the Bulgarian-backed Slav Macedonians in status quo Greek Macedonia targeted with exclusionary policies rather than intense assimilationist ones? These and some more puzzles emerge from the incorrectly predicted cases from Chapter 4's statistical analysis (see Table 5.1).

Examination of these outliers reveals a few pertinent issues: the sensitivity of results to the time horizon of the study, the presence of mixed policies that undermine scholars' efforts to classify them, the distinction between nation-building policies that are terminal versus those that are transitional and actually have a different ultimate goal, as well as the role of external powers' foreign policy priorities and how symmetrical alliances are in the decision making process of host states. I also identify a divide-and-rule strategy that Balkan governments pursued both to fragment large groups and to prevent subnational assimilation of small non-core groups to larger ones. I discuss all of these issues in separate sections directly addressing each case but also using other examples from the twentieth-century Balkans.

TIME HORIZON

The time horizon of an analysis affects the conclusions we draw from it. Many existing works in political science evade this important issue. Hypotheses are

TABLE 5.1. *Incorrect Predictions*

Country	Non-Core Group	Group Larger Than 1%	Prediction	Policy
Albania	Greeks	Yes	Exclusion	Accommodation
	Montenegrins/ Serbs	No	Exclusion	Assimilation
Bulgaria	Gypsies	Yes	Assimilation	Accommodation
	Jews	No	Assimilation	Accommodation
Greece	Jews, Sephardim	Yes	Assimilation	Accommodation
	Muslims (Turks)	Yes	Assimilation	Accommodation
	Pomaks	No	Assimilation	Accommodation
	Slavs, "Bulgarian leaning"	Yes	Assimilation	Exclusion
Romania	Germans	Yes	Assimilation	Accommodation
	Hungarians	Yes	Assimilation	Accommodation
	Jews	Yes	Assimilation	Accommodation
The Kingdom of Serbs, Croats and Slovenes	Germans	Yes	Assimilation	Accommodation
	Greeks	No	Accommodation	Exclusion
	Hungarians	Yes	Assimilation	Accommodation
	Slovenes	Yes	Assimilation	Accommodation
	Jews	No	Assimilation	Accommodation
Turkey	Jews	No	Assimilation	Accommodation

tested in specific places and historical instances but sometimes processes take time to unfold. How can one decide the appropriate time horizon for testing certain hypotheses? Is it a year, a decade, or a generation? These are difficult but pertinent questions in the social sciences.

The short answer is that the appropriate time horizon for testing hypotheses depends on the phenomenon under study. If we want to test a theory about the rate of assimilation, then the appropriate time horizon is probably a generation or more. If our research question concerns the rate of acculturation – the acquisition of certain traits by a specific group – then a decade might be enough. Similarly, in the study of state-planned nation-building policies the time horizon depends on the aspect of the process on which we focus. If our aim is to understand policy choices by the ruling political elites of a state, our efforts should focus on the period of policy planning immediately after a critical event such as an annexation, a war, or a regime change. However, if our aim is to evaluate which nation-building policies are successful and under what circumstances, then we would have to allow for several decades to pass.

In this book I seek to identify the logic of state-planned nation-building policies toward non-core groups across states and over time. The research strategy I followed in Chapter 4 was to look at state policies immediately after World War I, an event that affected all societies in the region. This research strategy works well in cases where the initial conditions that propelled the policy do not change during the period of study. However, there are cases in my analysis where the initial conditions change profoundly during the first five years after the end of World War I.

For example, the Greek-Turkish War of 1919–1922 and the subsequent Turkish victory had a significant effect on the nation-building policies of the two states involved. In particular, whereas the Muslims in Northern Greece – foremost candidates for agitation by Turkey – were more or less accommodated until 1923, they became part of an obligatory population exchange thereafter.[1] Depending on the time horizon of our analysis we would code this case differently. This shift was not because the Greek government just changed its mind but rather because the values of important independent variables changed after Greece's defeat in the Greek-Turkish War.

Another example is that of the Jews in Turkey. According to my argument the Jews in Turkey should have been targeted with assimilationist policies since they did not enjoy the external support of any state and resided in a status quo state. However, the Jews were initially accommodated. As a result, this case is one of the outliers in my analysis. The first systematic effort for assimilation of the Jews in Turkey did not begin until late into the 1920s. In this example, if I had chosen a ten-year period for coding I would have coded the Jews in Turkey as being targeted with assimilationist policies – which is consistent with my prediction – but having chosen a five-year period I coded it as a case of accommodation.

A similar situation emerges when we look at the policies toward the "Bulgarian-leaning" Slavs in northern Greece (an enemy supported non-core group in a status quo state).[2] I predict assimilationist policies but code the case as one of exclusion. Again, a change in the time horizon of the analysis would result in different coding. This non-core group was initially targeted with assimilationist policies. However, with the treaty of Neuilly a voluntary population exchange led to the emigration of a significant part of this population to Bulgaria between 1919 and 1924. By 1924, the number of people who had emigrated was high enough to consider this a case of exclusion. But in 1919 or 1920, this was not the case and we would still code it as a case of assimilationist policies.

The Greeks in Albania (a non-core group supported by a hostile state and residing in a revisionist host state) should have been targeted with exclusionary

---

[1] Clark 2006; Hirschon 2003; Ladas 1932; Pentzopoulos 1962; Yıldırım 2006.
[2] I describe this category in more detail in Chapter 6. Eliakis referred to this group as Boulgarizontes, I translate this term as "Bulgarian-leaning" Slavs.

policies according to my argument, but they were accommodated instead. Albania was a new state whose existence was not guaranteed after the end of World War I. Italy had been promised significant portions of Albania in order to enter the war, Greece claimed the southern provinces, and the Serbs were occupying territories bordering Kosovo. The Allies – with the exception of the United States – were sympathetic to these plans. The Albanian reaction to these partitioning plans was decisive.

Early in 1920 the pro-Italian government was overthrown and replaced by a new government determined to secure the independence of Albania. At this point the Albanian authorities put pressure on the Greek community to declare that they preferred Albanian to Greek rule. According to the Greek General Governor of Epirus, Achilleas Kalevras,

[B]eing in a helpless situation these Christians are obliged, in order not to be subjugated by force, to flee their homes; thus the first significant exodus to the villages on our side of the border.[3]

However, Albania – or better the ruling elites in the south of the country – shifted from an enemy to an ally within a couple of days. In late May 1920, Prime Minister Venizelos was waiting for the final approval from Britain before he ordered the Greek military to annex southern Albanian territories –promised to Greece by the Allies during the January talks of the same year. Southern Albania had been under French administration up to that point. On 27 May 1920 the British government advised Venizelos not to occupy these territories because such an occupation would enrage the Albanians.[4] According to Kontis, the discovery of oil was the reason behind the British change of policy over Albania.[5] Considering that Venizelos was at that time negotiating for the Dodecanese Islands and Thrace and fighting in Asia Minor it is understandable that Greece was not in a position to occupy southern Albania without British approval. A principle emerges from this case: The ally of my ally is my friend.

The main concern of the Albanians at the time was ousting the Italian troops from Albanian soil. Albanians knew that Greece had military superiority and the Greek government did use its leverage to secure rights for the Greek community. In the absence of the British mediation and the consequent accord between Greece and Albania, the enemy-supported Greek population would have been left unprotected against the revisionist Albanian authorities and may have been targeted with exclusionary measures.[6]

As a result of Greek diplomatic maneuvering, however, a protocol was indeed signed on 28 May 1920 declaring friendly relations between Albania and Greece and obligations on the Albanian side to respect the Greek population in Albania

---

[3] AYE, 1920, A/5, no. 312, Achilleas Kalevras, General Governor of Epirus to Ministry of Foreign Affairs, Ioannina, 28 March 1920 (quoted in Kontis 1994: 123).

[4] Kontis 1994: 136.

[5] 1994: 137.

[6] Ibid., p. 139.

and allow the unobstructed operation of schools and churches.[7] This sudden change in diplomatic relations between the two countries surprised the Italian consul in Ioannina who wrote to the Greek Governor-General of Epirus:

We Italians are surprised by the Albanian pro-Greek demonstration at a moment when Greece has not given up her claims on Northern Epirus and has no interest in following a bunch of foolish Albanians in their anti-Italian policy.[8]

On 5 June 1920, a few days after the Albanians began their fight against the Italians, the Albanian government sent "a confidential circular announcing to the local Albanian authorities that the relations with Greece were cordial and that the Greek government was friendly."[9] The British intervention in favor of Albania and Venizelos's compliance prevented a military confrontation between the two states. Acting as a Great Power, Britain was trying to include the new Albanian state into its sphere of influence; thus, by extension, its allies would become Albania's allies.

To be sure, the balance of power between Greece and Albania also affected the interstate relations between the two countries. For example, as soon as the Albanians managed to successfully contain the Italians they also altered their diplomatic approach toward Greece. The emerging international context undermined Greek claims in Albania. By August 1920 the Albanians signed a protocol with the Italians that resulted in the latter withdrawing their troops from Albania and recognizing its independence. As a result of this Italian-Albanian reconciliation, the Albanians ended up refusing the validity of the Greek-Albanian protocol signed in May 1920. By December 1920, Albania had become a member of the League of Nations and in October 1921 its representative, Fan Noli, declared that his country would respect the rights of the Greek population. It is worth noting, however, that the Albanian government recognized a Greek minority only in the province of Argyrokastro (Gjirokastër) and not outside of that area.

From the discussion of the above cases it becomes clear that the values of crucial independent variables do not all change at the same time or with the same pace for every observation. This problem can be addressed in the context of a case study through meticulous process tracing; however, it is much harder to resolve when we conduct a cross-national analysis. Often important explanatory variables are not held constant over arbitrarily chosen periods of time. Five- or ten-year period intervals are commonly used for testing hypotheses but they are open to such problems. I address the problem of time horizons in this book by combining the cross-national test in Chapter 4 with carefully selected case studies in all other empirical chapters.

---

[7] Ibid., p. 143.
[8] AYE, 1920, A/5, no. 7122, Kalevras to Ministry of Foreign Affairs, Ioannina, 11 June 1920 (quoted in Kontis 1994: 145).
[9] AYE, 1920, A/5, no. 7154, Kalevras to Ministry of Foreign Affairs, Ioannina, 10 June 1920 (quoted in Kontis 1994: 145).

MIXED POLICIES

Another issue that stems from the analysis of the outliers is that ruling political elites did not always apply policies uniformly to all the members of a non-core group. Although non-uniform application of nation-building policies was unusual, it did occur. In some cases, the application consisted of a strategy of divide and rule, which I discuss separately in the last section of this chapter. In other cases, variation in application was merely a function of capabilities and military expedience.

The Slav Macedonians in Greek Macedonia (discussed as "Bulgarian leaning Slavs" in Chapter 6) are a case of nonuniform application of nation-building policies by the ruling political elites. The policies toward this non-core group were harsher for those living close to the borders with Bulgaria, many of whom were internally displaced.[10] Moreover, young people were targeted with intensive assimilationist policies while older ones were not. According to my theory, "Bulgarian-leaning" Slavs in Greece should have been targeted with intense assimilation policies and indeed they were for a couple of years before the Treaty of Neuilly was signed (1919) and the voluntary population exchange between Greece and Bulgaria began.

Archival research allowed me to study this case in depth. As I discuss in Chapter 6, my theory correctly predicts the intentions of the Greek administration. "Bulgarian-leaning" Slavs were supported by a revisionist enemy power while the Greek administration wanted to preserve the international status quo in Greek Macedonia. Consequently, assimilationist policies, taking the form of colonization and internal displacement of the non-core group, were the preferred choice. After World War I, however, a voluntary population exchange between Greece and Bulgaria under the treaty of Neuilly was decided upon by the respective governments. As a result, about 56,000 Bulgarians left Greece for Bulgaria, "in many cases being forced to emigrate by the Greek authorities."[11] However, the picture is complicated by IMRO's efforts to discourage "Bulgarian-leaning" Slavs from leaving in order to preserve Bulgarian territorial claims in Greek Macedonia and further complicated by some voluntary departures to Bulgaria. Nevertheless, the members of the group who remained in Greece continued to be targeted with assimilationist policies and were not granted minority status. Thus, this case has elements of both exclusion and assimilation.

This case highlights an important caveat for my argument. Governments may intentionally follow mixed policies toward non-core groups. How often this is the case is an empirical question. In my statistical analysis I necessarily simplified the picture and focused on the "dominant" strategy. However, as the case of the "Bulgarian-leaning" Slavs in Greece shows, the ruling political elites might

---

[10] This is consistent with James Ron's argument; see Ron 2003.
[11] Michailidis 2005: 94.

choose to follow a mixed strategy of assimilation toward one part of a non-core group and exclusion of another part of the same group.

Turning to another of my outliers, the Hungarians in Romania, we see a similar pattern. Coding this case was challenging, as the initial intentions of the Romanian elites seemed to be rather assimilationist – if not exclusionary – in an effort to "Romanize" Transylvania, but their consequent policies were accommodationist. Romanians granted minimal minority rights to the Hungarian population that remained in Romanian Transylvania. Nevertheless, around 200,000 Hungarians from Transylvania fled to Hungary between 1918 and 1922, followed by another 170,000 over the remainder of the interwar period.[12] But the majority of Hungarians stayed in Romania and their differences were perpetuated through separate schools, associations, and their own political party. The case of Hungarians in Romania again raises the issue of coding policies based on an arbitrarily chosen threshold.

The threshold one sets in coding is crucial in such cases. Almost 23 percent of the total population of Hungarians left Romanian Transylvania for Hungary during the interwar period. Thus 77 percent of the Hungarians stayed in Romania but 23 percent fled the nationalizing policies of the Romanian state. If we set a coding threshold of 20 percent we could conclude that the Hungarians were targeted with exclusionary policies. I set a higher threshold and thus code this as a case of accommodation. Actually, the intentions of the Romanian administration were – at least initially – assimilationist but the policies granted minority rights to the Hungarians. Hungarians were discriminated against and targeted with nationalizing policies but ultimately they were accommodated. This was of course related to the treaties that Romania had signed after World War I that required accommodation as a policy toward the Hungarians. This international constraint definitely mattered. But at the same time as I show later accommodation was a transitional policy, not a terminal one.[13]

Moving from Romania to the Kingdom of Serbs, Croats and Slovenes we find another community of Hungarians. Again in this case we have a relatively large group supported by an enemy state[14] and living in a host state that wants to preserve the international status quo. As Sajti put it, "Hungarian governments never gave up hopes of securing a revision of the terms of the Treaty of Trianon, although they were all too aware that the international climate for attaining that was unfavourable."[15] Given that the newly-founded kingdom of the Serbs, Croats, and Slovenes was on the side of the winners and wanted to preserve

---

[12] Kovrig 2000: 34.

[13] For more on this distinction, see the next section.

[14] "In order to provide support for Hungarian communities outside the country's borders, Bethlen [Prime Minister of Hungary from 1921 to 1931] in 1921, established a supposedly secret ministry to exercise political influence on those communities through an openly operating blanket organisation called the Federation of Social Associations (TESZK), through which fairly generous financial support was given to Hungarian political and cultural organisations in Slovakia, Transylvania and the Voivodina" (Sajti 2006: 117).

[15] 2006: 116.

the status quo, my argument predicts that the Hungarians should have been targeted with assimilationist policies.

Indeed, after the annexation of Vojvodina to the Kingdom of Serbs, Croats and Slovenes, primary and secondary level Hungarian-language schools were all closed down.[16] The extensive land reform implemented in the new Kingdom was very much felt in Vojvodina as well. "[T]he avowed goal of such resettlements was to populate the territories lying along the northern borders of Yugoslavia with 'reliable Slavs' to offset the majority, the 'unreliable Magyars.'"[17]

Nevertheless, the Hungarians of Vojvodina had their own party and cultural associations, and some Hungarian-speaking schools reopened in the region. Sajti provides an explanation of the public accommodation of Hungarians in the interwar period:

The League of Nations mechanism for the protection of minorities may have offered some safeguards of minority rights (elementary education in the mother tongue, etc.) and, as a creation of the post-1918 European order, Yugoslavia[18] was in no position to reject the basic principles of the international regime for the protection of minorities that the victorious Allies had established.[19]

But the Hungarian population living in Vojvodina was also targeted with an extensive colonization campaign as well as some measures aiming at the nationalization of the economy and of the administration of the region. The Kingdom of Yugoslavia, however, did not try to eradicate the cultural differences and way of life of this non-core group. A mixed policy was pursued.

Although I extensively discussed the case of the Greeks in southern Albania in the previous section, it also deserves treatment here. The Albanian government's policies toward the Greeks, during the Greek-Albanian dispute over the delimitation of the territorial borders of Albania, were exclusionary. As we have seen, however, as soon as the interstate relations between the two countries changed, the policy shifted to one of accommodation. Notably, when Fan Noli referred to the Greek population and its accommodation he meant only the Greeks inhabiting a specific region in southern Albania. The Albanian government tried to assimilate Greeks living outside the designated area and accommodated only the ones concentrated within that area. According to Kontis:

---

[16] Ramet 2006: 51. As Sajti put it, "Hungarian civil servants and railwaymen were dismissed *en masse*, the judiciary was replaced, and the Hungarian secondary school system was dismantled, followed by the primary system. The nationalist character of the Yugoslav land reform, which dragged on to the end of the 1930s, weakened the traditional Hungarian gentry class while doing nothing to help the peasantry, who made up the bulk of the population in the Voivodina: landless agricultural labourers of Hungarian ethnicity were not given any land" (2006: 112).

[17] Sajti 2006: 112.

[18] King Aleksandar changed the name of Kingdom of Serbs, Croats, and Slovenes into Kingdom of Yugoslavia in the beginning of 1929. In an effort to avoid anachronisms, I use the appropriate name for the period I am discussing.

[19] Sajti 2006: 117.

The Albanian government allowed the operation of Greek schools only in the areas where the presence of a Greek population was officially recognized and prohibited Greek language instruction in all other Albanian-speaking areas.... Concerning education, the goal of the Albanians was to ban private education and to impose an absolute state monopoly.[20]

These efforts were not limited to the educational establishments of the Greek community but extended to its religious organization as well. Albanian nationalists tried to establish an Autocephalous Christian Orthodox Church of Albania in order to prevent either the Greek-dominated Ecumenical Patriarchate in Istanbul or the Autocephalous Orthodox Church of Greece from interfering in the domestic politics of Albania.[21] The attempts to assimilate the Greek population, though largely unsuccessful, were indicative of the Albanian government's intentions.

But the Albanian government had also undertaken certain obligations under the supervision of the League of Nations in order to achieve international recognition of its independence in the early 1920s; it had to respect the minority rights of the Greek non-core group, among other things. As a result of this commitment the Albanian government did recognize a Greek minority in Albania but only in designated parts of the country. The members of this non-core group that resided outside of those parts were targeted with assimilationist policies that potentially aimed at forcing them to return to Greece. This latter point brings us to the issue discussed in the next section.

TERMINAL VERSUS TRANSITIONAL POLICIES

A third insight arises from a careful study of nation-building policies in the Balkans, the distinction between terminal and transitional policies. We should therefore try to discern when long-term goals and short-term policies coincide and when not. This distinction between terminal and transitional policies is linked to a broader consideration concerning the impact of the international standard of minority rights protection in each era. For example, following World War I Britain was a proponent of the League of Nations and the protection of minority rights but its ultimate goal at the time was not the creation of multinational states. The British government's rationale was that such guarantees for national minorities would facilitate the initial coexistence of core and non-core groups and would pave the way for future assimilation to the dominant culture.

Ruling political elites in the Balkans were attuned to these realities and international norms surrounding nation-building. Given this context, in some cases Balkan states chose to follow a policy of accommodation for a certain period before they applied assimilationist policies. Cases of this sort include the Jews in Turkey, who were initially accommodated but toward the end of the

[20] 1994: 154–155.
[21] Kontis 1994: 157–158.

1920s were targeted with assimilationist policies, as well as the Muslims in Greek Macedonia, who were initially accommodated but with an intention to ultimately assimilate them as Greek officials indicated in their confidential reports (see Chapter 6). The important point to note here is that in both cases the host state's intention was assimilationist from the beginning.

According to my theory, the Muslims in Greece should have been targeted with assimilationist policies after World War I since they were members of an enemy-supported group living in a state that favored the international status quo. In the five-year period before the obligatory population exchange between Greece and Turkey occurred we observe a policy of accommodation and only a few selectively targeted exclusionary measures. Without archival material it would have been impossible to discern whether the ultimate goal was their assimilation or not. However, from the evidence I have gathered,[22] we find that accommodation in this case was in fact mainly a transitional policy.

It is in this connection that my incorrect predictions with respect to the five Jewish communities in the Balkans are not surprising. According to my coding criteria the Jews in the Balkans were a non-core group with no external state supporting them and as such they should have been targeted with assimilationist policies. In reality, they were all granted minority rights – at least in the period under study. This clearly contradicts my predictions. What accounts for the accommodation of most Eastern European Jewish communities immediately after World War I? Why weren't they targeted with assimilationist policies? Coding the Jewish communities in the Balkans as a non-core group with no external support – as I did in Chapter 4 – is problematic. My hypothesis is that the Jews were actually accommodated because they were perceived as being supported by the British – the victors of World War I – as well as a rapidly growing Zionist movement. Here, I briefly probe this hypothesis, but a comprehensive answer to this set of questions is beyond the scope of this book.

Around seven million Jews lived in Eastern Europe at the time and the fact that there was no Jewish homeland yet complicated the picture and added to the uncertainty surrounding the future fate of Jews in Europe.[23] The participants in the Paris Peace Conference in 1919 knew well that the British had promised to support the creation of a Jewish state. Everyone was familiar with Balfour's Declaration.[24] The endorsement of the declaration by the Supreme Council of the Peace Conference during the first days sent a clear signal to everyone that the Jews were to be treated as a national minority in the post–World War I world.[25]

Let us take a closer look at this transformation of the Jewish people from religious to national minority. A characteristic incident dates as far back as 1912

---

[22] See Chapter 6.
[23] For more on the link between the Jewish Question and the protection of minority rights in Europe, see Janowsky 1966.
[24] "Palestine for the Jews. Official Sympathy," *The Times*, 9 November 1917.
[25] MacMillan 2002.

when Dr. Adolf Friedemann[26] traveled to Vienna – sent by the Berlin-based Zionist
Actions Committee – to lobby on behalf of the Jews of Thessaloniki. There he met
with the First Director of the Ministry of Foreign Affairs of Austria-Hungary, Baron
Karl Macchio, and argued for the coincidence of interest between the Austro-
Hugarian Government and of the Jews in the internationalization of
Thessaloniki.[27] In his presentation, Dr. Friedemann informed the Baron, "[w]e
[the Zionist Actions Committee] are interested in the Salonikan Jews from a
nationalist point of view."[28] The Baron, baffled by the treatment of the Jews as
a nationality, asked for an explanation. Dr. Friedemann replied:

The Jews of Salonika are Sephardim. They have never assimilated and have always
retained their particular characteristics and maintained contacts with the Jews of
Palestine. Incidentally, we are interested in the Jews of the East [in general] from the
stand-point of nationality.[29]

The internationalization of Thessaloniki did not materialize but on 18 January
1913, Dr. Friedemann was informed that "the joint Austro-Hungarian cabinet
had decided to demand at the peace conference political guarantees for the Jews
in the captured territories."[30]

The combination of Zionist activism illustrated above and Balfour's
Declaration – endorsed by the Supreme Council of the Paris Peace
Conference – invited state elites to consider the Jewish communities in Europe
as "national minorities" supported by the victors of the war. Mark Levene notes
that already in October 1918, the Zionist leadership had voiced its demands for
"national autonomy in the diaspora" as a necessary corollary to "a national
home in Palestine" next to the demand that the Jewish people should be admitted
to the League of Nations.[31]

The fate of Jews in the Balkans would more or less be decided at the Paris
Peace Conference. The solution first developed with respect to the Jews in Poland
functioned more or less as a prototype for the other cases. One of the national
autonomy clauses of the Minorities Treaty signed in Paris mentioned the Jews by
name.[32] This arrangement was to be protected in two ways: First, international
treaties and safeguards provided civil and political rights as well as cultural

---

[26] "The Berlin lawyer Dr. Adolf Friedemann (1871–1932) . . . An aide of Herzl, he was a member of
the Zionist Action Committee and the co-founder of the 'Kommittee fur den Osten.' He published
Reisebilder aus Paldstina (Berlin 1904), Herzl's first biography, Das Leben Theodor Herzls
(Vienna 1919) and Dawid Wolffsohn. Biographie (Berlin 1915)" (Gelber et al. 1955: 107).

[27] Austria supported this plan in an effort to preserve the rights it had secured from the Ottoman
Empire to connect Vienna with Thessaloniki by a railroad passing through Budapest. For a
thorough presentation of the involvement of the Zionist movement in this affair, see Gelber
et al. 1955.

[28] Zionist Archives, Jerusalem, Files of the Berlin Zionist Bureau [=ZBB], 538, Quoted in Gelber
et al. 1955: 111.

[29] Ibid.

[30] Gelber et al. 1955: 112.

[31] 1993: 520.

[32] Levene 1993: 523.

rights to the Jews and other minorities in all the new states, guaranteed by the League of Nations. The Jews and other recognized minorities had the right to run their own schools and cultural organizations in their own language.[33] Second, "a series of negotiations leading to private arrangements with senior East European statesmen" also protected this arrangement.[34]

The British Foreign Office had already endorsed this latter method since November 1918 with the following guidelines:

> In all countries with Jewish inhabitants but especially in East and South-East Europe where the Jews form a large and more separate element in the population than elsewhere, the spokesmen of this Jewish element, if they put forward demands for cultural autonomy as well as individual citizen rights, should be recommended in the first instance to discuss the question with the government or other representative parties of their respective countries. They should be discouraged from referring this question to outside Powers of the Peace Conference before they have done their utmost to arrive at a settlement with peoples among whom they respectively live.[35]

From the discussion it becomes clear that the various governments – at least in Eastern Europe – had plenty of reasons to treat the Jews as a national minority. For example, it was in an effort to impress the peacemakers that the governments of Ukraine and Lithuania introduced national autonomy programs for the Jews in their lands. With similar ends in mind they included Jewish elites in their delegations at the Peace Conference.

Eastern European leaders reacted negatively to what they perceived as favoritism toward a newly constructed Jewish national minority mostly using state sovereignty arguments. The new system lacked the means to enforce its decisions but in many cases it accounted for the initial accommodation of Jewish communities. Despite these policies of accommodation, however, the pogroms of Jews in Ukraine that took place in 1919 were instructive. As Lucien Wolf,[36] a British journalist and Jewish leader, put it in his diary of the Paris Peace Conference:

> For us [British Jewry] to give any advice to the Jews of the Ukraine is impossible. We cannot advise them to be good Ukrainians without the risk that we are setting them against the Entente and asking them to be traitors to Russia. We cannot ask them to support the cause of an undivided Russia without pillorying them as enemies of their country's national cause. We cannot recognize them to be neutral without recognizing a Jewish nationality and setting both Russians and Ukrainians and probably also

---

[33] Ibid., 523–524.

[34] Ibid., 524.

[35] Quoted in ibid., 530.

[36] "Lucien Wolf (1857–1930), English historian and Jewish leader, was editor of the Jewish World (1874–93) and of the Daily Graphic (1890–1909). He was a founder of the Jewish Historical Society of England in 1893 and secretary of the Conjoint Foreign Committee." "The Conjoint Foreign Committee of the Board of Deputies of British Jews and of the Anglo-Jewish Association was established in connection with the Congress of Berlin (1878) and was most active during the peace conferences after World War I" (Gelber et al. 1955: 114).

Bolshevists, Poles and Rumanians against them ... the problem is an extremely difficult one. It shows how dangerous it is to mix up *raison d'etat* with a *politique des principes.*[37]

A closer look at one of the Jewish communities in the Balkans – that of Thessaloniki, Greece – can prove instructive. The center of Jewish life in the Balkans was Thessaloniki. Up to the annexation of Thessaloniki to the Greek state, the Greek authorities perceived the Jews as Turcophiles, "anti-Greek, disloyal, and untrustworthy"[38] and plans for the internationalization of the city were popular amongst the Jewish community.[39] Following the annexation three camps emerged within the Jewish community of Thessaloniki: the Zionist, the Socialist (later Communist), and that of the supporters of assimilation.[40] The first two camps constituted the overwhelming majority and opposed assimilation.

According to my argument the Jews of Thessaloniki should have been targeted with assimilationist policies since they had no external state supporting them and the Greek state was dominated by ruling political elites with a clear national character in mind. However, immediately after Greece annexed Thessaloniki the Jews were accommodated, although the terminal policy was assimilation.[41]

Although it seems counterintuitive that the Greek government did not pursue at first assimilationist policies, upon consideration of the international context described above the case becomes less puzzling. Greece was an ally of the Entente powers and its territorial expansion had been supported and legitimized by Britain and France. Britain was arguably the most important external supporter of Venizelos and by extension of Greece at the time. Once again, your ally's ally is your friend.

According to the Balfour Declaration in 1917, the Jews were promised their own national home in Palestine and therefore had been officially discussed as a national minority.[42] Greece did not want to jeopardize its alliance with Britain. Greece had to recognize minority rights for the Jews in order to retain support from its allies. Moreover, the Greek government could not say one thing and do another because the Jewish community lived in an urban center with many consuls and much international attention. Moreover, the Chief Rabbi had important international connections himself – aside from the international Zionist movement.[43] Regardless, the Greek administration had a clear view at the time: its ultimate goal was assimilation.

---

[37] 1919: 510–11.
[38] Fleming 2008: 57.
[39] Mazower 2004.
[40] Mavrogordatos 1983: 263.
[41] Rena Molho. *The Jerusalem of the Balkans: Salonica 1856–1919.* The Jewish Museum of Thessaloniki: http://www.jmth.gr/web/thejews/pages/pages/history/pages/his.htm. URL accessed 23 April 2008.
[42] For the reasons behind the Balfour declaration, see Friedman 1973, Sanders 1984, Stein 1961.
[43] For more information on the important activities of the Zionist movement on behalf of the Jews of Thessaloniki, see Gelber et al. 1955.

Finally, we have to further distinguish transitional policies from policy changes resulting from a learning process. Ruling political elites might consciously pursue one policy toward a group with the ultimate intention of another as described by the Governor-General of Macedonia in his report to the Ministry of Foreign Affairs.[44] However, there are cases where the ruling political elites have tried assimilation, decided at some point that it cannot work, and, as a result, changed their policy to exclusion or even accommodation. It is very difficult to discern which of these different paths is at play without detailed archival research. Such an effort is nonetheless worthwhile, as it is the only way to resolve these instances of observational equivalence. A failure to address this problem could lead to policies predicted correctly, but for the wrong reasons, which in turn would keep us from falsifying incorrect hypotheses and consequently improving our understanding of the process of nation-building.

FOREIGN POLICY PRIORITIES AND ASYMMETRIC ALLIANCES

The Greeks in the Kingdom of Serbs, Croats and Slovenes were a non-core group supported by an ally and residing in a status quo host state. According to my argument they should have been accommodated. Instead, the Greek community of Monastir was targeted with intense assimilationist policies that led to the ultimate migration of most of the group to Greece. This counterintuitive case highlights two important dimensions of the dynamics of external support that were not directly discussed in my theory chapter: foreign policy priorities and asymmetrical alliances.

Greece at the time was operating as an external supporter of a few non-core groups in the near abroad. The Greek government had to make choices about which of these groups were the most strategically important. In this calculation the preservation of a Greek minority in Southern Serbia was not a priority for the Greek government when compared with the Greek community in Asia Minor.[45] The Greek government had given up any effort to preserve a Greek minority in Southern Serbia by the end of World War I. Prime Minister Venizelos was looking primarily eastward to Asia Minor and Thrace and northwest to Northern Epirus (or Southern Albania). In both cases Venizelos relied on Greece's alliance with the Kingdom of Serbs, Croats and Slovenes to achieve these goals.

An additional consideration is that Greece may have been relying on this alliance more than Yugoslavia. This raises another important point about the nature of interstate relations. It suggests that the role of an alliance, that is, accommodation of non-core groups supported by allies, may depend on the extent to which this alliance is symmetrical. As Walt points out: "Alliances may ... be symmetrical or asymmetrical, depending on whether the members possess roughly equal capabilities and take on broadly identical commitments

[44] AYE, 1921, 41/2, Governor-General of Macedonia to Ministry of Foreign Affairs, 29 August 1919, Thessaloniki.
[45] Llewellyn-Smith 1998.

to each other."[46] Thus, we may need to relax that assumption for cases of asymmetrical alliances or cases where the commitments and goals of the allies diverge.

Given the situation, the Serbian authorities – operating within the context of a status quo Kingdom – pursued assimilationist policies toward most non-core groups in southern Serbia including the Greeks.[47] This option was available because of the asymmetric nature of the alliance with Greece but also because Greece had clearly signaled that it would not go out of its way to protect the rights of this group. The actual implementation of these policies was harsher than planned because of principal-agent problems between the Serbian political elites and the military establishment.[48] This, coupled with the limited interest of the Greek government in this minority ultimately led to the mass migration of Greeks to their "homeland" across the border.

A "DIVIDE AND RULE" STRATEGY

A few groups that should have been targeted with assimilationist policies according to my theory were accommodated instead. In half of these cases (six out of twelve) a "divide and rule" dynamic appears to be operative. With this term I refer to the counterintuitive minority proliferation aiming either at the fragmentation of a large group or the reversal of a subnational assimilation pattern. For example, Seton-Watson points out that the Romanians granted minority rights to the Germans in order to reverse the process of Magyarization that had taken root within the German community of Romania.[49]

This divide and rule policy was a systematic pattern in the twentieth-century Balkans with respect to Muslims in Christian-dominated countries. Scholars have discussed the accommodation of Gypsies (nowadays referred to as Roma) and Pomaks – Muslims speaking a Bulgarian dialect – in Greece and Bulgaria at specific periods during the twentieth century as an attempt to weaken the Muslim communities in both countries and prevent the subnational assimilation of these groups into their respective Turkish minority.[50]

This pattern was not special to the interwar period. For example, in 1962 after a trend of Turkification of Gypsies had emerged, the Bulgarian Politburo decided to intensify its assimilation policies. The first step it took was to stop the Turkification trend by ensuring that Gypsies, Tatars, and Bulgarian-speaking Muslims were "registered with their real nationality"; prohibiting Turkish language instruction of non-Turkish children, banning their internal migration to Turkish-dominated villages, and so on. Following this Politburo decision,

---

[46] 1997: 157.
[47] Vasiliadis 2004. BNA, FO 371/14317 [C5316,/82/7] "The Origins of the Macedonian Revolutionary Organization and Its History since the Great War," 1 July 1930, p. 9,
[48] For more on principal-agent problems in nation-building, see Chapters 7 and 8.
[49] 1962.
[50] Kostopoulos 2009; Tsitselikis 2012.

around 100,000 Gypsies who had identified themselves as Turks in the census were forced to change their names to Bulgarian ones.[51]

Similarly, during the 1990s and after the collapse of the Soviet bloc the Greek government once again recognized the presence of Pomaks in Western Thrace as a non-core group separate from that the rest of the "Muslims." For most of the Cold War the Pomaks were submerged into the larger "Muslim" minority of Western Thrace. This submersion was a way to prevent the Pomaks from being used by the Bulgarian government (member of the Soviet bloc) in order to interfere in Greek (member of NATO) internal affairs. After the collapse of the Soviet Union the Greek government was no longer considering Bulgaria an enemy power and could thus recognize the Pomaks as a distinct Muslim group and thus fragmenting the Turkish-dominated Muslim minority of Western Thrace.[52] More empirical work is necessary to study this pattern through the archives in Bulgaria and Greece.[53]

CONCLUSION

In Chapter 4, I have shown that whether a non-core group enjoys external support or not and the interstate relations between host states and external powers account for the variation in nation-building policies in the interwar Balkans. But here I focused on the incorrect predictions of my theory and identified important methodological caveats in the study of nation-building policies. To sum up, the periodization we choose affects the results we get; policies are not always mutually exclusive; a mix of policies can be pursued in some cases toward the same non-core group; often the initial policy pursued by governments is merely a transitional strategy aimed at achieving a distinct long-term objective; and external powers' foreign policy priorities and the degree to which alliances are asymmetrical significantly impact the decision making process of host states with respect to nation-building. Furthermore, from the analysis of the outliers, a counterintuitive "divide and rule" strategy also emerges. Balkan ruling elites often chose to strategically accommodate certain non-core groups in order to prevent their subnational assimilation to larger and more threatening non-core groups. Finally, there are a few cases where change of policy is the result of learning through failure of a previous policy but a *longue durée* approach is necessary to explore such patterns.[54]

[51] Eminov 1997.
[52] Kostopoulos 2009.
[53] Aarbakke 2000; Anagnostou 2005 and 2007; Troumbeta 2001.
[54] Braudel 1980.

6

Subnational Variation

Greek Nation-Building in Western Macedonia, 1916–1920

How well does my theory explain state policies toward non-core groups at the subnational level? What accounts for variation in nation-building policies toward different non-core groups within one state? Using both secondary sources and archival material, I focus on the province of Western Macedonia, annexed by Greece during the Balkan Wars, and account for the variation in the nation-building policies planned by the ruling political elites administering the region. I find that the Greek government chose its nation-building policies based not on objective measures of cultural distance or deep-rooted ethnic hatred, but on security and geostrategic concerns. The diplomatic relations between competitor states and Greece within the context of World War I largely determined both the perception of the non-core groups inside Greece and their consequent treatment.

My analysis is based on archival research conducted in Greece in 2006 and 2007. For the purposes of this chapter, I rely mostly on a compilation of reports written by Ioannis Eliakis between 1916 and 1920. To contextualize Eliakis's reports I use both secondary sources and archival material.[1] Ioannis Eliakis was a close friend of Prime Minister Venizelos from the island of Crete. Born in 1878, he was an MP in autonomous Crete, worked in Venizelos's newspaper, and published his own newspaper "Crete" from December 1912 to August 1913. Prime Minister Eleftherios Venizelos sent Eliakis to the recently annexed Macedonia in July 1916 as a representative of the Liberal Party. On 16 September 1916 he led the Revolutionary movement in Western Macedonia. A month later the Provisional Government in Thessaloniki appointed Eliakis as their representative in Kozani and Florina prefectures and later on Governor-General of

---

[1] For this chapter I conducted research in Greece at the Museum of the Macedonian Struggle, Pavlos Kalligas Archive (PKA), Thessaloniki; the Historical and Diplomatic Archives of the the Ministry of Foreign Affairs; Municipal Library, Kozani; the Eleftherios Venizelos Archive, Benaki Museum, Athens; General State Archives, Florina; General State Archives, Kozani; General State Archives of Macedonia, Thessaloniki; Gennadius Library, Athens; and the Hellenic Literary and Historical Archive, Thessaloniki. All translations from the archival material are mine.

Western Macedonia.[2] He remained there until 1 November 1920, when Venizelos was defeated in the election.[3]

From 1916 to 1920, Eliakis was the ultimate authority in that region. His decisions overrode those of any other state official, including military officers. His reports had a wide range of recipients: the Prime Minister, the Ministries of the Interior, Foreign Affairs, and, last but not least, the Ministry of Military Affairs.[4]

More importantly, Eliakis was part of a like-minded political elite surrounding Venizelos at the time including Governor-General of Epirus Aristeidis Stergiadis,[5] Governor-General of Eastern Thrace Harisios Vamvakas, Minister of Interior and Deputy Prime Minister Emmanuel Repoulis, Minister of Foreign Affairs Nikolaos Politis, member of the Greek-Bulgarian Mixed Commission Alexandros Pallis, Governor-General of Macedonia Adosidis and many more.[6]

The focus of Eliakis's work was the national integration of Western Macedonia to the Greek nation-state. This nation-building effort took place during the turbulent period following the Balkan Wars and during World War I in a region that was under the Ottoman administrative system for centuries and was composed of a linguistically, religiously, and culturally heterogeneous population.

The scope conditions of my argument are met, but more importantly from the perspective of testing my argument Greece's foreign policy goals shifted over this period. During World War I, Greece was fighting for the preservation of its gains from the Balkan Wars and for redeeming its co-ethnics in Asia Minor.[7] Following World War I, Greece was trying to secure its territorial gains. Moreover, some non-core groups had no external links, while some were supported by allied states and others by enemy states.

The combination of the rich archival material I have unearthed and the important variation in my main independent variables render this region an ideal location to study the politics of nation-building and test my theory. This type of analysis has two key benefits: first, the material allows me to detect the intentions behind the inception and planning of the various policies concerning the non-core groups residing in this region; second, it serves as a test for the micro-foundations of my theory. We rarely have the opportunity to access the reasoning behind the planning of such measures. Yet this type of evidence is crucial to address issues of observational equivalence and allows me to test the causal mechanisms I laid out in Chapter 2.

[2] Western Macedonia is delimited by mountains: Pindos and Grammos in the west; Vitsi, Peristeri, and Kaimaktsalan in the north; Olympus, Kambounia, and Chassia in the south; and Vermion in the east. The largest cities at the time were Florina, Kastoria, Kozani, and Grevena (see Map 6.2). See Kontogiorgi 2006, p. 13.
[3] Eliakis also became the President of the Council of Greek Scouts during the short-lived Pangalos dictatorship and later on the representative of the Mount Athos Monasteries to Athens (from 1929 to the late 1930s). For more information on Eliakis and his life, see Eliakis 1940.
[4] PKA, Eliakis to Greek Ministry of Foreign Affairs, 22 January 1920.
[5] Later on Stergiadis became the High Commissioner in Smyrna (1919–22).
[6] For more, see Glavinas 2008 and Llewellyn-Smith 1998.
[7] Llewellyn-Smith 1998.

Studying a specific region in depth allows me to trace the logic behind the nation-building policies proposed by the Greek administration. Focusing on one region I can control for many state- and regional-level hypotheses such as levels of economic development, regime type, elite understandings of nationhood, and international norms, and test the plausibility of my argument against three main alternative arguments: the cultural distance, status reversal, and homeland arguments.

THE CONTEXT

World War I and the National Schism in Greece

When World War I broke out, geographic Macedonia – "a distinct geographic region of rugged mountains, high intermontane basins, and fertile lowland plains"[8] – once again became the center of controversy (see Map 6.1).[9] As described in Chapter 3, Serbia and Bulgaria had entered World War I on opposite sides of the conflict. Bulgaria allied with the Central Powers, and in October 1915 Entente forces landed in Thessaloniki to assist Serbia.[10]

Around the same time, a national schism had developed in Greece, which was the culmination of an ongoing domestic conflict between pro-German King Constantine and pro-Entente Venizelos. Venizelos's government pushed for the entry of Greece in the war on the side of Entente; King Constantine's plan was to stay out of World War I and to sustain a "small but honorable Greece."[11] This disagreement between Venizelos and the King led to the resignation of the former in February 1915 and the formation of a government led by the Anti-Venizelists. The elections of 31 May 1915 turned into a referendum to decide Greece's position in World War I. Venizelists, Independents, and Anti-Venizelists exchanged accusations with regard to promises – especially in terms of land rights – made to Muslim voters in order to gain their electoral support.[12] The result was an overwhelming support for the Anti-Venizelists in Greek Macedonia and the dispute of the electoral result by the Venizelists. The central claim of the latter was the fact that the Muslims voted regardless of their citizenship status.[13]

However, Venizelos's victory in the 31 May elections did not suffice and a new round of bickering led to his second resignation within a year in September. New elections were scheduled for 6 December but the Venizelists decided not to participate. With the Entente powers already operating in the north of Greece

---

[8] Kostanick 1948: 6.

[9] Barker 1950.

[10] During World War I, Russia aimed for Istanbul and, according to many observers of the day, wanted to conquer the southern shores of the Black Sea as well. Italy wanted to secure control of both sides of the Adriatic. Germany supported Austria-Hungary in its effort to weaken Serbia and hold its Slavic lands in the Balkans. For the military events of the period, see General Staff of the Army 1958.

[11] Mavrogordatos 1982 and 1983.

[12] For more on this, see Glavinas 2008: 230.

[13] Ibid., 231.

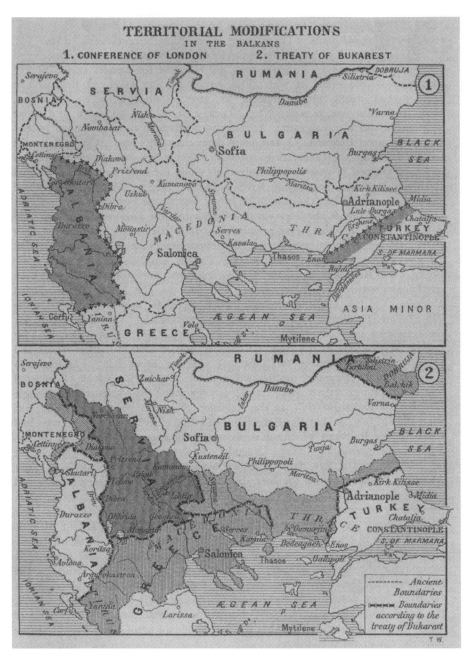

MAP 6.1. Boundary changes after the Balkan Wars, 1912–1913.
Source: Report of the International Commission to Inquire into the Causes and Conduct of the Balkan Wars, Carnegie Endowment for International Peace, 1914. www. CarnegieEndowment.org.

and Venizelos's Liberal Party not participating, the 6 December elections were peculiar to say the least. Regardless, in Western Macedonia they turned into a headcount between the Anti-Venizelist party led by Gounaris – that kept courting the Muslims – and the National Slate (Ethnikos Syndyasmos) Party – a splinter of the Anti-Venizelist coalition together with some Independents – which claimed to represent the Greeks of the area and tried to polarize the vote along ethnoreligious lines.[14] The Anti-Venizelists won, of course, but so did abstention. In Kozani, the capital of Western Macedonia and later Eliakis's post, only 7,000 out of 25,000 registered Greeks voted in the election following Venizelos's request to abstain.[15]

Skouloudis formed an Anti-Venizelist government following the 6 December 1915 election; however, Great Britain and France reacted to the capitulation of Fort Roupel – an important military stronghold – to German and Bulgarian forces in May 1916 by demanding the demobilization of the loyalist elements in the Greek army and pushing for new elections in the fall.[16] To enforce their will they also implemented blockades on Greek ports.[17] In the midst of these developments Ioannis Eliakis moved to Greek Macedonia in July 1916, as a representative of Venizelos's Liberal Party, and was faced with a challenging situation.

Entente forces had been stationed in northern Greece since September 1915, and yet another pre-election period began. The non-core groups of the area supported the Anti-Venizelists in the 1915 elections. Foreign propaganda had been extremely active in the recent past in an attempt to influence the vote of the local population. But in the end, none of Eliakis's campaigning efforts was put into test – not until 1920 – since the planned election never took place.

In August 1916, Bulgarian and German troops occupied both Eastern and much of Western Greek Macedonia. This was a final blow to the territorial integrity of Greece. The internal fighting between Venizelists and Anti-Venizelists and the Entente reactions led to the National Defense revolt, orchestrated by Venizelist forces in Thessaloniki, and to the peculiar situation of two governments in Greece. In fact, Eliakis had already led a revolutionary movement in Western Macedonia on 16 September 1916 in response to fears concerning Serbian plans for Greek Macedonia.[18] Eliakis knew that Greece's neutrality under King Constantine had allowed discussions between the Allies and Serbia concerning the future role of Serbia in Macedonia. This is yet another example of how precarious alliances can be and how they change in ways that are not endogenous to nation-building policies.

---

[14] Glavinas 2008: 232–238.

[15] *Iho tis Makedonias*, 9 December 1915.

[16] Leon 1974: 362–369.

[17] Tucker et al. 1999: 103.

[18] Ibid. A combination of factors worried Eliakis. The exiled King of Serbia had moved to Thessaloniki with his government and in May 1916 more than 100,000 Serbian troops arrived from Corfu to Greek Macedonia to fight in the Macedonian front. This situation was the result of the Serbian Army retreat following the Serbian Campaign.

ILLUSTRATION 6.1. French General Sarrail with Prime Minister Venizelos.
Source: Library of Congress Prints and Photographs Division, Washington, D.C.

A month later the provisional government in Thessaloniki appointed
Eliakis as its representative in Kozani and Florina prefectures and later on
Governor-General of Western Macedonia. Eliakis's party was pro-Entente, so
a cooperative relationship was initially formed with the French Army and
General Sarrail in particular (see Illustration 6.1).[19] By 1917, the Entente
forced King Constantine to leave Athens and Venizelos governed over the
reunified Greek Kingdom. Venizelos's agenda had prevailed: Greece, on the
side of Entente forces, regained Eastern Macedonia in September 1918 and,
with the Treaty of Sevres in 1920, annexed Eastern Thrace and formed a
provisional administration in Smyrna/İzmir. Until November 1920, when
Venizelos lost the elections, Eliakis remained the Governor of Western
Macedonia. These events form the general context within which Eliakis
operated in Western Macedonia.

---

[19] Eliakis 1940: 51. Maurice-Paul-Emmanuel Sarrail (1856–1929) was a French general in World
War I. He was in command of the French Army of the Orient deployed in Thessaloniki in October
1915. In January 1916 he became the commander of all Allied forces in the Macedonian front
where he stayed until December 1917. Sarrail did not hide his support for Venizelos and actively
supported the Venizelist camp. General Guillaumat (1863–1940) replaced General Sarrail in the
end of 1917. Guillaumat was in turn replaced in June 1918 by the last commander of the Allied
armies in Thessaloniki General Franchet d'Esperey (1856–1942).

Integrating Western Macedonia: Intentions and Policies

The population residing in Greek Macedonia was far from being linguistically, ethnically, religiously, or culturally homogeneous. The inhabitants were mostly peasants who lived in a world of corporate privileges for religious groups rather than individual rights. More specifically, in Western Macedonia, industrial development was almost nonexistent (see Map 6.2).[20] The inhabitants were mostly illiterate, living in more or less homogeneous villages but overall culturally, religiously, and ethnically mixed eparchies.[21]

National identities were present in the Balkans, but we should also not forget the fluid character of these identities at the time. The Greek administration, for instance, discussed the various groups in their confidential reports and often referred to people of "fluid national consciousness." Table 6.1 provides us with a categorization of non-core groups in Greek Macedonia at the time. Despite the fluidity of identities and the superficial character of some identifications, Greek policymakers were convinced that in the 1910s the "pure Greek element" was a minority in Western Macedonia. According to Eliakis, with the exception of the eparchies of Servia and Anasselitsa, in all eparchies when you combined the non-core groups Greeks were a minority. In Kozani, the Muslims were predominant and in Kailaria – today's Ptolemaida – Muslims and Bulgarians prevailed. In the eparchies of Kastoria and Florina, the majority was of the Bulgarian element together with a group of people with a fluid national consciousness. In the eparchy of Grevena, according to Eliakis, the influence of "Romanian-leaning" Vlachs was so great that one was not sure if there were any "pure Greeks" there.[22]

Given the ethnic makeup of Western Macedonia, nation-building policies were a top priority. The Greek government had been thinking of nation-building policies for the population of these lands for over forty years before their actual incorporation; however, officials had to finalize and recalibrate them after 1913.[23] As Mazower put it, "Much time, money and effort was required by disciples of the new nationalist creeds to convert its inhabitants from their older, habitual ways of referring to themselves, and to turn nationalism itself from the obsession of a small, educated elite to a movement capable of galvanizing masses."[24]

But what was the dominant understanding of nationhood in Greece at the time? The definition of the national type had crystalized around the end of the nineteenth century. To be Greek, one had to be born in Greece or be of Greek

---

[20] Gounaris 1996; Karavidas 1931; Kontogiorgi 2006: 19.
[21] An eparchy (*eparcheia*) is a political subdivision of a prefecture (*nomos*) of Greece.
[22] PKA, *Other Peoples*, Eliakis to the Venizelos, Abstract of No. 5359 report 18 October 1917. See also PKA, *The State of Affairs of the Population in Western Macedonia*, Eliakis to the President of the Council of Ministers, Abstract of No. 7861 report, 19 October 1918). For detailed statistics of the regions, see Aarbakke 2003 and Glavinas 2008.
[23] Carabott 1997: 59–78; Gounaris 1996: 409–425; Karakasidou 1997; Michailidis 1998: 9–21; and Michailidis 2003.
[24] Mazower 2004: 256.

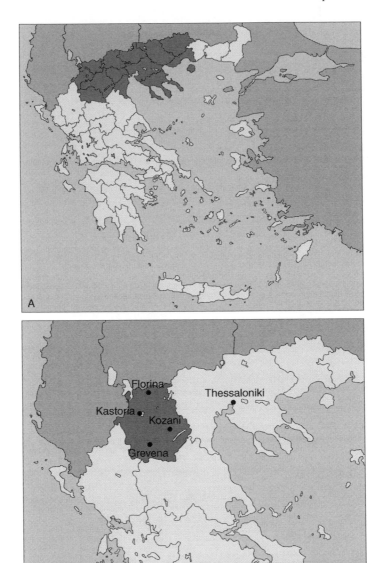

MAP 6.2. (A) Greek Macedonia, http://commons.wikimedia.org/wiki/File:PosGreek
Macedonia.png; (B) Western Greek Macedonia, http://commons.wikimedia.org/wiki/
File:Periferia_Dytikis_Makedonias.png.

TABLE 6.1. *Non-Core Groups in Greek Macedonia (c. 1915)*

Non-Core Groups	Religion	Language[a]
Koniareoi	Muslim	Turkish
Valaades	Muslim	Greek
Albanians	Muslim (and Christian)	Albanian
Muslim Vlachs	*Muslim*	*Vlach*
Pomaks, Çitaklar	*Muslim*	*Slavic*
Donmehs	*Muslim*	*Ladino/Turkish*
"Bulgarian-leaning" Slavs	Christian (Exarchate)	Slavic
"Greek-leaning" Slavs	Christian (Patriarchate)	Slavic
"Romanian-leaning" Vlachs	Christian (Romanian)	Vlach
"Greek-leaning" Vlachs	Christian (Patriarchate)	Vlach
Greeks	Christian (Patriarchate)	Greek
Greek Refugees	*Christian (Patriarchate)*	*Greek*
Sarakatsans	Christian (Patriarchate)	Greek
Armenian	*Christian (Gregorian)*	*Armenian*
Gypsies	Christian (Patriarchate) and Muslim	Gypsy/Romany
Jews (Sephardim)	*Jewish*	*Ladino*

Note: Italicized non-core groups are not discussed in Eliakis's reports.
[a] I list the primary language of the group. Many members of these groups were bilingual or even trilingual at the time using different languages for different purposes and in different contexts.

ancestry, had to usually speak Greek, and had to be an Orthodox Christian. During the Balkan Wars, and faced with the heterogeneity of the "New Lands" they were incorporating, Greek ruling political elites strategically emphasized the importance of national consciousness over language or religion. The views of the Greek elites around Venizelos concerning the matter were very close to Ernest Renan's ideas as expressed in his 1882 lecture at the Sorbonne.[25]

Venizelos clearly stated his understanding of nationhood both before and after he became Prime Minister. The first instance goes back to October 1906 when Venizelos, addressing the Second Constituent Assembly of Cretans, argued that "it is of great interest for Hellenism to propagate that its understanding [of nationhood] is so broad and so foreign to religious doctrines so that within Hellenism can fit not only Christian believers, but also the believers in any other known or unknown religion."[26] Venizelos remained on message following World War I, at the Paris Peace Conference in 1919, saying, "[R]eligion, race, language cannot be considered as reliable indications of nationality. The only unmistaken indicator is national consciousness, the purposeful desire of individuals to self determine their luck and to decide which national family they desire to belong to."[27] Finally, even after the Greek defeat in the Greek-Turkish War following World War I, Venizelos insisted

[25] Renan 1996.
[26] Stephanou 1965: 288–290 and 1969: 282–283 .
[27] Quoted in Glavinas 2008: 289.

that an important element of the foundations of a society is "respect of all religious doctrines, even those that oppose all religious doctrines."[28] The political elites surrounding him, and definitely Eliakis, shared this understanding of nationhood.[29]

In the rest of this section, I describe Eliakis's thoughts and policy recommendations about each non-core group under his jurisdiction. I structure the discussion based on the religious divide between Muslims and Christians, which was the oldest and most salient cleavage in the region.[30] Within each religious group, there were groups speaking different languages and having different national leanings (see Table 6.1). Moreover, some non-core groups had no external links, some were supported by allied powers, such as Romania, and others were supported by enemy states, such as Bulgaria. During this four-year period, from 1916 to 1920, Greece moved from being a revisionist state to a status quo state within the context of the Macedonian front, and in certain cases Eliakis's recommendations changed as well (see Tables 6.2 and 6.3).

MUSLIMS

In 1915 more than one third of the inhabitants of Greek Macedonia were Muslims, prime candidates for external support by the Ottomans.[31] According to a census, Muslims in Western and Central Macedonia were more equally divided between mixed (225) and pure (288) settlements, while in Eastern Macedonia Muslims were mostly living in pure settlements (250 to 112).[32] In terms of the type of settlement, 20 percent lived in urban centers while 80 percent lived in rural areas.[33] Turning to Western Macedonia, in its two prefectures of Kozani and Florina Muslims formed 27 percent and 20 percent of the total population, respectively.

After the incorporation of southern Macedonia into the Greek kingdom in 1913, Muslims had to choose the Ottoman or the Greek nationality. In particular, the Treaty of Athens provided for a period of three years to choose a nationality.[34] This was a policy clearly differentiating the Muslim religious community from the other communities by "encouraging" the Muslims who felt strong attachments to

[28] *Eleftheron Vima*, 18 February 1929.
[29] Glavinas suggests that the Greek administration was downplaying the importance of linguistic differences but he is more skeptical about religion (2008: 44). However, Eliakis's and Venizelos's private and public statements contradict this view. I draw a similar conclusion by looking at other confidential reports from the period. For example, see the report written by Adosidis describing a meeting he had with the Chief Rabbi of the Jewish Community of Thessaloniki, AYE, 1921, 41/2, Report of the Governor-General of Macedonia to Ministry of Foreign Affairs, 20 August 1919, Thessaloniki.
[30] Braude and Lewis 2000; Tsitselikis 2007: 354–372.
[31] Glavinas 2008: 13, 261.
[32] Ibid., p. 20.
[33] Ibid., p. 15.
[34] The Treaty of Athens was signed between Greece and the Ottoman Empire on 14 November 1913. For more on this treaty, see Glavinas 2008: 133–139. See also Tsitselikis 2012.

TABLE 6.2. *Explaining Nation-Building Policies in Western Macedonia, 1916–1918, Greece Revisionist*

Non-Core Groups	External Support?	External Power: Enemy or Ally?	Predictions	Intentions	Policy
"Greek-leaning" Slavs	No	–	Assimilation	Assimilation	Assimilation
"Greek-leaning" Vlachs	No	–	Assimilation	Assimilation	Assimilation
Sarakatsans	No	–	Assimilation	Assimilation	Assimilation
Valaades	No	–	Assimilation	Assimilation	Assimilation
Albanians	Yes	Neutral	Accommodation	Accommodation	Accommodation
"Romanian-leaning" Vlachs	Yes	Ally	Accommodation	Accommodation/ Assimilation	Accommodation
Koniareoi	Yes	Enemy	Exclusion	Exclusion/ Assimilation	Exclusion/ Accommodation
"Bulgarian-leaning" Slavs	Yes	Enemy	Exclusion	Exclusion/ Assimilation	Exclusion/ Assimilation

TABLE 6.3. *Explaining Nation-Building Policies in Western Macedonia 1918–1920, Greece Status Quo*

Non-Core Groups	External Support?	External Power: Enemy or Ally?	Predictions	Intentions	Policy
"Greek-leaning" Slavs	No	–	Assimilation	Assimilation	Assimilation
"Greek-leaning" Vlachs	No	–	Assimilation	Assimilation	Assimilation
Sarakatsans	No	–	Assimilation	Assimilation	Assimilation
Valaades	No	–	Assimilation	Assimilation	Assimilation
Albanians	Yes	Future Ally	Accommodation	Accommodation	Accommodation
"Romanian-leaning" Vlachs	Yes	Ally	Accommodation	Accommodation/ Assimilation	Accommodation
Koniareoi	Yes	Enemy	Assimilation	Assimilation	Accommodation/ Assimilation
"Bulgarian-leaning" Slavs	Yes	Enemy	Assimilation	Assimilation	Assimilation/ Voluntary Exchange

the Ottoman Empire to leave. There was variation in the effectiveness of this mechanism of "ethnic unmixing."[35] To begin with, the Greek administration did not pursue its implementation.[36] The emigration of Muslims to the Ottoman Empire could – and many times did – lead to a justification of further persecution of Greeks in Asia Minor. At the same time, keeping the Muslims in the "New Lands"[37] was beneficial in two more ways: first, it was good for agricultural production, and second, it demonstrated the administration's competency in governing over many more Muslims in light of the Greek territorial aspirations in Asia Minor.[38]

On top of this contradictory set of incentives from the state's perspective, the status of Muslims during the elections of 1915 was in flux and their Anti-Venizelist vote invited the criticism of the Venizelist newspapers and supporters. When Eliakis arrived in the summer of 1916, he attempted to divide the Muslim vote by forming alliances with personal enemies of the Muslim candidates from the Anti-Venizelist party. The Entente powers were also natural allies of the Venizelist party in this campaign and were used in order to keep Anti-Venizelist Muslims in check.[39]

In Western Macedonia, fewer Muslims chose the Ottoman nationality than did Muslims in other parts of northern Greece.[40] Eliakis attributed this fact to the timely arrest of the Mufti[41] in Kailaria and of certain Beys[42] by the French Army in 1916, as well as to his own personal efforts. He summoned all the Mukhtars[43] of the region and explained the program of the Greek authorities, and asked them to accept Greek rule. These Mukhtars submitted to the new sovereign, and Eliakis promised to protect their human and community rights from both Greek and foreign authorities.[44]

---

[35] I have adopted this term from Brubaker 1998.

[36] For example, between 1914 and 1915 Muslim emigration was prohibited. Moreover, when the deadline arrived in November 1916 the treaty was not enforced because of World War I. In general, with the exception of cases where there was evidence of anti-Greek activity (see Glavinas 2008: 286–287), even Muslims who had chosen the Ottoman citizenship were allowed to change their status and remain in Greece just by filing out their papers for Greek citizenship. For more, see Glavinas 2008: 105–106.

[37] This is the designation that the Greek government used for the territories annexed in the Balkans Wars and World War I.

[38] For more, see Llewellyn-Smith 1998.

[39] Glavinas 2008: 240–241.

[40] And fewer issues emerged with the emigration of Muslims after the end of World War I.

[41] A Mufti is a Muslim cleric who gives opinions on Islamic law.

[42] A Bey was a provincial governor in the Ottoman Empire. By the end of nineteenth century, however, the term Bey is used for local notables, and military officials.

[43] Mukhtar was the Turkish word for community leader, later mayor. They were appointed by the Ottomans in each community and were usually wealthy. The Mukhtar was responsible for enforcing law and order, collecting taxes, and calling the police when necessary. His house also functioned as the base for any visiting government officials.

[44] PKA, *The Attitudes of Aliens toward the Movement: Voting Rights*, Eliakis to the Provisional Government, Abstract of No. 564 report, 11 November 1916. To be sure, Eliakis wrote this report in 1916. Glavinas informs us that the Provisional Government replaced Anti-Venizelist Muftis with the help of the Entente troops.

It is important to remember that Eliakis – just like Prime Minister Venizelos – was from the island of Crete where he had experienced the coexistence of Muslims and Christians. This experience informed Eliakis's attitude toward the Muslims. More importantly, the Greek Prime Minister shared this experience and attitude. Venizelos, as we have demonstrated, had a very inclusive understanding of Hellenism. Just after the end of the second Balkan War he argued, "it is to our great interest to keep the Muslim population of the recovered territories. They are an excellent group, a first class agricultural group, exemplar and obedient citizens."[45] Thus, despite the fact that there were many negative stereotypes against Muslims in Greek society, an important part of the Greek administration and ruling political elites, both Venizelist and Anti-Venizelist,[46] shared a positive view, the former based on principles and the latter possibly for electoral purposes.

In a report to the Ministry of Military Affairs in 1917, Eliakis wrote:

With respect to the Muslims of my jurisdiction I am in the pleasant position to stress that because of my stance toward them, although they have been asked to satisfy many military needs, they understood that the State is protecting everyone irrespectively of race or religion, and this made them even more loyal subjects of our State. Holding the view that we should not grant political rights to the Muslims, since this would corrupt them, I have always argued we will not be able to sever their bonds with the Ottoman State unless we respect their human rights and their religious beliefs. Following this policy will allow us to use them as an important factor in every respect, but more importantly, it will prove that we are able to govern alien people, something necessary in order to enforce order in Macedonia.[47]

Not much later Eliakis noted that the above policy produced amazing results. The Muslims had demonstrated their trust to the state by enthusiastically enlisting in the Greek army. The benefits from this were clear, because the army needed these "obedient and healthy soldiers." Eliakis drew a parallel between them and the "Moroccan Spahis"[48] fighting for the French and suggested specific policies to ensure the success of this endeavor:

1. create Muslim battalions with their own flag, which should include the half moon in one of its corners; 2. allow each battalion to have an Imam[49] for prayer; 3. promote the best to non-commissioned officers; 4. allow them to wear the *fez*; 5. insert Greek soldiers fluent in Turkish to monitor the behavior of these battalions and spy on them if necessary.[50]

In general, Eliakis believed Muslims were easy to deal with *because* of their religion. It was enough to protect their life, honor, and property, respect their religion, and treat them equally. Having political rights was not a concern for

---

[45] *Ai Agoreuseis tou Ellinikou Koinovouliou, 1909–1956* 1957: 46.
[46] Glavinas 2008.
[47] PKA, *Conscription of Muslims*, Eliakis to the Ministry of Military Affairs, 25 August 1917.
[48] Spahis regiments were light cavalry regiments in the French Army recruited primarily from the indigenous populations of French Morocco. The name comes from *Sipahi*, an Ottoman cavalryman.
[49] An Imam is a Muslim prayer leader.
[50] PKA, *Conscription of Muslims*, Eliakis to the Ministry of Military Affairs, 25 August 1917.

them, he believed, as long as they could freely regulate their communal affairs. According to Eliakis, if the policy he outlined were to be followed, the Muslims would gradually become "civilized" and understand themselves to be an indispensable part of the Greek nation. This would happen especially after the Muslims realized that the Ottoman state would not be able to recapture these territories. No government ever implemented his proposal restricting Muslims of their political rights, but it was clearly regarded as a possibility – at least during the turbulent times of World War I. A prominent alternative to what Eliakis suggested was the establishment of separate electoral colleges.[51] Regardless, in the 1920 election that overlapped with Venizelos's defeat and Eliakis's removal from office, none of the above took effect and 38 Muslim MPs were elected.[52]

The Muslims of Western Macedonia were not a homogeneous ethnic group. Eliakis distinguished between three main non-core groups: Koniareoi, Valaades, and Albanians. Koniareoi were the Turkish speaking conquerors of Macedonia who came from Anatolia and, according to Eliakis, were still in an "animal state." The ones that felt closer to the Ottoman Empire would choose the Ottoman nationality and would be "encouraged" to leave. For the rest, he believed that they could be ruled easily through the Koran. During the Balkan Wars and World War I exclusionary policies were pursued but not fully implemented toward this group. The "state of siege" law,[53] instituted by the 1864 constitutional revision and reaffirmed in the 1911 one, and the 1871 law "on the persecution of banditry," which was extended to the "New Lands" in December 1913, provided the legal basis for the selective exclusionary policies.[54] Glavinas informs us that the Provisional Government replaced many Muftis with the help of the Entente troops and Muslims that exhibited "Anti-Greek" activity were deported or internally displaced.[55]

The second group was Valaades, Greek speakers who had converted to Islam and lived in villages near Anasselitsa. According to Eliakis, many of them were aware of their Greek origin and most did not even speak Turkish. They would be easy to assimilate. As Eliakis put it: "Their assimilation will be complete once they are convinced that religion is not the attribute of Nations, but national consciousness and origin."[56]

---

[51] See Glavinas 2008: 257.

[52] Glavinas 2008: 255. After the Greek defeat in Asia Minor and the Venizelist takeover in 1922, separate electoral colleges were established for the Muslims of Macedonia and Thrace that could elect only 19 MPs; see Mavrogordatos 1983: 239.

[53] The "state of siege" law was voted on 20 July 1917 and with the Law 755 voted on 18 August 1917 the Greek authorities could internally displace individuals that provided information on Greek military affairs to the enemy, instigate desertion, or was otherwise causing suspicion to the authorities. Similar laws were in effect during the Provisional Government's rule in Thessaloniki. The "state of siege" law was officially lifted after the Sevres Treaty was signed in 1920.

[54] Law "on the persecution banditry" TOD 27 February 1871 and the law that extended the 1871 law to the New Lands was Law 121, voted on 31 December 1913.

[55] 2008: 85–86, 423–424.

[56] PKA, Eliakis to the President of the Council of Ministers, Abstract of No. 7861 report, 19 October 1918.

After World War I, Eliakis's intentions with respect to Valaades and Koniareoi were far from exclusionary. Valaades were perceived and treated as if they were Greek. Koniareoi were accommodated in the short term, but the ultimate goal was to assimilate them within an expanded Greece. Given that they were perceived as a group supported by an enemy power, the Ottoman Empire,[57] and that Eliakis wanted to preserve the favorable status quo, my theory also predicts assimilationist policies. Moreover, the exclusionary land and property policies followed by Venizelos's government toward the Muslims during World War I were, consistent with my argument, reversed in their favor following the end of the war. Thus Eliakis and the Greek administration at large shifted their policy following World War I toward one of assimilationist long-term objectives, even though the actual policies they pursued initially looked more like accommodationist than assimilationist (see Illustration 6.2).

Finally, there was also the third group, the Muslim Albanians.[58] According to Eliakis, religion did not matter to them and their Albanian consciousness prevailed.[59] The Albanians differed from the Koniareoi, since the latter were looking toward Istanbul for protection. Many Albanians had economic interests in the Greek territories, emphasized the common origins of Greeks and Albanians, and worked for Greek-Albanian cooperation.

Two factors made Eliakis suggest a different treatment of Albanians: his desire to ensure friendly relations with the newly born state of Albania, and the distinct Albanian consciousness of this population, which dissociated them

ILLUSTRATION 6.2. Governor Ioannis Eliakis addresses Muslims in Florina, 1920.

[57] According to confidential reports cited by Glavinas, Istanbul and Ankara also got involved supporting the Anti-Venizelist camp encouraging the Muslims to vote Muslim candidates and against Venizelos (2008: 249).

[58] There were three other groups of Muslims that lived in Greek Macedonia at the time: the Muslim Vlachs (primarily from Meglen region), the Gypsies, and the Slavic-speaking Muslims (Pomaks). Eliakis, however, does not refer to them.

[59] He also noted there were few Christian Albanians sharing this Albanian consciousness.

from other Muslims and thus diminished the likelihood of external support by the Ottomans. He wrote:

If there is an Albanian State after the War it is to our benefit that this State is friendly to us. Thus, I think we should not take the same measures toward the Albanians ruled by our regime that we take against the other Muslims. We should not for example confiscate their land as if it was abandoned, even if it really is, as long as they do not emigrate to Turkey. The confiscated land of the Albanians, who emigrated for a while but came back and declared their loyalty to our regime has to be returned to them even if their loyalty is not sincere.[60]

Albania, established in 1913 but not yet a functional entity due to the outbreak of World War I, would be a new state that Greece had many reasons to befriend.[61] The Albanians in the Greek kingdom could operate as guarantors of friendly relations with Albania. The national interest would be better served by making this small material sacrifice of not confiscating Albanian land. Eliakis's proposal was implemented by the government a year and a half later. Thus the Albanians, members of a non-core group supported by a neutral power in World War I and a prospective ally, were accommodated by the Greek administration, consistent with my theory.

The alternative hypotheses (see Tables 6.4 and 6.5) all incorrectly predict exclusionary policies toward the Albanians because they spoke a different language and had a different religion, had a newly minted homeland, and had been traditionally allied with the Turks within the dominant Muslim *millet* during Ottoman times. Similarly, all three alternative hypotheses predict that the Greek administration should have excluded the Koniareoi population because it was Muslim, spoke a different language, and had a privileged position during Ottoman times. While this was partially true during the Balkan Wars and World War I, it certainly does not appear to be in Eliakis's intentions and actions following World War I. Of course, the Greek defeat in Asia Minor changed these calculations.

CHRISTIANS

Slavic-Speaking Christians

Having tested my theory on non-core groups with a different world religion from the core group, I now turn to non-core groups that shared the same religion (although not necessarily the same denomination) with the core group, but in many cases spoke a different language. The largest Christian group in the area was the Slavic-speaking population. This group consisted of "Bulgarian-

---

[60] PKA, *Alvanistai*, Eliakis to the Provisional Government, Abstract of No. 389 report, 27 January 1917. Note: The date for Abstract of No. 389 report appears as 1918 in the original document but this must be a mistake. First, the report is addressed to the Provisional Government, which did not exist in 1918; second, this Abstract appears between reports from 1916 and 1917.

[61] According to Eliakis, the Albanians could be Greece's allies in case of a pan-Slavic alliance in the Balkans.

TABLE 6.4. *Evaluating Existing Explanations in Western Macedonia, 1916–1918*

Non-Core Groups	Language	Religion	Status Reversal	Homeland	Policy
"Greek-leaning" Slavs	*Exclusion*	Assimilation	Assimilation	*Exclusion*	Assimilation
"Greek-leaning" Vlachs	*Exclusion*	Assimilation	Assimilation	*Exclusion*	Assimilation
Sarakatsans	Assimilation	Assimilation	Assimilation	Assimilation	Assimilation
Valaades	Assimilation	*Exclusion*	*Exclusion*	Assimilation	Assimilation
Albanians	*Exclusion*	*Exclusion*	*Exclusion*	*Exclusion*	Accommodation
"Romanian-leaning" Vlachs	*Exclusion*	*Assimilation*	*Assimilation*	Exclusion	Accommodation
Koniareoi	Exclusion	Exclusion	Exclusion	Exclusion	Exclusion/ Accommodation
"Bulgarian-leaning" Slavs	Exclusion	Exclusion	Assimilation	Exclusion	Exclusion/ Assimilation

Note: Incorrect predictions are shown in italics.

leaning" Slavs,[62] loyal to the Bulgarian Exarchate and considered a Bulgarian national minority by the Bulgarian state, and "Greek-leaning" Slavs, loyal to the Orthodox Patriarchate in Istanbul.

"Bulgarian-Leaning" Slavs

Although Eliakis was not as worried about the loyalty of the various Muslim groups, he was less optimistic with respect to the Christian Orthodox, "Bulgarian-leaning" Slavs. These were people who sided with the Bulgarian Exarchate after its establishment in 1870. His reasoning, however, was not one of cultural differences or affinities but rather of diplomatic relations and war dynamics. He believed that if there had been no Second Balkan War in Macedonia, then:

> the local Bulgarians would be so audacious that [Greek] Macedonia would be everything but Greek, since the "Bulgarian-leaning" Slavs would be able to freely express their Bulgarian feelings. However, the second war followed and the local "Bulgarian-leaning" Slavs were discouraged and converts to the schism [the Exarchate] presented themselves as orthodox [loyal to the Patriarchate] and Greeks, supposedly forced to convert religiously and consequently to change their nationality as well. In the midst of that terror, our state should have put aside everything else and focused its efforts on cementing in the hearts of the population these [national] ideas.... It did almost nothing instead.[63]

[62] The term Eliakis uses is *Boulgarizontes*.
[63] PKA, *The State of Affairs of the Population in Western Macedonia*, Eliakis to the President of the Council of Ministers, Abstract of No. 7861 report, 19 October 1918.

Eliakis criticized the Greek government because it did not send its best civil servants and educators to Macedonia. He strongly believed that if there were schools in every village and Greek priests took the place of those backing the Bulgarian Exarchate, then the population would have been assimilated quickly. However, the civil servants were below average and many of them came in order to make a fortune; moreover, only a few schools started operating right away, and no priests were sent to the villages which returned to the jurisdiction of the Patriarchate. Despite all of these complaints, Eliakis was optimistic following World War I:

[I]f we try to change the souls of the population, it should be easy to do, since they are used to being changed. They tell me that in one trial which took place in Florina during Turkish rule . . . a witness was asked by the President of the Court what his nationality was and he replied that eight years ago he was Bulgarian, two years later he became a Greek and remained such for three years, after which he became Bulgarian again. . . . And he found this identity change unproblematic and really believed in each period that he was what [nationality] he thought he was. Thus if we work not spasmodically . . . but systematically, it would be possible to make the local population believe they have become Greeks and if they maintain this conviction for a long time it will be possible that they will really become such.[64]

The grave results from the government's inaction with respect to the assimilation of the local population were obvious during the Bulgarian attack in Western Macedonia, when many Slavic speakers welcomed Bulgarian soldiers as liberators. A further indicator of the pro-Bulgarian sentiment from a part of the local population was that even when the Entente (French and British) forces pushed out the Bulgarian troops, many believed they would come back. Some of them followed the defeated troops, hoping they would return as victors.

Following the Bulgarian defeat in the area, the Entente forces treated the people residing in Western Macedonia badly because they had demonstrated pro-Bulgarian feelings. The only refuge for these people was to adopt the Greek national identity and demonstrate their loyalty to the Greek state. According to Eliakis, this was an opportune moment for the Greek administration to achieve in two years what it would otherwise not be able to achieve in ten. The Slavic-speakers of Western Macedonia were trying to prove their "Greekness" by protesting the lack of schools. Once again, the Greek government did not act upon this opportunity because of administrative failures. While Eliakis was writing his report in 1918, most schools remained closed and Athens did not provide schoolbooks.

Eliakis was not optimistic about assimilating the older Slavic-speaking population in the region, and he suggested that most policies should focus on the younger generation. He expected the best results to come from orphanages and girls' boarding schools. He also insisted that, based on experience, the assimilation of "Bulgarian-leaning" Slavs could not entail solely cultural and educational measures; it had to entail terror as well.

[64] Ibid.

During World War I, methods such as deportations, arrests, and even killings were legitimized by the fact that Bulgaria was an enemy power fighting on the side of the Central Powers (the German, Austro-Hungarian, and Ottoman Empires). During peacetime – when Eliakis was writing this report – violent measures were harder to justify and pursue without attracting the attention of the international community. Furthermore, Greece was in favor of the international status quo and did not want to jeopardize it. Nevertheless, Eliakis suggested that selective violent measures were essential even in peacetime in order to neutralize any obstruction to peaceful assimilation policies.

Indeed, the Greek government had passed a law during World War I that facilitated the deportation of individuals considered dangerous to the public order.[65] Eliakis built on that law and suggested it had to be enforced when necessary. He thought that Greek authorities should deport not just the guilty party but their whole family. Moreover, the deportation and the reasons for it should be made known to the community.

The possibility of deporting all of the "Bulgarian-leaning" Slavs from Macedonia was suggested and described as a more "radical" measure of nationalizing the territory. However, Eliakis quickly dismissed this idea because "on the one hand, this would make a terrible impression to the liberal people of the civilized world, and, on the other, because we do not have those [Greeks], with whom we could replace them."[66] In 1919, the emigration of Greeks from Anatolia was unlikely, especially because their presence was the primary justification for the Greek campaign to the Asia Minor.[67] Under such circumstances, a mass deportation of all the Bulgarian-speakers would lead to a severe depopulation of Macedonia. This would make Greece look weak.

Moreover, the Greek government had to act as a civilized liberal polity in the eyes of the international community. This was the first concern of the Governor-General of Western Macedonia. Before the Treaty of Neuilly was signed and while considering a deportation proposal made by Alexandros Mazarakis-Ainian,[68] Eliakis writes:

In case of a deportation of "Bulgarian-leaning" Slavs there will be a terrible manipulation of the affair. If we listen to the advice of the [local] Greeks then there is a danger either of turning Northern [Greek] Macedonia into a deserted land, which would call for the intervention of Europe and would damage our reputation in the eyes of the civilized world, or of providing the opportunity to these Greeks of all sorts of blackmail that would disturb human consciousness.[69]

---

[65] See n. 54.

[66] PKA, *The State of Affairs of the Population in Western Macedonia*, Eliakis to the President of the Council of Ministers, Abstract of No. 7861 report, 19 October 1918.

[67] Venizelos 1919.

[68] Alexandros Mazarakis-Ainian (1874–1943) participated in the Macedonian Struggle and later on in the National Defense Movement. During the Peace Conference he served as special advisor to Prime Minister Venizelos.

[69] PKA, *Deportation of Bulgarians*, Eliakis to the Ministry of Interior, Abstract of No. 4164 report, 12 June 1919.

For the above reasons, Eliakis concluded that the most sensible policy was assimilation. He argued that if the right measures were taken only a few would not be assimilated:

We are obliged to follow the hard and rough way of proselytizing, through good and expensive administration, systematically in all sectors of the administration. I am certain that with such administration we will rapidly have results. And instead of transplanting the local population with the danger of not replacing them, through this kind of administration, we will implant in them our ideas and turn them into fanatic Greeks, more fanatic than the old Greeks.[70]

All in all, with respect to the "Bulgarian-leaning" Slavs, my theory correctly predicted Eliakis's preferred policies. During World War I, terror and intensive assimilationist policies would have achieved the exclusion of the pro-Bulgarian population and successfully assimilated the rest of the Slavic-speaking population. "Bulgarian-leaning" Slavs were agitated and mobilized by an enemy power while the Greek administration was fighting a war to recapture its lost territories. Following World War I, Greece wanted to preserve the international status quo in Macedonia, thus intensive assimilationist policies were the preferred choice and exclusionary policies would only target specific families of agitators.[71]

For the whole period under study, 1916–1920, external interference never stopped. Bulgarian agitators were present in all of Macedonia. Toward the end of the period under study, as I discussed in Chapter 5, a voluntary population exchange between Greece and Bulgaria was decided under the Treaty of Neuilly in 1919. After 1919, a mix of assimilationist and selectively targeted exclusionary policies was the actual policy followed toward this group.

All but one of the alternative hypotheses predict exclusionary policies toward the "Bulgarian-leaning" Slavs since they spoke a different language; were organized under a different religious organization, the Exarchate; and had a national homeland. The status-reversal argument is the only one that predicts assimilationist policies, because the "Bulgarian-leaning" Slavs were also disadvantaged during the Ottoman times, along with the rest of the Christians. Because of the mixed strategy followed toward the "Bulgarian-leaning" Slavs, one way or another all hypotheses find support, although the mechanisms they posit do not appear to be operative. Significantly for my argument, however, the group was not accommodated.

"Grecomanoi" or "Greek-Leaning" Slavs
"Grecomanoi" was a term used to indicate Slavic speakers with Greek national consciousness. These people had sided with Greek guerrilla bands during the Macedonian Struggle (1903–1908) and had opposed the influence of the Exarchate.[72] They were not perceived as mobilized by a competing claim and were, as expected, targeted with assimilationist policies. In fact, the dominant

---

[70] PKA, *On the Ownership of the Fertile Lands*, Eliakis to the Ministry of Interior, Abstract of No. 4164 report, 12 June 1919.
[71] Hassiotis 2005.
[72] Dakin 1966.

ideology amongst the Greek ruling elites was that these people were only linguistically Slavicized but ethnically Greek.

Looking solely at the cultural differences of this non-core group from the core group could lead to a prediction of exclusion, because they spoke a different language and most likely were of Slavic origins. The homeland argument likewise incorrectly predicts exclusion because Bulgaria could be understood as their homeland. The status-reversal argument accurately predicts this policy, because "Greek-leaning" Slavs were a politically disadvantaged group under Ottoman rule.

Vlach-Speaking Christians

Another Christian non-core group that Eliakis discussed is that of the Vlachs. Many Vlachs were primarily herders living a nomadic life, while others were sedentary farmers. A few had settled in larger towns in the Balkans and had become merchants or artisans. They spoke a Latin dialect akin to modern Romanian. Most of them lived in the Pindus mountain range, but some also resided in the hills near trading centers such as Monastir, Grevena, Kastoria, Koritsa, Moskopol, Veroia, and Edessa.[73] Looking at the archival material we find that the Vlachs were divided into two subgroups by the Greek administration: "Romanian-leaning" and "Greek-leaning" Vlachs.[74]

"Romanian-Leaning" Vlachs

The Romanian government began its efforts to "awaken" a Romanian identity in the Vlachs of Macedonia in the late 1860s. To gain Romania's support during the conference in Bucharest, Prime Minister Venizelos declared in 1913 that Greece would provide autonomy to the Koutsovlach[75] schools and churches in the newly acquired Greek lands.[76] The group was recognized as a national minority, and their schools and churches were funded by the Romanian state.[77] This was the first time that minority provisions of a treaty signed by Greece referred to a national minority. It was up to the different Vlach communities to decide if they were "Romanian" or "Greek." Despite their alliance, the governments of the two countries competed for their allegiance.

In the eparchy of Grevena there were a few "Romanian-leaning" Vlachs, who during Ottoman times were under the protection of Romania. Their main incentive to identify with Romania was to facilitate herding and commerce

[73] For more on this area, see Alvanos 2005.

[74] The terms Eliakis uses are *Roumanizontes* and *Hellinovlachoi*, respectively.

[75] Koutsovlachs is another name used for Vlachs in Greece. The language of this group was Vlach, a Latin based language close to modern day Romanian. Most of these people were bilingual at the time and most of them only speak Greek in contemporary Greece.

[76] For more on the Romanian support for and links with this population, see Vlasidis 1998.

[77] Mavrogordatos 2003: 16. In Chapter 2, I discussed the logic behind externally supporting a non-core group in an allied state with special reference to the case of Romania in the Balkans.

with Romania.[78] Romania had pursued a national agitation campaign in European Turkey during the late nineteenth century, and with the Treaty of Bucharest in 1913, Romania achieved the recognition of Romanian minorities in Serbia, Bulgaria, and Greece. Romanian propaganda in Macedonia waned immediately after its occupation by the Greek army, despite the treaty provisions; however, it was spurred during World War I under the temporary French military administration. The civil servant for finance at Grevena, Askarides, wrote to Eliakis:

If the French Administration lasts longer and if the *National Defense* [government] does not incorporate the eparchy of Grevena soon, then they ["Romanian-leaning" Vlachs] will prevail over the Greek element since they are working systematically and intensely in order to establish a precedent which I hope will not be recognized as a permanent situation.[79]

During World War I Eliakis was mostly worried about the spread of "Romanian propaganda." Unlike most Muslims and "Bulgarian-leaning" Slavs, who were perceived to be supported by enemy powers, Romania was an ally; therefore, the only reasonable policy toward the pro-Romanian Vlachs was to accommodate them while presenting Greece as a better and more prestigious protector of their rights. Eliakis firmly believed that as soon as the "Romanian-leaning" Vlachs realized that they no longer had a need for external protection, then with the help of school, military service, and church, they would become "pure Greeks."

In 1917, Eliakis warned Venizelos's government that the Italian authorities there had approached the "Romanian-leaning" Vlachs in Grevena in order to change them into "Italian-leaning" Vlachs. The Italians presented the idea of self-determination to the Vlachs living in the Pindus mountain range, and while the Italian troops were withdrawing, many locals expressed such desires. The Greek police arrested some of the rebels who were against Greek sovereignty. However, the ambassadors of both Italy and Romania protested to the Greek government over these arrests. Eliakis interfered and asked to meet with the prisoners before they were taken to the court-martial in Thessaloniki.

I asked them why they were arrested and they pretended that they had no clue or attributed their arrest to defamations by their enemies. I asked them if they are Greek, and they hesitated to deny the Greek national identity; some even said "if only more were like us...." Following these questions, I talked to them for a long time in this manner: I told them, that since I hear that they speak Greek, I consider them Greek. And they should boast for being Greek since they have the most glorious history in the world.[80]

---

[78] PKA, *"Romanian-leaning" Vlachs*, Eliakis to Venizelos, Abstract of No. 5359 report, 18 October 1917.
[79] PKA, *"Romanian-leaning" Vlachs*, Eliakis to the Provisional Government, Abstract of No. 389 report, 27 January 1917.
[80] PKA, *"Romanian-leaning" Vlachs*, Eliakis to Venizelos, Abstract of No. 5359 report, 18 October 1917.

This is a typical example of Eliakis's cultivation of the local population. He would emphasize the superiority of Hellenism and Greek culture in general, while at the same time he would attempt to convince them of their Greekness. Sometimes he highlighted the linguistic attributes of the population he addressed, other times their religious affiliation, and sometimes even their dress, like in the following report:

The inhabitants of upper Grammatikovon, where the liturgy is in the Romanian language, are "Romanian-leaning" Vlachs and almost Romanians. The potential military recruits of this village are so fanatical that they did not enlist in the last draft; instead they went to work for the English service station. Because of this, the committee of grain storage in Kailaria did not want to supply grain to this village. So the head of this village came to complain. I asked him if he is a Greek and he replied "Don't you see what I am wearing?" pointing to his dress. I answered that I saw him wearing the Greek fustanella[81] and that I heard him speak Greek, which means that he is Greek, and one of the best for that matter, since the Evzones that also wear the fustanella are the best soldiers of the Greek Army. On this basis and with the above spirit I spoke to him and I could tell the powerful impression it produced. I made him wonder how he could have been unaware that he is Greek.[82]

More important for my argument, Eliakis moderated his assimilationist tendencies because of the geopolitical situation. Although he tried to instill Greek feelings in the "Romanian-leaning" Vlachs, he also told a group of them:

If any of you has Romanian feelings, if he is Romanian, I respect his feelings, because Romania is a friend and allied power. We share both friends and enemies with her and we have no conflicting interests since Romania is not considering jumping over the Balkan Peninsula to come and conquer the territories you inhabit.[83]

Eliakis was willing to respect their Romanian feelings, both because he had to, and because he considered them to be geopolitically harmless, because Romania was an ally. Accommodation was the policy toward the "Romanian-leaning" Vlachs. A population exchange between Greece and Romania was not considered at all. Greece needed Romania as an ally, and Bulgaria was the common enemy. Finally, the absence of a common border with Romania minimized the perception of threat for the Greek side.

"Greek-Leaning" Vlachs
"Hellenovlachoi" was the term used to refer to the second Vlach-speaking non-core group identified by the Greek administration that had Greek national consciousness; it stood for "Greek-leaning" Vlachs. These people had sided

---

[81] A fustanella is a skirt-like garment worn by men in the Balkans up to the end of the nineteenth century. It was the uniform of the Evzones (light infantry) until World War II; today it is worn by the Greek Presidential (formerly Royal) Guard in Athens.

[82] PKA, *"Romanian-leaning" Vlachs*, Eliakis to Venizelos, Abstract of No. 5359 report, 18 October 1917.

[83] Ibid.

with the Greek guerrilla bands during the Macedonian Struggle (1903–1908) and had either resisted or escaped the influence of the Romanian and Italian propaganda. They were not mobilized by a competing claim and were thus good candidates for assimilationist policies. The policies toward both subgroups conform to the expectations of my theory.

Looking at the Vlach-speaking population and its two subgroups, we observe that focusing on cultural differences alone does not help us account for the variation in nation-building policies. Both groups spoke a Latin-based language and they should thus be excluded. Instead, the former non-core group, the "Romanian-leaning" Vlachs, was accommodated while the latter, the "Greek-leaning" Vlachs, was targeted with assimilationist policies. Moreover, the homeland argument cannot help us distinguish between the two subgroups of Vlach-speakers either, because Romania viewed both groups as potential co-ethnics. The status-reversal argument correctly predicts a policy of assimilation toward the "Greek-leaning" Vlachs, but is incorrect in the case of the "Romanian-leaning" ones, who were accommodated instead. Both groups were disadvantaged during the Ottoman times, and based on this fact, we would expect the Greek administration to pursue assimilationist policies toward both of them.

Finally, focusing on the religious affiliation of the two subgroups leads to similar predictions. Because both groups were Christian Orthodox, they should be targeted with assimilationist policies; however, only the "Greek-leaning" Vlachs were targeted while the "Romanian-leaning" ones were accommodated. To be sure, assimilationist tendencies were expressed by Eliakis, but the policy during that period was one of accommodating their differences of the latter group through the state's acceptance of Romanian schools and Romanian churches operating in Greece.

Greek-Speaking Christians

Within the "Greeks," the Greek-speaking or Greek dialect-speaking Christian Orthodox population, there was a group referred to by Eliakis as "Skenitai" or "Sarakatsans." They dressed like Vlachs and lived nomadic lives, but they were considered by everyone, including Eliakis, to be Greeks. There were approximately 40,000 in Greek Macedonia, referred to as Skenitai (tent-people) for their way of life. In the winter they settled in the lowlands, especially Chalkidiki, while in the summer they tented up in the mountains. This group apparently made no claims to the communal property of the places it inhabited and it did not interfere with their administration.[84] Eliakis suggested the settlement of this population among groups who had foreign national leanings and recommended its conscription into the Greek army.[85] Not surprisingly, all

---

[84] In contrast to the Sarakatsans, according to Eliakis, the explanation behind the emergence of "Romanian-leaning" Vlachs was that they were people who emigrated to Romania, but when they came back they were in constant competition with the sedentary local population.

[85] PKA, *Skenitai*, Eliakis to Venizelos, Abstract of No. 5359 report, 18 October 1917.

theories make the same prediction for the Sarakatsans: assimilation. They were indeed targeted with standard assimilationist policies such as schooling and military conscription.

WHAT EXPLAINS VARIATION IN NATION-BUILDING POLICIES?

The evidence provided largely supports my geostrategic argument. Granted, a set of reports written by a particular administrator over a four-year period is not a representative sample of the Greek government as a whole – not to mention governments in general; however, this level of analysis is crucial if one wants to test the microfoundations of an argument. A theory might make the right predictions, but fail to identify the correct causal mechanisms at work. In this chapter, historical contextualization coupled with rich archival material allowed me to test both the predictions and the causal logic underlying my theory.

The different combinations of interstate relations with external powers and foreign policy goals, lead to different predictions of my theory. Looking at Tables 6.2 and 6.3 we see that, consistent with my argument, non-core groups without any external power supporting them and claiming their allegiance were targeted with assimilationist policies, and were the least likely to get minority rights protection. Groups supported by current or prospective allies were accommodated ("Romanian-leaning" Vlachs and Albanians, respectively).

During World War I, we find that Eliakis's goal was securing Western Macedonia for the Greek kingdom by neutralizing both internal and external enemies (see Table 6.2). Besides dealing with direct security concerns, he had to counteract the propaganda of the various competitors in the region. Under these circumstances, exclusionary policies were pursued toward enemy-supported non-core groups (Koniareoi and "Bulgarian-leaning" Slavs). Toward the end of World War I, however, Eliakis became more optimistic about the assimilability of certain non-core groups.

Following World War I, the Greek administration was in favor of the international status quo and adopted an assimilationist policy toward enemy-supported non-core groups with an emphasis on political equality and egalitarianism toward the population regardless of cultural, religious, or linguistic differences (Koniareoi and "Bulgarian-leaning" Slavs). Consistent with my theory, the perception of these non-core groups was to a great extent endogenous to the external interference by competing states. The past political behavior of the various non-core groups vis-à-vis the Greek cause in the region prior to the annexation of the territories was also central in the planning of nation-building policies.

Another shortcut the Greek administration used in order to determine whether a non-core group was assimilable was not the particular marker that differentiated it from the core group but rather the incentives and constraints put in place by international and bilateral treaties with neighboring states and Great Powers (France and Britain). For instance, the linguistic assimilation of

Koniareoi is a quite different case from that of "Bulgarian-leaning" Slavs since, first, the linguistic and educational rights of the Muslims were protected by international treaties and, second, the Greek state was in the process of annexing more areas with significant Muslim population and thus had to prove itself to them and the Great Powers. Even though Muslims could get an education in Turkish, Greek was also introduced as an obligatory language in their curriculum. To be sure, besides the constraints – which my theory emphasizes – there were also perceived opportunities, as in the case of the Albanians. Interstate alliances had an effect on the planning of nation-building policies in two ways: through a retrospective assessment based on existing alliances, and a prospective one based on future opportunities for useful alliances.

How well do alternative arguments do in this context? State- and regional-level hypotheses such as levels of economic development, regime type, understandings of nationhood, international norms, and so forth are held constant by design. There is, however, group level variation. Looking at Tables 6.4 and 6.5, we see that cultural-distance arguments cannot explain most of the variation. For example, with respect to the "Bulgarian-leaning Slavs" and "Romanian-leaning" Vlachs, Eliakis's reasoning was not one of cultural differences or affinities, but rather on diplomatic relations and war dynamics. The former group was supported by an enemy power and was thus targeted with intense assimilationist and ultimately exclusionary measures, while the latter was

TABLE 6.5. *Evaluating Existing Explanations in Western Macedonia, 1918–1920*

Non-Core Groups	Language	Religion	Status Reversal	Homeland	Policy
"Greek-leaning" Slavs	*Exclusion*	Assimilation	Assimilation	*Exclusion*	Assimilation
"Greek-leaning" Vlachs	*Exclusion*	Assimilation	Assimilation	*Exclusion*	Assimilation
Sarakatsans	Assimilation	Assimilation	Assimilation	Assimilation	Assimilation
Valaades	Assimilation	*Exclusion*	*Exclusion*	Assimilation	Assimilation
Albanians	*Exclusion*	*Exclusion*	*Exclusion*	*Exclusion*	Accommodation
"Romanian-leaning" Vlachs	*Exclusion*	*Assimilation*	*Assimilation*	*Exclusion*	Accommodation
Koniareoi	*Exclusion*	*Exclusion*	*Exclusion*	*Exclusion*	Accommodation/ Assimilation
"Bulgarian-leaning" Slavs	Exclusion	Exclusion	Assimilation	Exclusion	Assimilation/ Voluntary Exchange

Note: Incorrect predictions are shown in italics.

supported by an ally and was accommodated. Even where such arguments make correct predictions, it is for the wrong reasons. Koniareoi were not targeted with exclusionary policies during World War I due to their cultural difference, but because of their links to the Ottoman Empire, which was fighting on the side of the Central Powers.

The status-reversal argument does better. This argument, however, can only differentiate between conflict and no conflict and thus has little to say about instances of assimilation or accommodation. For example, although the Koniareoi were members of the dominant group before the Greek occupation, Eliakis pursued a policy of accommodation in terms of their culture and language. This policy directly contradicts the status-reversal argument. It also contradicts my argument, which predicts exclusion during and assimilation after World War I for this group, but the archival material helps us to understand this policy choice. As Eliakis stated, this phase of accommodation (coupled with a certain degree of internal displacement and colonization) was just a step before assimilationist policies.[86]

The homeland argument does worse than the status-reversal argument. Whether a non-core group has an external homeland or not is important, but it does not help us predict which nation-building policy the host state will pursue. My theory suggests that looking at the degree to which the homeland interferes with the fate of its "ethnic kin," as well as the interstate relations of the host state with the homeland, is crucial. Moreover, besides the existence of external involvement (covert or overt), the foreign policy goals of the host state are an important factor in the planning of nation-building policies.

CONCLUSION

Overall, while the members of the core group were less tolerant of previously dominant groups and tried to undermine their assimilation so that they would not have to share the national wealth with them, the ruling political elite pursued policies according to geopolitical and security concerns.

Non-core groups without an external power supporting them and claiming their allegiance were targeted with assimilation and were the least likely to receive minority rights protection. External interference and support for specific non-core groups by competing states affected the core group elites' perception of threat and the nation-building policies they pursued. When interstate relations changed, policy changes followed suit.

The devastating military defeat of the Greek army by Mustafa Kemal's forces in 1922, however, led to the Agreement of Moudania in October, which resulted in the incorporation of Eastern Thrace into Turkey. The Lausanne Conference (December 1922–May 1923) brought about the largest "peaceful" compulsory population exchange in history.[87] The 1922 disaster in Asia Minor symbolized

---

[86] For a discussion of the distinction between transitional versus terminal policies, see Chapter 5.
[87] Clark 2006; Ladas 1932; Yıldırım 2006.

the end of Greek irredentist politics, but not of Greek nation-building. Territorial expansion was no longer on the agenda; however, national integration was.[88] National, religious, ethnic, and cultural minorities, as well as refugees from Turkey, had to be integrated into the society and assimilated into the Greek nation.

The borders drawn after the Balkan Wars, World War I, and the Greek-Turkish War and the treaties that followed them brought most Christians, who were previously under Ottoman Muslim rule, under the jurisdiction of Christian nation-states (the KSCS, Greece, or Bulgaria). However, the population was so mixed, the territorial competition so bloody, and the propaganda so intense that non-core groups still existed. People who sided during the war with the "wrong" side were acutely aware that they were perceived by their host state as disloyal. This situation of mutual distrust in and of itself would have been hard to overcome with even the best-planned policies, but it was worsened by continued external involvement, even after the signing of the peace treaties, by revisionist states dissatisfied with the international status quo. Building trust was a challenging enterprise.

[88] Mavrogordatos 1983.

7

Temporal Variation

Serbian Nation-Building toward Albanians, 1878–1941

[F]or us Serbs Kossovo is much less a geographical and strategical term than a term of our national psychology, a term announcing a historical synthesis, proclaiming to the world that the Serbs have been able to transform a military defeat into a moral victory, to develop a national tragedy into a national glory.[1]

We have explored the explanatory power of my argument across the Balkan states immediately following World War I and probed it at the subnational level in one Greek province during and after World War I, but how well does my argument explain variation over longer periods of time? In this chapter, I trace the logic underlying the policies followed by the Serbian ruling political elites[2] toward the Albanians in Toplica and Kosanica at the end of the nineteenth century and in Kosovo and Metohija[3] from 1912 to 1941. I test my theory against archival material, secondary sources, and memoirs, as well as available newspapers and

---

[1] Mijatovich 1917: 219.
[2] Serbia did not formally exist as an administrative unit within the Kingdom of Serbs, Croats and Slovenes or later within the Kingdom of Yugoslavia. However, we can definitely talk about the Serbian political elites as well as the "Serbian lands" during the Interwar period. For more, see Petranović 2002: xxiii-48.
[3] Under the Ottomans modern-day Kosovo was part of three *vilayets*: Bosna, Kosova, and Monastir before 1877 and part of Kosova *vilayet* after 1878 (Magocsi 2002: 85, 119). During the early twentieth century this territory was split between Serbia (Zvečan, Kosovo, and southern Metohija) and Montenegro (northern Metohija). In 1922 internal borders changed again and Kosovo was split between three oblasts: Priština/Kosovo, Čačak/Raška, and Cetinje/Zeta. In 1929, with the transformation of the Kingdom of Serbs, Croats, and Slovenes (KSCS) to the Kingdom of Yugoslavia, Kosovo was divided among three *banovinas*: Zeta Banovina, Morava Banovina, and Vardar Banovina. This is the area that corresponded to the *Autonomous Province of Kosovo and Metohija* part of the constituent republic of Serbia in Communist Yugoslavia. The "Metohija" part was dropped in the 1974 Constitution, and thus the *Socialist Autonomus Province of Kosovo*. Today this territory is still claimed by the Serbs, but a new state, the Republic of Kosovo, has declared its independence in 2008 as a result of the 1999 Kosovo War. In this book, when I refer to Kosovo I refer roughly to the present-day territory of Kosovo unless otherwise stated in the text. For more on the changing boundaries of Kosovo and Metohija, see Krstić-Brano 2004: 27–34. For more on ethnographic maps of the region during Ottoman times, see Grimm 1984: 41–53.

journals from the period under study. I find that nation-building policies were not chosen based on objective measures of cultural distance, non-core group preferences, domestic political developments in the host state, or deep-rooted ethnic hatred between the non-assimilated and the core-group but rather based on a combination of other factors: the level of danger of secessionist claims by externally backed non-core group elites as perceived by the host government, bilateral state relations of the latter with the external power supporting the group, and the foreign policy goals of the host state.

Studying Serbian policies toward Albanians for a period of fifty years allows me to keep important regional-, state-, and group-level characteristics constant and isolate the effect of my main variables of interest. The region experienced successive annexations and the Albanian population residing there was exposed to a variety of nation-building policies, ensuring variation in both my dependent and independent variables. Many historians and political analysts read this period – if not the whole modern history of Serb–Albanian relations – as a period of repression and do not analyze the fluctuations in policy.[4] I offer a novel interpretation of events.

The main independent variables – perceived level of external support for the non-core group, interstate relations between the host state and the external power, and foreign policy preferences of the host state – vary during this period. In particular, there was important variation in external support of the non-core group under study. Initially, the Albanian national movement agitated parts of the population; later on the Albanian state took over that role. For a short period when the interstate relations between the Kingdom of Serbs, Croats and Slovenes (KSCS) and Albania normalized, external involvement in Kosovo ceased. But once again the Italian involvement during the late 1920s in the region – through the capture of Albania – and its plans to undermine the Yugoslav state brought about a new era of externally sponsored agitation in Kosovo. Interstate relations between the external backers of the Kosovo Albanians (Albania and Italy) and the Serbian ruling elites (Kingdom of Serbia and, later, within the KSCS) varied over time and so did the latter's perception of the involvement by external powers in their internal affairs.

Serbian elites' foreign policy goals also shifted during this period: from dissatisfied with the international status quo – no access to the Adriatic and unredeemed co-ethnics – before World War I, to working for its preservation after the "Great War" – when they achieved both South-Slav unification and access to the Adriatic. The important variation in my dependent and main independent variables together with the host of variables that are held constant by design render this region an ideal location to study the politics of nation-building and test my theory.

I organize this chapter in four sections. In the first, I describe the exclusionary policies of the expansionist Serbian Kingdom toward Albanians before World

---

[4] For example, see Babuna 2000; Malcolm 1998; Poulton 2003; Stefanović 2005.

External Power Support

		Yes		No
		Interstate Relations		No
		Ally	Enemy	
Host State (Foreign Policy Goals)	Lost Territory (Revisionist)	Accommodation	Exclusion 1878–1912 1912–1915	Assimilation
	Gained Territory (Status Quo)	Accommodation c.1924	Assimilation/Colonization 1918–1923 1925–1941	

FIGURE 7.1. Serbian nation-building toward Albanians, 1878–1941.

War I (see Figure 7.1). In the second, I describe the assimilationist policies that were implemented in the KSCS after World War I, when the Serbian elites were in favor of the international status quo. I also focus on a fascinating turn of events that transformed interstate relations between Albania and the KSCS circa 1924 and as a result led to a brief period of accommodation of Kosovo Albanians. In the third section, I explore the effect of internal political developments in the Kingdom of Yugoslavia on the choice of nation-building policies toward the Albanians in Kosovo. Finally, I conclude with a discussion of the fit between my theory and the patterns identified in the previous sections in light of alternative explanations.

THE REVISIONIST KINGDOM OF SERBIA

Serbian-Albanian Relations Prior to 1912: Exclusion

The Serbian national revival focused on language and Orthodox Christianity, both of which separated them from their Ottoman rulers. Before Serbia's independence in 1878, Serbian elites focused largely on two categories of Muslims: the Islamized Slavs, who in their view should convert back to Christianity or be excluded from the nation, and the Turkish speaking Muslim settlers, who had come into the area after the conquests of the fifteenth and sixteenth centuries and who should return to Anatolia.

During the nineteenth century Serbian animosity toward Muslims – and primarily the urban Muslims who were seen as exploiting the rural Serbs and as an obstacle to national independence – manifested itself in various writings but also in Serbian uprisings.[5] However, this animosity was rarely channeled toward Albanian Muslims until late in the nineteenth century – except when Albanians would offer their military services to the Ottomans against Serbs.[6]

Toward the end of the nineteenth century, the Serbian army – pursuing a Greater Serbia – decided to deport the Albanian population living in Toplica and Kosanica, two regions incorporated into the newly independent Serbian state in 1878 (see Map 7.1).[7] The Albanian national movement claiming the loyalties of these Albanians had competing territorial claims to Serbia and thus accommodating the Albanians was also precluded as a possibility. The Albanian national awakening was in full swing[8] and the Serbs would not allow a potential security threat within their newly drawn borders.[9] Consistent with my theory, exclusion was the policy pursued by the Serbian ruling political elites (see Table 7.1).

As an upshot of these exclusionary policies in the late nineteenth century, "The Albanians expelled from these regions moved over the new border to Kosovo, where the Ottoman authorities forced the Serb population out of the border region and settled the refugees there."[10] Consequently, relations between Albanians and Serbs deteriorated to unprecedented levels. According to Stefanović this was the turning point that influenced all future interactions between the two groups.[11] We will see that this view of the interethnic relations in Kosovo, although consistent with the events in 1912, cannot account for variation in state policies toward Albanians in the first half of the twentieth century.

The Initial Occupation of Kosovo: Exclusion

After the occupation of Kosovo and part of Metohija by the Serbian forces the ruling elites had to come to a decision about how to treat the Albanians living there.[12] The Serbian elites at the time were still motivated by revisionist foreign policy goals[13] aiming at the creation of a Greater

[5] Edwards 1969; Garašanin 1998; Karadžić 1972; Njegoš 1930.
[6] For more on the nineteenth-century history of the relations, see Banac 1984; Stefanović 2005: 465–492.
[7] Horvat 1988: 71; Stefanović 2005: 469.
[8] Austin 2004: 235-253; Skendi 1967. The Albanian national movement first developed in modern-day Kosovo during the Great Eastern Crisis of 1875–1878. For more, see Zavalani 1969: 55–92.
[9] Bogdanović 1986.
[10] Popović 1987: 80.
[11] Stefanović 2005: 470.
[12] For the Serbian perspective, see Jagodić 2009 and 2010. For the Austrian perspective, see the reports of a Jewish Parliamentarian member of the Social-Democratic Party in Vienna, Freundlich 1997: 332–360.
[13] To put it in International Relations terms, Serbia was a limited aims revisionist, see Schweller 2006: 88. Unlike Hitler, Napoleon, or Alexander the Great, Serbia was not a major power and therefore was incapable of becoming an unlimited aims revisionist state where the complete domination of all of the Great Powers is the aim. For a Croatian perspective, see Beljo 1992.

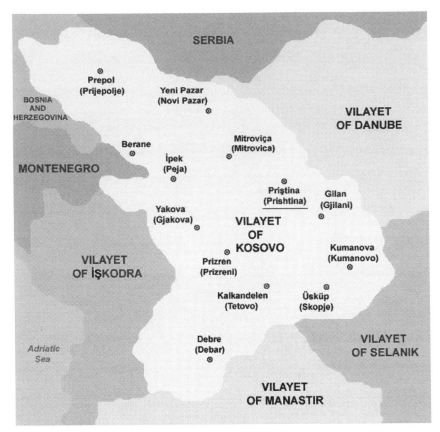

○ - Vilayet of Kosovo within Ottoman Empire from 1875 to 1878

○ - semi-independent states within Ottoman Empire

∞ - other Ottoman territories

MAP 7.1. *Vilayet* of Kosova, 1875–1878. *Source*: http://en.wikipedia.org/wiki/File: Kosovo02.png.

Serbia.[14] In particular, the goal of the Serbian government was the annexation of parts of the Kosova *vilayet*[15] and parts of geographic Macedonia,[16] but also

[14] Serbian nationalism had taken a hold of the soldier's imagination as well. Čedomilj Mijatović (1842–1932), a Serbian statesman and leader of the Progressive Party who served as Minister of Finance and Minister of Foreign Affairs, informs us in his memoirs that Serbian leaders did not have to make long and stirring speeches in order to motivate their soldiers; they only uttered, "Let us avenge Kossovo!" Mijatovich 1917: 220; for an Albanian perspective, see Verli 1999.

[15] Bataković, *"Kosovo and Metohija: A Historical Survey."*

[16] Wilkinson 1951; Stefanidis et al. 2010.

TABLE 7.1. *Serbian Nation-Building toward Albanians, 1878–1941*

Period	State	Host State	Albania	Prediction	Policy
1878–1912	Kingdom of Serbia	Revisionist	No State	Exclusion	Exclusion
1912–1915	Kingdom of Serbia	Revisionist	Enemy	Exclusion	Exclusion
1918–1923	KSCS	Status Quo	Enemy	Assimilation	Assimilation
c.1924	KSCS	Status Quo	Ally	Accommodation	Accommodation
1925–1937	KSCS/ Yugoslavia	Status Quo	Enemy	Assimilation	Assimilation
1937–1941	Yugoslavia	Status Quo	Enemy	Assimilation	Plans for Exclusion

of a significant part of contemporary Northern Albania, which would guarantee access to the Adriatic Sea.[17]

Albanians in Kosovo were mobilized by the Albanian national independence movement, which actually began in the Kosova *vilayet* in the late nineteenth century with the support of Austria-Hungary and Italy.[18] Albanian territorial aspirations, expressed by the Prizren League in 1878, extended to territories from four different *vilayets*, including that of Kosova.[19] Austria-Hungary and Italy were prepared to do anything to prevent Serbian access to the Adriatic Sea, while Russia and France operated as protectors of Serbia in the international scene. The Serbian government realized that it had to change the ethnic balance of the population in the region in order to legitimize its territorial aspirations.[20]

Given this setting, my theory predicts that nation-building policies toward the Albanians should have been exclusionary (Table 7.1). Indeed, in the period following the annexation (1912–1915), it is estimated that around 25,000 Albanians were killed and approximately 120,000 were forced to flee from Kosovo as a result of acts of intimidation and violence pursued by the Serbian army.[21] Many of the existing explanations that I discussed above would also

---

[17] Statements indicating this desire can be found from the early twentieth century in the work of Jovan Cvijić (1865–1927), a famous Serbian geographer. Cvijić served as president of the Serbian Royal Academy of Sciences and was also rector of the University of Belgrade.

[18] Kola 2003; Skendi 1967; Zavalani 1969.

[19] Hadri 1995; Skendi 1967.

[20] Mazower 2001: 124.

[21] Malcolm 1998: 254, 258. Freundlich (1997) claims that the Serbian government aimed at the extermination of the Albanians in the lands they were annexing.

predict exclusion in this situation; however, as we will see below, Albanians were also targeted with assimilationist policies and even granted minority rights in subsequent periods. Existing arguments cannot account for this variation since their predictions remain constant over time. My argument does account for these shifts because it focuses on variation in interstate relations and host states' foreign policy goals.

To understand the logic of this policy choice and test the microfoundations of my argument it is necessary to take a closer look at the events that preceded this exclusionary policy decision. By the beginning of the twentieth century, nationalism as an ideology was at its peak. During the Balkan Wars, Serbia expanded significantly. Not surprisingly, armies of nation-states that wanted to secure territories had to ensure the right "ethnic balance" on the ground. Serbian nationhood – like that of most Christian Balkan states at the time – had been built in opposition to the Ottoman Muslims. In the case of Kosovo, which was primarily inhabited by Albanian Muslims but annexed by Serbia, the initial strategy was a mix of violence and intimidation. This was the first time that the Serbian expansion reached a region inhabited primarily by an alien population (see Map 7.2).[22]

The situation was not that different from what took place in 1878. The Albanians, however, had a more developed national movement by 1912[23] and were embittered by the centralization efforts of the Young Turks that also aimed at their assimilation into the stillborn Ottoman identity.[24] In the meantime, Albanian militants – pursuing their own nation-building project – had been attacking and intimidating Serbs living in the Ottoman Empire around the turn of the twentieth century under the protection of the Sultan. According to Jovan Cvijić, as many as 150,000 Serbs fled from Sandžak and Kosovo during that period, 1876–1912.[25] These developments guaranteed an explosive mix.

Despite this background, faced with the Ottoman forces during the first Balkan War, Pašić – the Serbian Prime Minister at the time and a close friend of the Tsar and the Russian Government[26] – tried to take the Kosovo Albanians on his side by offering in return guarantees for religious freedom and cultural rights within the Serbian state. The Albanian leaders refused to collaborate; many were backed by Austria-Hungary,[27] and a few actually fought on the side of the Ottomans.[28] It is hard to know what would have happened if Albanian leaders had decided to collaborate with the Serbs during the first Balkan War.

---

[22] Banac 1984: 293.
[23] Skendi 1967.
[24] Findley 2010; Ülker 2005: 617.
[25] Stefanović 2005: 472.
[26] Mijatovich 1917: 232. For more on Pašić, see Djokić 2010; Dragnich 1974.
[27] Vickers 1998: 77.
[28] Bataković 1991: 173; Lampe 2000: 92, 97; Stefanović 2005: 474.

MAP 7.2. Territorial development of Serbia, 1817–1913. *Source*: http://en.wikipedia.org/wiki/File:Serbia1817_1913.png.

Assuming that Pašić's offer was sincere, the fact that Pašić made this offer suggests that things could have turned out otherwise and ethnic cleansing might have been averted. Not surprisingly given the situation, the policy of the Serbian forces when they annexed Kosovo in 1912 was to kill or force to emigrate as many Albanians as possible and colonize the territory with Serbs.

ILLUSTRATION 7.1. Üsküb: King of Serbia welcomed by mayor. *Source*: Library of Congress Prints and Photographs Division, Washington, D.C.

The Serbian authorities were trying to establish control, disarm disloyal groups, and force unwanted aliens to leave (see Illustration 7.1).[29]

In a memorandum that Mary Edith Durham[30] compiled for Aubrey Herbert[31] – a British MP for Somerset – we read that at least 25,000 Albanians were killed in the *vilayet* of Kosova. According to McCarthy, between 7,000 and 10,000 Albanians were killed in the areas of Kumanovo and Pristina,[32] while over 25,000 refugees fled to Northern Albania.[33] Durham reported that:

The Servian [*sic*] officers declared in the intoxication of victory that the best way to pacify Albania was to exterminate the Albanians. Between Koumanoval and Üsküb, they

---

[29] Naturally, there were dissenting voices to almost all of the Serbian and Albanian strategies I am discussing in this chapter; but for the sake of brevity and a more coherent narrative I do not cover them here. For more on alternative Serbian views, see Banac 1984: 296–297 and Stefanović 2005.

[30] Mary Edith Durham (1863–1944) was an English reporter on the Balkans and Albanian and Montenegrin affairs in particular. She was also a relief worker and a lobbyist for the Albanian cause. For more, see Harry Hodgkinson's introduction in Durham 2001: i–xx.

[31] Aubrey Nigel Henry Molyneux Herbert (1880–1923) was a conservative member of Parliament for the southern division of Somerset from 1911 to 1918 and for Yeovil from 1918 to 1923. He was a supporter of Albania and often corresponded with Edith Durham. Twice he was offered the throne of Albania.

[32] McCarthy 1995: 141.

[33] Durham 2001: 29, Nikolić 2003.

massacred over three thousand people; in the vicinity of Prishtina five thousand Albanians were killed.[34]

Although this seems like evidence of deep-rooted ethnic hatreds at work, contemporary observers suggested that these efforts had little to do with religious or cultural difference. In a confidential report by the British chargé in Belgrade Dayrell Crackanthorpe[35] to the Foreign Secretary Sir Edward Grey[36] we find further evidence supporting my argument.[37] Crackanthorpe, reporting on civil and religious freedoms in the new territories of Serbia, writes:

The signal lack of religion noticeable among the large minority of Servians precludes the possibility of this uncompromising attitude being due to religious intolerance; the real explanation seems to be that Servians look upon their national Orthodox Church as a means of propagating not the Kingdom of Heaven, but the Kingdom of Servia.[38]

The dominant policy was one of exclusion as the archival material demonstrates and as eyewitness accounts such as those included in the Report of the Carnegie Endowment for International Peace and even that of Trotsky testify to.[39] The Carnegie Report quotes a letter of a Serbian soldier to the Socialist paper *Radnitchké Noviné*:

Appalling things are going on here.... Liouma (an Albanian region along the river of the same name), no longer exists. There is nothing but corpses, dust and ashes. There are villages of 100, 150, 200 houses, where there is no longer a single man, literally *not one*. We collect them in bodies of forty and fifty, and then pierce them with our bayonets to the last man.[40]

From the available accounts, Serbian violence toward the local Albanian population appears to have been strategic rather than motivated by ethnic hatred or antipathy. The Kaçaks[41] were a serious security concern. The Carnegie Report mentions that these incidents were part of an effort to repress the Albanian revolts instigated by Albanians from autonomous Albania and/or by Bulgaria.[42] Crackanthorpe corroborated this logic of Serbian policies when he wrote in May 1914:

---

[34] Memorandum researched by Mary Edith Durham for Aubrey Herbert, MP for Somerset: "The Albanians must be exterminated," 1913 Somerset Records Office (DDR/o).

[35] Dayrell Crackanthorpe (1870–1950) was a diplomat and at the time British Chargé d'Affaires at Belgrade.

[36] Sir Edward Grey (1862–1933) was British Secretary of State for Foreign Affairs from 1905 to 1916.

[37] For the views in the British Foreign Office at the time, see Evans 2008: 105–107.

[38] Dayrell Crackanthorpe, Belgrade, to Sir Edward Grey, 26 May 1914, civil and religious freedoms in the new territories of Servia [FO 371/2110].

[39] Carnegie Endowment for International Peace 1914; Lampe 2000: 97; Trotsky 1980: 267.

[40] Carnegie Endowment for International Peace 1914: 149.

[41] Albanian rebel group. From the Turkish word "kaçaklar," which means outlaw.

[42] Carnegie Endowment for International Peace 1914: 149.

It is this constant dread of political propaganda that has coloured, and is still colouring, the attitude of the Servian Government toward religious minorities in the annexed territories.... It seems ... that their attitude toward the Moslems has been considerably coloured by apprehensions lest the indigent Moslem population may become a prey to political propaganda and a dangerous element of unrest in the event of further trouble with Albania or Bulgaria, and the desire therefore is to force them to emigrate.[43]

In a later report, Crackanthorpe adds more information that he received from the Vice-Consul in Monastir. Interestingly, Crackanthorpe hesitates to believe this additional information wholeheartedly, as he recognizes that a great deal of it could be the product of political propaganda. He writes:

I cannot personally guarantee, from information gathered here, the accuracy of the lurid horrors Greig describes. I think some account should be taken of local exaggeration and of the fact that the Moslem population, led by Albanian priests, have undoubtedly been painting things in the blackest colours in the hopes of promoting autonomy. I have found even the Austrian Legation inclined to accept these reports with a grain of salt, and I cannot conscientiously recommend their publication in a despatch to be laid before Parliament.[44]

Less-studied aspects of these events have to do with the degree of control of the Serbian administrative apparatus in the newly annexed territories as well as the quality of implementation of state policies. In other words, it is unclear what percentage of the actions observed on the ground in Kosovo were dictated by Belgrade and what was part of a micro-level story of opportunism on the part of individuals pursuing their private agendas. With respect to administrators, we do know that they were often selected on the basis of patronage and were not trained at all. Overall, the conditions of relative anarchy on the ground coupled with low salaries from the Serbian government were conducive to abuses of office. Crackanthorpe again illuminates this aspect:

Testimony has reached me from every source of the corrupt and venal character of Servian administration, the one endeavour of Servian subordinate officials being apparently to supplement their insufficient pay by every means within their grasp. The principal sufferers have been the Moslems, who, if local reports are to be believed, have been subjected for some time past to systematic persecution of a callously cruel description by the local officials. It is difficult to say how far this persecution has taken place with the consent and connivance of the Central Government.[45]

---

[43] Mr Dayrell Crackanthorpe, Belgrade, to Sir Edward Grey, 26 May 1914, civil and religious freedoms in the new territories of Servia [FO 371/2110].

[44] Mr Dayrell Crackanthorpe, Belgrade, to Sir E. Crowe, Asst. Under Secretary for Foreign Affairs, 2 June 1914, covering Mr Dayrell Crackanthorpe, Belgrade, to Sir Edward Grey, Foreign Secretary, 2 June 1914, enclosing despatch from Vice-Consul Greig, Monastir, 25 May 1914, on Serbian occupation and its effects [FO 371/2110].

[45] Mr Dayrell Crackanthorpe, Belgrade, to Sir Edward Grey, 26 May 1914, civil and religious freedoms in the new territories of Servia [FO 371/2110].

A report by Peckham, British Vice-Counsel in Üsküb, however, suggests that the Serbian government directed a great deal of what was going on in Kosovo. Reporting on 14 December 1913, he writes:

I learn on reasonably good authority that a former prefect of Prishtina was relieved of his duties because he had too much conscience to carry out the Government policy of the removal of the Albanian population. This, coupled with other indications given in my previous reports, seems to me to fix the responsibility in pretty high quarters.[46]

Given the number of killings and forced migrants on the Albanian side following the annexation of Kosovo (25,000 and 120,000, respectively, according to most estimates)[47] we can conclude that Serbia's initial nation-building strategy was that of physical removal of Albanians and colonization with Serbian settlers.[48] The Kingdom of Serbia was a small revisionist state faced with a relatively large and enemy-backed non-core group, which it perceived as a potential threat to its future territorial integrity. As a result, exclusionary policies ensued.[49]

Forced assimilation – although not the dominant policy in this period – was also pursued toward Albanians. According to Banac, Serbian propaganda "simultaneously dehumanized Albanians, presenting them as utterly incapable of governing themselves and as the sort of element that ought to be exterminated, and elevated them to the standing that warranted their assimilation." The justification behind the assimilationist policies followed toward some of the Kosovo Albanians was that many of them were Islamized Serbs who had eventually become Albanians. The fundamental belief behind this policy was that the "Albanians had no nationhood and their nationalism was the product of Austrian and Italian intrigue." World War I followed soon thereafter, Kosovo was occupied by Bulgaria and Austria-Hungary, and the Serbian ruling political elites had to deal with more pressing concerns until 1918.

THE STATUS QUO KINGDOM OF SERBS, CROATS AND SLOVENES

Albania Supporting the Kaçak Movement: Assimilation and Colonization

In 1918, the Serbian army assumed control over Kosovo once again. The KSCS was in favor of the international status quo and wanted to consolidate it.[50] The implementation of exclusionary policies, like the ones pursued during the Balkan Wars, toward the Kosovo Albanians would not serve this purpose. It would just add another front. Albanians in Kosovo were still mobilized by a secessionist

---

[46] Vice-Consul Peckham, Üsküb, to Mr Crackanthorpe 14 December 1913, reporting on Serbian Government policy of the removal of the Albanian population [FO 421/286].

[47] Malcolm 1998: 254, 258.

[48] For an Albanian perspective, see Verli 1995.

[49] Banac 1984: 293–295.

[50] Petranović 2002: 11.

movement linked to their "brothers" in Albania (the Kaçak movement),[51] which was supported financially by Italy. Given this context, my theory predicts assimilation (see Table 7.1).[52]

Indeed, the policies followed by the new government of the KSCS were not as violent as those of the 1912–1915 period. State policy toward the Albanians was one of assisted assimilation through the Serbian language education system.[53] The elites of the new state wanted to preserve the favorable international status quo and decided to colonize the territory by giving land to Serbs who wanted to move there and also used the political system to co-opt local elites.[54]

Let us take a closer look at the events that took place during this period. After World War I and the brief administrative split of Kosovo, with Austria ruling in the north and Bulgaria in the South,[55] the territory was incorporated into the newly formed KSCS. The creation of the KSCS was the outcome of World War I and the consequent collapse of Austria-Hungary and the Ottoman Empire.[56] In particular, the Slovenian and Croatian fears of Italian domination, coupled with the long-lasting Serbian desire to unite all of the Serbs into a single state, led to the unification of the South Slavs.[57] The unification took place under the Serbian Karadjordjević dynasty in 1918 and was recognized by the Paris Peace Conference in May 1919. The new state, on the side of the winners in World War I, was in favor of the international status quo.

Before World War I, irredentism and the pursuit of a Greater Serbia clearly drove Serbian politics. After the end of the war, the political situation was quite different. Nearly all of the Serbs in the Balkans were included in one state, which finally had access to the Adriatic. Serbian revisionist goals subsided; however, the energies of Serbia's political leaders were now focused on turning the new kingdom into a centralized state under Serbian hegemony.[58]

The newly established Kingdom engaged in several territorial disputes with its neighbors: Italy, Austria, Hungary, Bulgaria, Romania, and Albania – in other words with all of its neighbors except Greece. Italy supported extremist movements of Croatians, Slav Macedonians, and Albanians, "hoping to stir unrest and hasten the end of the new kingdom."[59] Bulgaria supported the "Macedonian" movement in Southern Serbia. Hungary also envisioned reclaiming its lost territories. Unrest broke out in Vojvodina as early as 1919. And, of

---

[51] For more on the complicated domestic situation in Albania at the time, see Fischer 2007: 21–28; Kola 2003: 18–19; Pearson 2004: 110–224.
[52] For an account of KSCS policies toward minorities during the interwar period, see Janjetović 2005.
[53] Poulton and Vickers 1997: 146.
[54] Banac 1984: 155–156; Krstić-Brano 2004: 80–81.
[55] Austrian rule was clearly accommodative to the Albanians; see Vickers 1998: 261.
[56] For more on the Kingdom of the Serbs, Croats, and Slovenes (later Yugoslavia) in the interwar period, see Banac 1984; Biondich 2007: 203–213; Djilas 1991; Djokić 2003 and 2007; Dragnich 1983; Lampe 2000; Petranović 2002; Ramet 2006.
[57] Sørensen 2009: 70.
[58] Tomasevich 1955; Banac 1984.
[59] Curtis 1992.

course, Albania supported the Kaçak movement in Kosovo. The main task of Yugoslav Ministers of Foreign Affairs in the interwar period was addressing these threats with the help of Balkan (Little Entente[60] and later on the Balkan Entente[61]) and European alliances (primarily with France and the Great Britain) in an effort to secure the favorable status quo.

Exclusionary policies would have jeopardized this status quo. Intimidation, persecution, and assassinations of Kosovo Albanians were prevalent, but targeting was selective. Between 1918 and 1921 a small-scale war occurred in Kosovo between the Serbian military forces and its *četas*,[62] on the one hand, and the "Committee for the National Defense of Kosovo" and its Kaçaks, on the other.[63] The Kosovo Committee, which fought for the liberation of Kosovo and the unification of all Albanian lands, "was assisted financially by Italy and led by Hoxha Kadriu from Pristina, and consisted mainly of political exiles from Kosovo."[64]

According to the 1921 census there were 436,929 inhabitants in Kosovo at the time. Sixty-four percent of them (280,440) were Albanian speakers.[65] Given this context, the KSCS government had good reasons to fear the development of a secessionist movement in Kosovo. The Kosovo Albanians were backed by Albania and could have threatened the territorial integrity of the KSCS,[66] thus accommodation was also out of the question.[67]

The Serbs reacted to what they perceived as an externally supported secessionist non-core group,[68] which had killed "since the liberation in December 1918 until the present day 800 Orthodox Serbs ... more than were killed in Turkish days during a full ten years."[69] In the summer of 1920 the KSCS waged a small war against Albania.[70] Extensive internal displacement of suspected Kaçaks and their families took place but the KSCS government offered an amnesty in early 1921.[71] The consequent internationalization of this crisis forced the Great Powers to speed up the delimitation of the Albanian-Yugoslav border process, which was fueling the conflict.

The KSCS was a status quo power that was faced with a non-core group, the Kosovo Albanians, supported by an enemy power, Albania. Exclusion might have led to a war where Italy – and maybe a revived Austria in the future – would back Albania against the KSCS. Accommodation would only prolong – if not

---

[60] Czechoslovakia, Yugoslavia, and Romania.
[61] Greece, Yugoslavia, Romania, and Turkey.
[62] *Četas* were small paramilitary units.
[63] Banac 1984: 298, 303–304.
[64] Vickers 1998: 93.
[65] The Albanian side claims that there were around 700,000 Albanians in Kosovo at the time; see Ramet 2006.
[66] For more on the KSCS concerns regarding the foreign invasion of the country, see Todorović 1979.
[67] Austin 2004: 241.
[68] Banac 1984: 304.
[69] Mr. W. Strang, Belgrade to Earl Curzon 30 August 1921, reporting on colonization under government auspices in Southern Serbia (FO 371/5725).
[70] Banac 1984: 298.
[71] Malcolm 1998: 275.

exacerbate – the problem. The Kosovo Albanians could be used as an "enemy within" to destabilize the KSCS. Consistent with my argument, assimilationist policies – in the form of colonization and internal displacement – were the only available responses to address this situation (Table 7.1).

The use of Albanian was prohibited for any official purposes,[72] Albanian schools were closed down,[73] Albanian children were sent to Serbian schools, and mosques were used for military and government purposes. "To aid [the assimilation] Bosnian Serbo-Croat-speaking Muslim teachers were used" in the schools.[74]

Electoral politics were also marshaled in the assimilationist project. The Radicals "supplanted the assimilationist role of the Serbian church under new increasingly secular circumstances and stimulated a Serb consciousness in newly acquired southeastern Serbia, where it formerly had not existed."[75] The Radical Party co-opted the local Muslim organization *Cemiyet*.[76] However, this only lasted until the late 1920s when the *Cemiyet* ceased to exist because its leader was accused of plotting a secessionist movement.[77] Parallel to these measures, the government arranged the electoral districts in such a way that Serbs were the majority in all of them (see Map 7.3).[78]

Finally, as predicted, the KSCS followed a colonization policy. On 24 September 1920 the government launched its colonization effort in Kosovo with the Decree on Settlement.[79] Serbs and Montenegrins were encouraged to move into Kosovo and by 1921 "[n]early 7,000 families ha[d] received grants of land in Southern Serbia, the total area of their holdings being 57,531 hectares, or about 8 hectares per family." The selective implementation of the land reform in the areas contributed to the grievances of the local Albanian population.[80] The same year William Strang[81] informed the British government that

This colonization is doubly advantageous from a national point of view: regarded as economic redistribution, it should bring contentment to many who have either lost their homes or who have found it impossible to subsist without distress on the barren lands they have hitherto occupied ... and in the second place it establishes a sound and loyal population in a region where races and religions are mixed and loyalty doubtful.... At whose expense these lands are found, it is not easy to say.... It is certain, however, that in

[72] Vickers 1998: 103.
[73] Banac 1984: 298–299.
[74] Poulton and Vickers 2007: 146.
[75] Banac 1984: 155–156.
[76] Islam Muhafazai Hukuk Cemiyet (Society for the Preservation of Muslim Rights) was a Muslim organization for the Turks and Albanians of Southern regions of the KSCS.
[77] Banac 1984: 378.
[78] Stefanović 2005: 479.
[79] For more on the colonization policy, see Banac 1984: 299–301; Krstić-Brano 2004: 80; Marmullaku 1975: 138.
[80] Sørensen 2009: 70.
[81] William Strang (1893–1978) served in the British embassy in Belgrade from 1919 to 1922.

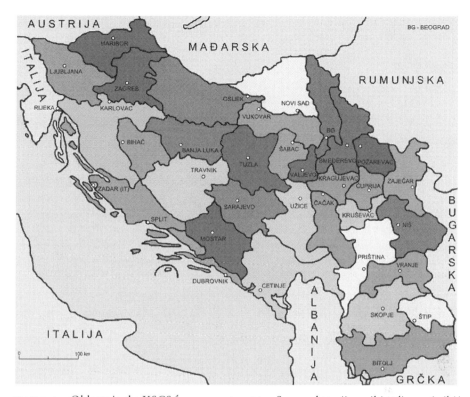

MAP 7.3. Oblasts in the KSCS from 1922 to 1929. *Source*: http://en.wikipedia.org/wiki/
File:Podjela_Kraljevine_SHS_na_33_oblasti.jpg.

some cases a deliberate attempt has been made to drive out or destroy Albanian
Mussulman population and install loyal Serbs in their place.[82]

Ahmet Zogolli (later renamed King Zog) became Prime Minister of Albania
in 1922 but his rule encountered intense opposition. A great deal of the dis-
contentment had to do with his lack of enthusiasm on the Kosovo issue, that is,
liberating Kosovo and annexing it to Albania. He favored focusing first on
domestic problems that Albania faced and then pursuing an irredentist agenda
with respect to Kosovo.[83] This position earned him many enemies. According to
others[84] his position on the Kosovo issue was the result of his rivalry with leaders
such as Hasan Prishtina.[85]

---

[82] Mr. W. Strang, Belgrade to Earl Curzon 30 August 1921, reporting on colonization under
government auspices in Southern Serbia (FO 371/5725).
[83] Fischer 2007: 19–49.
[84] Kola 2003: 19.
[85] Hasan Prishtina (1873–1933) was an Albanian national leader and briefly became Prime Minister
of Albania in 1921. Hasan Prishtina together with Hoxhë Kadriu, Bajram Curri, and others
created the Committee for the National Protection of Kosovo.

Regardless, Bishop Fan Noli[86] and his Democratic Party managed to take over the government for six months and forced Zog to flee to Yugoslavia. As we will see in the next section, accommodation of the Kosovo Albanians – contrary to the predictions of all alternative arguments – became possible when Zog reestablished his rule and ceased supporting the Kosovo Albanian secessionist movement, but only for a little while.

Albania from an Enemy to an Ally: Accommodation

For a couple of years during the mid-1920s the KSCS remained in favor of the status quo and Albania ceased supporting the Kaçak movement in Kosovo and was an ally of the KSCS. Under such circumstances, my theory predicts that Albanians in Kosovo should be accommodated (Table 7.1). Indeed, as we will see below, in the mid-1920s Belgrade issued an extensive amnesty decree, permitted religious schooling conducted by Muslim imams in Muslim mektebs (primary schools) and medreses (secondary schools), and permitted the use of the Albanian language.[87]

A closer look at this counterintuitive shift is warranted. In December 1924, Zog invaded Albania with the help of the Yugoslav army – and Wrangelite White Russian troops – and managed to overthrow Fan Noli.[88] Zog prevailed over the Kosovo politicians in Albania and persecuted his enemies.[89] Kola describes the situation well:

Zog chose Yugoslavia, of all places, to retreat to. There he was supplied with money and men and returned to stage a coup six months later. From then onwards, he became a virtual vassal of the Serbs, and the question of Kosova was buried.[90]

By the mid-1920s the Kaçak movement had been almost eradicated. At that moment, Albania ceased acting as a national homeland. Albania was now a friendly state that did not interfere and Kosovo Albanians were no longer perceived as a threat by the government in Belgrade.[91] In response to these developments in Albania – and consistent with my argument – the government in Belgrade "issued a sweeping amnesty decree."[92]

At around the same time that Zog reestablished his power in Albania, the Cemiyet elected fourteen members in the Yugoslav parliament and was in a coalition with the ruling Serb-dominated Radical Party.[93] As an otherwise

---

[86] Fan Noli (1882–1965) was the founder of the Albanian Orthodox Church and serve as a Prime Minister and Regent of Albania from June 1924 to December 1924. For more, see Austin 1996: 154.
[87] Vickers 1998: 103.
[88] Banac 1984, pp. 302, 305; Fischer 2007: 31–32; Swire 1971: 445.
[89] Kola 2003: 19.
[90] Ibid., p. 20.
[91] Burgwyn 1997: 25.
[92] Vickers 1998: 101.
[93] Banac 1984: 377.

scathing Albanian memorandum to the League of Nations put it, "[t]he Albanians hoped for one moment in 1925–1926 that they would be as free as the other citizens of Yugoslavia to occupy political positions in the country."[94]

Given the geopolitical situation and domestic politics in Albania, however, the Yugoslav favoritism in Tirana did not last for long. Zog faced an Italian-backed revolt in 1926 but managed to crush it.[95] Faced with externally supported opposition and a difficult economic situation Zog decided to change his stance toward Italy.[96] As we will see, Italy successfully penetrated Albanian political life in the late 1920s and changed Albanian foreign policy toward the Kosovo Albanians and the KSCS once again.

Albania from Ally to Enemy Again: Back to Assimilation

The alliance with the KSCS did not last long under the increased pressure from financial problems that led Zog closer to Italy.[97] For the KSCS soon enough Albania turned into an enemy power agitating the Kosovo Albanians once again. Assimilation policies ensued (Table 7.1).

By 1929, Zog's turn from the KSCS to Italy[98] and King Aleksandar's dictatorship altered the geopolitical situation. According to Burgwyn's research in the Italian archives, Zog "was ready to turn to the Italians, but only on the condition that they provide him substantial support for Albania's irredentist claims on the Kosovo region."[99] Zog signed the Pact of Friendship and Security in November 1926 and since then Albanian foreign policy ceased being independent.[100] A second pact, signed a year later, solidified the alliance and thus the dependence on Mussolini's Italy.[101] Zog was also tellingly named "Zog I, King of the Albanians" in August 1928 (see Illustration 7.2).[102] The Yugoslavian government feared that Zog's new title meant that secessionist claims would once again be propagated amongst the Albanians in Kosovo.[103]

The dictatorship imposed by King Aleksandar on 6 January 1929 brought with it a new approach of the nation-building policies in Kosovo and the KSCS as a whole. The period that followed was marked by strict internal security

[94] Bisaku et al. 1997: 389.

[95] Fischer 2007: 35–36.

[96] Andrić 1997: 444.

[97] Kola 2003: 20.

[98] According to Fischer, Zog could not trust Belgrade and relying on Italy had the advantage that they had no common land borders and that Italy could help Albania financially (2007: 37). For more on Mussolini's foreign policy in the Balkans, see Burgwyn 1997; Steed 1927; Villari 1956.

[99] Burgwyn 1997: 40.

[100] Burgwyn 1997: 41; Miller 1927; Sereni 1941.

[101] Armstrong 1928.

[102] Documenti Diplomatici Italiani (DDI), Series 7, Vol. 6, document no. 41, 22 January 1928; Longworth 2007.

[103] Italy was aiding at the same time the Croatian movement and the Internal Macedonian Revolutionary Organization (IMRO); see Burgwyn 1997: 44–48.

ILLUSTRATION 7.2. King Zog. *Source*: Library of Congress, Prints and Photographs Division, Washington, D.C.

measures and the curtailment of civil liberties. On 3 October of the same year the Kingdom of Serbs, Croats and Slovenes was renamed the Kingdom of Yugoslavia; the banovine (administrative units) were created, conveniently dividing Kosovo into three new banovine,[104] (see Map 7.4); and the various legal systems were unified. Leaders of various non-core groups (ranging from Muslims to Slovene) were imprisoned and persecuted for sedition and terrorist activities. This was, in other words, the apogee of centralization under Serbian hegemony that ultimately solidified Croatian – and in general minority – opposition. The royal dictatorship lasted up until 1931 when King Aleksandar promulgated a new constitution. The 1931 attempt at democratic governence was a parody, with only one electoral list participating in the election. Thus, while the royal dictatorship formally ended in 1931, the subsequent period cannot be considered as democratic. Only in 1935 were there the first regular elections.

During this transformation, colonization and assimilation policies ensued toward Kosovo Albanians. This policy change also coincided with the increasing

---

[104] Lampe 2000: 167.

MAP 7.4. *Banovinas* in the Kingdom of Yugoslavia, 1929–1941. *Source*: http://upload. wikimedia.org/wikipedia/commons/e/eb/K%C3%B6nigreich_Jugoslawien.jpg.

influence of Italy on Albanian internal affairs and the proclamation of Zog as "King of the Albanians." Longworth summarizes this process well:

Italy financed a national bank for him [Zog]; arranged to lend Albania 50 million gold francs at 13 per cent, but interest-free for five years; provided a moratorium on the interest for 1925 and 1926 and paid over further large sums in 1928 and 1935, including £1 million for economic development. There were concessions in return, of course. The Friendship and Security Pact signed at Tirana in November 1926 heralded Albania's descent to the status of an Italian vassal. Step by step Italy not only gained the right to intervene at Albania's request (a device to keep Zog in power), but influence in military affairs, control over national assets, the replacement of British by Italian gendarmerie officers, acceptance of Italian advisers in a range of fields from civil engineering to physical training, control of air communications and *Lebensraum* provision for some of Italy's excess population. Cultural affiliation was indicated by provision for Italian in schools and the foundation of a fascist youth movement.[105]

[105] 2007: 163.

This increased influence of Italy in Albania was directly linked with the intensification of the Serbian colonization efforts in Kosovo. Decrees were passed in 1931 "forcing Albanians out of their lands, with ... new regulations requiring all land to pass into state property unless the owner could produce Yugoslav title-deeds."[106] Naturally, the Albanians in Kosovo were less likely to produce the necessary documentation. According to Verli, by 1938 every Albanian-inhabited area had been targeted with this policy.[107] Dérens reports that by 1939 around 59,300 Serbs had settled in the region, which accounted for approximately 9 percent of the total population.[108] Other estimates bring this number up to 100,000.[109]

From a memorandum presented to the League of Nations in 1930 we learn, among other things, that the Albanian private school in Skopje closed in 1929, the last in a series of private schools that were closed down. Albanian cultural associations were prohibited around the same time, and in regard to public schools "there is not a single school or a single class among the 545 referred to by the Yugoslav Government in which teaching is conducted in Albanian."[110]

As if this was not enough, the economic situation in Yugoslavia was difficult in the beginning of the 1930s as a result of the global financial crisis. This was exacerbated by the fact that France – the main patron of Yugoslavia – stopped absorbing Yugoslavian exports. Geopolitically, things were not much better; both Britain and France attempted cooperative relations with Hitler's Germany and Mussolini's Italy. The result of these efforts was an agreement of the "Big Four" for the preservation of the territorial status quo in Europe (June 1933). Yugoslavia, surrounded by unfriendly states (with the exception of Greece) attempted to counteract the unfavorable geopolitical developments described above by entering in the Balkan Entente in 1934 together with Greece, Turkey, and Romania.

Following the assassination of King Aleksandar in 1934,[111] France was no longer as interested in Yugoslav affairs. Germany had already bought French and American interests in the country.[112] As a result, Yugoslavia signed trade agreements with Germany and became more and more dependent on it economically. In the spring of 1937 Yugoslavia signed a Pact of Friendship with Italy. On top of everything else, the *Anschluss* between Germany and Austria created a very difficult situation for Yugoslavia since it was now bordering Germany.

---

[106] Kola 2003: 21.

[107] 1995: 15.

[108] Dérens 2008: 65.

[109] Verli 1995.

[110] Bisaku et al. 1997: 395.

[111] King Aleksandar was assassinated by a member of Ivan Mihailov's Internal Macedonian Revolutionary Organization (a Bulgarian-backed separatist organization) in cooperation with Ante Pavelić's Ustaše (a Croatian separatist organization) – an action backed by Italy, Bulgaria, and Hungary – brought about fears of a breakup of Yugoslavia. Aleksandar was succeeded by his eleven-year-old son Peter II and a regency council headed by Aleksandar's cousin Prince Paul (or Pavle).

[112] Sørensen 2009: 78–79.

Plans for Exclusion

During the late 1930s the Serbian elites became increasingly concerned about the prospects of their nation-building policy in Kosovo. The colonization process did not achieve its goal of altering the ethnic balance in the region since the settlers were not adequate for the task, the administration was not efficient, and the land reform was following a pattern of dispersed settlement and not "the known model of taking possession of land piece by piece," thus not altering the demographic balance anywhere in particular.[113] Moreover, the national question in Yugoslavia – encapsulated in the Serb-Croat antagonism – became more pressing and the geopolitical situation untenable. It was in this context that the resettlement of Kosovo Albanians in Turkey surfaced as an option. However, this plan never materialized (Table 7.1).

As I discussed in the previous section, the geopolitical situation was changing rapidly in ways unfavorable to the Yugoslav Kingdom. Early in 1936, Turkey had expressed interest in signing an agreement with Yugoslavia for the resettlement of about 200,000 Muslims.[114] A year later, Vaso Čubrilović[115] suggested a radical solution to the Albanian question in a policy paper he presented to the Yugoslav government:

There is no possibility for us to assimilate the Albanians. On the contrary, because their roots are in Albania, their national awareness has been awakened, and if we do not settle the score with them once and for all, within 20–30 years we shall have to cope with a terrible irredentism, the signs of which are already apparent and will inevitably put all our southern territories in jeopardy.[116]

According to Čubrilović, the expulsion of the Albanians was necessary in order to "reestablish" the connection with the Slavs in South Serbia. Importantly for my argument, Čubrilović makes clear the geopolitical reasoning underlying his proposal. He was mostly concerned with the block of eighteen districts where the Albanians were concentrated and formed a compact settlement. Albanians and other national minorities in "other parts of the south are scattered and therefore constitute less of a threat to the life of our nation and state," he wrote in 1937.[117] Nationalizing the regions around the Shar mountains would prevent Albanian irredentism once and for all, and secure Kosovo forever. But his reasoning did not stop there: "[W]ith the elimination of the Albanians, the last link between our Moslems in Bosnia and Novi Pazar and the rest of the Moslem world will

---

[113] Krstić-Brano 2004: 82.
[114] Banac 1984: 301.
[115] Vaso Čubrilović (1897–1990). In 1914, he was a participant in the conspiracy to assassinate the Archduke Franz Ferdinand. During the 1930s, he was a professor of history in Belgrade and a political adviser for the government of Yugoslavia. After World War II, he became a member of the Communist Party and served as a Minister of Forests in Tito's government. He was a member of the Serbian Academy of Arts and Sciences.
[116] Čubrilović 1997: 407.
[117] Ibid., p. 405.

have been cut,"[118] and then the remaining Muslims would be an isolated religious minority ready for assimilation.

A year after Čubrilović's proposal, the Yugoslav Military Headquarters also "advocat[ed] the resettlement of the ethnic Albanians into Turkey"[119] because of growing security concerns. According to my argument, what should have kept the KSCS from pursuing exclusionary policies toward the enemy-backed Kosovo Albanians should have been their desire to preserve the international status quo. Indeed, Prime Minister Milan Stojadinović,[120] in his first term, had tried to keep Yugoslavia as a status quo power attempting to turn it into a neutral power – the Switzerland of the Balkans.

Late in the 1930s, however, when the international status quo was directly challenged and Italy's grip over Albania had reached its peak, the Serbian elites contemplated seriously pursuing exclusionary policies. As Andrić[121] put it, "[t] he presence of any of the great Powers in the Balkans means opening the floodgates to intrigue and invasion."[122] In this turbulent context, Stojadinović signed an agreement with Turkey – the latter aiming at its own ethnic engineering – in 1938 for the relocation of about 40,000 Muslim families – excluding nomads and Gypsies – over a period of six years (1939 to 1944).[123] However, this plan never materialized due to lack of funds and the outbreak of World War II.[124] In 1939, Andrić even considered the annexation of northern Albania to Yugoslavia in case of a partition. His rationale was consistent with the rationale of my argument: "[after the annexation of northern Albania] Kosovo would lose its attraction as a centre for the Albanian minority which, under the new situation, could be more easily assimilated."[125] All in all, consistent with my argument, assimilation was the dominant policy during this period but the geopolitical circumstances did provide incentives to contemplate exclusionary policies for significant parts of the Albanian population.

THE ROLE OF DOMESTIC POLITICS

Could the variation in nation-building policies be explained by the nature of domestic politics? A more systematic look at political life in the kingdom of

[118] Ibid., 406.
[119] Stefanović 2005: 482.
[120] Milan Stojadinović (1888–1961), a Serbian Politician who served as Prime Minister of Yugoslavia from 1935 to 1939.
[121] Ivo Andrić (1892–1975) was awarded the Nobel Prize for literature in 1961. Andrić joined the diplomatic service of the KSCS after World War I, his most important post being Ambassador of the Kingdom of Yugoslavia to Germany just before World War II (1939–1941).
[122] Andrić 1997: 446.
[123] For more on the Yugoslav-Turkish convention, see "Convention. Regulating the Emigration of the Turkish Population from the Region of Southern Serbia in Yugoslavia (1938)," in Elsie 1997; Institute of History 1993; Krstić-Brano 2004: 82–83.
[124] Lampe 2000: 192; Stefanović 2005: 482; Krstić-Brano 2004: 83.
[125] Andrić 1997: 448.

Yugoslavia is necessary to test this hypothesis.[126] King Aleksandar[127] was a central figure in the interwar politics of the Kingdom and did not hesitate to intervene in the political process. Three main political parties existed during the interwar period: The Radical Party under Pašić and the Democratic party under Davidović on the Serbian side, and the Peasant Party under Radić (and later Maček) on the Croatian side. There were also many smaller parties – some regional, others ethnic – vying for the majority in the Assembly. However, the main cleavage was that between the Serbs and the Croats, those in favor of centralization and those against it respectively.[128]

According to the Corfu Declaration in 1917, the Latin and Cyrillic alphabets as well as the three national names (Serbs, Croats, and Slovenes) and their flags were to be equally recognized. Moreover, the predominant religions (Orthodoxy, Catholicism, and Islam) were also officially recognized. However, the most problematic issue was whether the Kingdom would be centralized – a position supported by Pašić – or federalized – a position favored by Trumbić[129] and Radić.[130] In other words, the state was weak not because of its multinational character per se[131] but rather because of the disagreement between the three largest groups on the level of centralization of government. In addition, the largest political parties were all "ethnic" parties. As Ramet put it: "one could safely assume that only Croats joined the Croatian Peasant Party, only Slovenes joined the Slovene People's Party, only Serbs joined the (Serbian) Radical Party, and only Muslims joined the Yugoslav Muslim Organization (JMO) . . . a 'loyal' Croat was expected to vote for Radić, a 'loyal' Slovene to vote for Anton Korošec, leader of the Slovene People's Party, and a 'loyal Muslim' to vote for JMO leader Mehmed Spaho."[132]

A defining moment in the history of the Kingdom of Serbs, Croats and Slovenes was the Serbs' adoption of a centralist constitution in 1921 while all of the anti-centralist political forces boycotted the constituent assembly. The murder of the Minister of Interior and the Communists' attempted murder of King Aleksandar immediately after the new constitution's adoption were indicative of the political climate in interwar Yugoslavia. As a result of the violence the Communist Party was outlawed and many of its members persecuted.

---

[126] See Banac 1984; Djokić 2003 and 2007; and Troch 2010.
[127] King Peter I Karadjordjević was succeeded by his son Aleksandar in 1921, who had been already in control basically since the unification.
[128] Banac 1984.
[129] A Croatian leader who established the "Yugoslav Committee" in London during World War I. In 1918 he became foreign minister in the first government of the Kingdom but resigned in 1920. For more on Trumbić, see Djokić 2010.
[130] The leader of the Croatian Peasant Party.
[131] In the Kingdom there were Serbs (39%), Croats (23%), Slovenes (8.5%), Bosnian Muslims (6%), Macedonians/Bulgarians (4.8%), Germans (4.27%), Hungarians (3.98%), Albanians (3.68%), Turks, Greeks, and many smaller non-core groups (Banac 1984).
[132] 2006: 37.

The Croatian Peasant Party continued to voice its demands for regional autonomy and returned to the National Assembly only in 1924. In the meantime, the Radical Party had managed to reorganize the country into thirty three administrative districts (see Map 7.3), which undermined the pre-existing provincial administration in Croatia, Slovenia, Bosnia-Herzegovina, and Vojvodina.

In 1924, for the first time after unification, an anticentralist – but still Serbian – Prime Minister, Davidović, was appointed by the King. A coalition of Croats, Slovenes, Muslims, and Serbian Democrats had managed to wrest control from the Radical Party, but their control would not last for long (Davidović resigned on 17 July 1924); Pašić soon took over once again and led the country to new elections in February 1925.

On 2 July 1925 negotiations between the Radical and the Peasant Parties began, leading to the formation of a new government under Pašić. Radić became a Minister of Education on 17 November 1925.[133] The renunciation of any autonomist plans for Croatia by Radić had preceded this coalition.[134]

But even the coexistence of Serbs and Croats in the same government was shortlived. Pašić had to resign because of a corruption scandal, and a period of unstable political coalition governments under Uzunović – the new leader of the Radical Party – followed.

Given this narrative, one might argue that the short period of accommodation of Albanians in Kosovo around 1924 could have been the outcome of the influence that the Croatian Peasant Party had achieved through its participation in the government. However, these governments were dysfunctional and passed few important pieces of legislation. Moreover, the Serbian establishment in the military and the administration, with the king's support, did not allow non-Serbs to interfere with their policies within what was still viewed as "Serbian lands," which more or less corresponded to the pre-World War I Kingdom of Serbia.[135]

Nevertheless, despite the intense political conflict – especially between the Croats and the Serbs – democratic institutions lasted until 1929 when King Aleksandar imposed a royal dictatorship and renamed the state as the Kingdom of Yugoslavia (see Illustration 7.3). The dictatorship was a reaction to prolonged political instability. A critical event was the assassination of Radić – and two more Croatian deputies – by a Montenegrin deputy on 20 June 1928.[136]

Although the intense political conflict between Croats – and to a lesser extent Slovenes – and Serbs formed the main political cleavage in the country, it did not

---

[133] The government was formed on 18 July, the same day Radić was released from prison (Ramet 2006: 67).

[134] Radić was imprisoned during the elections in 1925 but immediately afterwards he renounced the autonomist plans for Croatia, accepted the Vidovdan Constitution (the first Constitution of the KSCS in 1921) and the dynasty, and declared his commitment to the unity of the state (Ramet 2006: 66).

[135] To be sure, hegemony in the political sphere did not prevent Croatian and Slovenian domination in the economic sphere; see Petranović 2002: 21.

[136] Radić actually succumbed to his wounds in August 1928.

ILLUSTRATION 7.3. King Aleksandar. *Source*: http://en.wikipedia.org/wiki/File:Kralj_ aleksandar1.jpg.

impact the planning of Serbian policies toward the Albanians in Kosovo, at least not directly. Most of the decisions relevant to nation-building were made by the king's court and the army's high command rather than the parliament. Issues of national security, such as Kosovo, were not to be decided by the parliament that had many members with questionable loyalties and who themselves had often fallen under the provisions of the Law on the Protection of Public Order and the State.[137] Moreover, Serbian politicians dominated the political scene almost exclusively in the interwar period.

Serbian hegemony over the Kingdom of Serbs, Croats and Slovenes manifested itself beginning with the adoption of a centralist constitution in 1921 and later with the administration of the state and the army, the way the institution of the Monarchy functioned, and the pre-eminence of the Serbian Orthodox Church. It is also captured in the following statistics:

[T]he prime minister's job went to Serbs for 264 of the 268 months that the interwar kingdom lasted (going to a Slovene for the other four months), the ministry of the army

[137] Ramet 2006: 64.

and navy was run by Serbs for all 268 months, the minister of internal affairs was a Serb for 240 out of 268 months, the minister of foreign affairs was a Serb for 247 months, and the minister of justice was a Serb for 237 of those months.[138]

Only very late in the interwar period, in 1939, the government negotiated the Sporazum (Agreement) with Maček, the Croatian leader who succeeded Radić, and created a semi-autonomous Croatian province (see Map 7.4).[139] Even then, although the new province was granted autonomy in internal matters, foreign policy, security, and taxation remained under the control of Belgrade. Maček actually became a Deputy Prime Minister in 1939 but World War II put a violent end to this cooperative period in Serb-Croat relations without any policy changes toward the Kosovo Albanians occurring during the Sporazum.

Before we turn to the conclusion of this chapter, it is worth discussing whether the Serbian nation-building policies pursued toward Kosovo Albanians were inspired by ethnic differences that generated mistrust. My findings indicate that the Serbian policy was attuned to the population's national loyalties rather than ethnic differences. The secondary importance of religious beliefs is demonstrated by the fact that the KSCS did not pursue the same policies toward Slav-speaking Muslims and Albanian-speaking Muslims.[140] The secondary importance of ethnicity is also supported by the fact that the Serbs pursued colonization in both Albanian Muslim-dominated Kosovo – which was under Albanian influence – and in Slav-dominated Orthodox Christian Vardar Macedonia – which was under Bulgarian influence. National loyalty and patterns of external involvement were key to government policies, not some specific set of ethnic attributes of the various non-core groups.

CONCLUSION

In this chapter, I used archival material as well as an extensive secondary literature on the history of interwar Yugoslavia in order to trace the logic underlying the policies followed by the ruling political elites in Belgrade toward Albanians from 1878 to 1941. Studying this case over time allowed me to keep many state- and group-level characteristics constant and isolate the effects of my main variables of interest, host state foreign policy goals and interstate relations between the non-core group's external power and the host state.

While Serbia fought for territorial expansion and redeeming its co-ethnics it pursued exclusionary policies toward the recently "nationally awakened" and externally supported Albanians. Following World War I, the Serbian elites had more or less achieved their national goals of territorial expansion. However, the Albanian nationalists continued to enjoy external support and to make

[138] Ibid., 38.
[139] This development was of course related to international pressures and events such as the German annexation of Sudetenland in 1938 and the growing economic dependence of the Kingdom on Germany; see Petranović 2002: 37 and Sørensen 2009: 70.
[140] Poulton and Vickers 1997: 146.

autonomy demands. In response to these circumstances the Serbian elites followed a policy of assimilation toward Kosovo Albanians.

Less than six years after the annexation of Kosovo by the KSCS, Ahmet Zog olli consolidated power in Albania – with Yugoslav help – and suppressed the Kaçak movement. Albania was now a friendly state and Albanians in Kosovo were no longer perceived as a threat. My theory predicts that Albanians should be accommodated. Indeed, in the mid-1920s Belgrade permitted religious schooling conducted by Muslim imams in Muslim mektebs and medreses.

By the end of the 1920s Italy's renewed interest in Albania altered the situation. King Zog was now "King of the Albanians," secessionist claims were once again propagated amongst the Albanians in Kosovo, and the Italian influence increased rapidly in Albania. For Yugoslavia, Albania was an enemy power once again. Assimilationist policies ensued. Due to the geopolitical changes in Europe prior to World War II, plans for exclusion emerged aiming at the resettlement of Kosovo Albanians to Turkey. However, these plans never materialized.

Overall, the choice of nation-building policies was not based on objective measures of cultural distance or deep-rooted ethnic hatred between the non-assimilated Albanians and the core group Serbs. Indeed, it was based on an interaction of the perceived danger of secessionist claims by the externally backed Kosovo Albanian elites and state relations between Albania and Serbia. In turn, the latter changed over time based on the geopolitical context and Serbia's foreign policy goals. None of the alternative explanations could have predicted all these shifts in policy since they either are time invariant or change at a much slower pace than the dependent variable. Lastly, macro historical explanations such as the rise of Fascism in Europe[141] or the impact of "Europeanization" on the Balkans[142] – although useful to understand the context – cannot account for the variation in the policies over time and across groups, either.

---

[141] See Alter 1994: 16–38; Stefanovic 2005: 483.
[142] Todorova 1997: 13.

8

Application of the Theory Beyond the Balkans

Can my argument help us shed light on shifts in nation-building policies toward non-core groups in other parts of the world? Does it provide us with insights beyond the interwar period? In Chapters 4 through 7 I have provided empirical support for my argument based on evidence from the early twentieth-century Balkans, a place described as chaotic, captivated by ethnic hatreds where there is a strong presumption against the logic of my argument. In this section I explore the extent to which the theory can help us explain variation in nation-building policies beyond the Balkan region and outside the interwar period.

The ideal – but hardly feasible or ethical – test would require me to conduct an experiment. A second best would be to construct a global panel dataset on nation-building policies toward all non-core groups living in states with ruling political elites of clearly defined core groups that were motivated by a homogenizing imperative. However, in order to identify the extent to which my argument may apply across space and time, challenging causal links have to be established. For example, we would need to determine whether there was external involvement in support of a non-core group – a particularly challenging task especially when dealing with covert or clandestine operations. Moreover, we would need data on whether this external involvement actually affected the choice of nation-building policies toward the non-core group. Existing secondary literature on nation-building policies is very limited and in most cases archival research is necessary to establish these causal links for a global dataset. Moreover, archival material is rarely accessible; most governments keep such information confidential for many years while others destroy it altogether.

Data collection problems are more pronounced in the most violent cases when the host government has pursued exclusionary policies. In such cases, there are incentives for both external supporters and host states to obscure the picture and forge the data in a way that absolves them of their responsibility. Cases of assimilationist policies are relatively easier to study but even this work has become increasingly difficult within an international environment that views assimilationist policies as "cultural genocide." Under such pressures, governments have incentives to disguise their policies and destroy evidence of such policies. Cases of non-core group accommodation are the easiest to study today. On the one hand, host states get an opportunity to publicize their multicultural arrangements; on the other, external supporters are eager to get credit for such progressive outcomes.

In addition to the lack of reliable data on such sensitive issues, researchers are often faced with propagandistic material. This type of material is most prevalent among secondary sources. Frequently, governments create "institutes of national history" or more specific centers studying certain periods or regions in an attempt to propagate their view of history and legitimize their claims. Moreover, such works are likely to be published in places where intense nation-building has taken place and this leaves us with very little data on cases that were less violent. Archival material is less likely to include propagandistic overtones, although researchers have to be careful of the biases – ideological or other – of the individuals writing the reports. In sum, sources on nation-building policies are difficult to find; even when they are available, they are often part of a nation-building strategy themselves. Researchers need to be cautious in their use of secondary sources and critical of primary ones.

With these limitations in mind, in the rest of this chapter I explore the extent to which my argument regarding policies toward non-core groups may be generalized to non-core groups which have inhabited different regional systems and highly diverse geopolitical environments over the last two hundred years. The cases I discuss below serve as illustrations of my argument outside of the interwar Balkans.

SAME REGION, DIFFERENT PERIODS

Two lessons emerge from the study of the Greek War of Independence in the early nineteenth century and ethnic relations in post–Cold War Balkans: Scapegoating is a special case of false accusation by the host state, and, with regard to the importance of one of my scope conditions, elites must be motivated by a homogenizing imperative for my argument to apply.

Nation-Building in Nineteenth-Century Balkans

Based on my scope conditions, the mechanisms I discussed in Chapter 2 should be operative only in the modern era. Thus, it is appropriate to look for the first instances of the *Politics of Nation-Building* in one of the first national awakenings that occurred in the Balkans: the Greek national awakening and the war of independence against the Ottomans.

The Rum *millet* within the Ottoman Empire was definitely accommodated in terms of its religious identity with the Orthodox Patriarch as its leader. Granted this was not the type of accommodation that is in place in Western liberal democratic states today; it was a rather hierarchical form of accommodation.[1] At the same time, however, the Ottoman Empire was not targeting the Rum *millet* with assimilationist – with the exception of the Devşirme system[2] – or exclusionary policies.

The Greek War of Independence followed the Serbian revolts, first against their local notables and then against the Ottoman Empire itself. The Ottoman Porte was now facing "the first all-out Christian uprising aiming at complete independence from the Imperial superstructure."[3] These events had a transformative impact on the nature of the Ottoman Empire itself. The religious cleavage became more and more salient and conflict ridden. At the same time, Ottomanism slowly emerged as a proto-national identity.

The Sultan, probably based on past experience,[4] operated under the assumption that the Russians were supporting the Greeks but he was wrong. Regardless, according to Ilicak, "one of the most determining factors in the Sublime's Porte's responses to the Greek Revolution was the Ottoman administrators' perception of a Russian conspiracy behind the insurgency." According to official Ottoman documents, the Sultan was convinced that Russia was "provoking and secretly assisting the Greek insurgents and that the Fanariots were a Russian fifth column."[5] The background of Alexandros Ipsilantis, the leader of the revolt in Moldowallachia, was seen as enough proof of the Russian connection. Ipsilantis was a Major General in the Russian army since 1817, a personal friend of Tsar Alexander I, and the son of a Phanariote who had been *voyvoda* of Wallachia and had defected to Russia.

The Russians tried to credibly signal that they were not backing this revolt in a variety of ways ranging from the discharge of Ipsilantis from the army to offering help in crushing the rebellion. These assurances and related actions did not appease the Ottoman administration. Ilicak unearthed from the Ottoman archives the Sultan's private notes during the first months of the rebellion. The Sultan wrote, "had the [Russians] not promised to help and interfere, the Greeks could not have dared [to revolt]." The reprisal on the Greeks of the Empire was extensive and brutal. Despite the fact that external support was not initially present, the Sultan perceived it as such and thus his reaction is consistent with my theory. To be sure, the Sultan would have reacted even if he was not convinced about the Russian involvement in the matter, but the extent of the reprisals would definitely have been smaller.

This case allows us to think about the ontology of scapegoating. A non-core group may be externally supported by an enemy or not and a host state may really perceive the group as threatening or not. In Figure 8.1 we may

---

[1] Kymlicka 2012.

[2] "A compulsory separation of [a select group of] boys from their families, their conversion to Islam and recruitment into the Ottoman service, a practice that extended well into the seventeenth century." Bieber 2000.

[3] Ilicak 2011, Chapter 3.

[4] See section "Motivations for External Involvement" in Chapter 2, where I discuss Russian Count Orlov's involvement in the Pelloponnese during the late eighteenth century.

[5] Ilicak 2011.

Enemy External Support	Perceived Threat	
	Truthful	Pretense
Yes	Not scapegoating	*Rare Event*
No	Not scapegoating	False Accusation (scapegoating)

FIGURE 8.1. Scapegoating.

discern two combinations that are clearly not cases of scapegoating: first, there is external support by an enemy and the host state perceives the non-core group as a threat; second, there is no external support but the host state still considers the group as a threat – this was the case of the Greeks in the early nineteenth century.

In a situation where there is no external support or any anti-government mobilization but the host state acts as if there were a real threat posed by the non-core group regardless, then this is a case of false accusation. Scapegoating is a special case within the category of false accusation and it refers to instances when the host state blames unfairly a non-core group for the problems faced by the host state. Finally, there is a small possibility that there is external support for a group by an enemy and the host state is unaware of that but has – for its own reasons – decided to act as if there is a real threat posed by the non-core group. This is a rare event since more often than not the external involvement soon enough manifests itself.

Nation-Building in Post–World War II Balkans

Attempts to account for variation in nation-building policies within the Post–Cold War Balkans also corroborate my interwar findings but highlight the importance of the international structure and the motives of the core group elites.[6] The rise of ethnic conflict in the Balkans, and the breakup of the former federal states in the 1990s (Yugoslavia and USSR), opened a lively debate among political scientists and commentators on what accounts for variations in the treatment of non-core groups.

For instance, why did Bulgaria pursue a forced assimilation policy in the mid-1980s while Greece, by recognizing a Muslim minority, facilitated the "Turkification" of its members? Why did Greece treat the Muslim minority as a unitary actor in the 1980s but not in the 1990s? Why did Bulgaria abandon its assimilationist policy in 1989 in favor of a policy of minority rights protection? Putting Greek and Bulgarian policies toward their Muslim minority groups in a comparative perspective reveals a pattern consistent with my theory.[7] The structure of the international system (unipolar, multipolar, bipolar) affected

---

[6] For more on this, see Chapter 9.
[7] For a thorough treatment of these cases, see Mantouvalou and Mylonas 2010.

interstate relations between these countries and ultimately impacted the treatment of the relevant non-core groups. I described some of these cases in Chapter 5 while discussing "divide and rule" policies in the Balkans.

Later on in the 1990s and into the 2000s Albanians in Kosovo and the former Yugoslav Republic of Macedonia were affected by very different policies from their respective governments.[8] These states both involve a South Slav core group and an Albanian non-core group; in both cases the non-core group was restless, large, and territorially concentrated; and both places have been parts of the Socialist Federal Republic of Yugoslavia. This is where similarities end; while the government in Skopje assumed a relatively accommodating stance toward its restive Albanian minority, the Serbian government switched from accommodation to repression. Why? Consistent with my argument, the absence of an enemy external power supporting the non-core group gave the government in Skopje no incentive for engaging in outright exclusionary policies. In fact the non-core group enjoyed support from the United States, a country that at the same time supported the government in Skopje. In contrast, in the case of Serbia, the fact that a similar non-core group started receiving external support from the United States toward the end of the 1990s resulted in Serbian ethnic cleansing since United States–Serbia relations had deteriorated significantly after the war in Bosnia. The differential patterns of external power support and interstate alliances between the host state and these backers best explain the treatment of these non-core groups.

Up to the 1980s accommodation was the dominant strategy toward Kosovo Albanians. However, in the 1990s things changed. This stark difference once again makes us appreciate the centrality of scope conditions, namely that for my argument to operate the core group must be clearly defined and its elites must be driven by a homogenizing imperative. Since World War II and until Tito's death in 1980, Yugoslavia was hardly conforming to my argument's scope conditions. Beginning in the 1980s and into the 1990s, however, the representation of nationalist core groups by leaders such as Milošević, Tuđman, and Gligorov, and the pursuit of homogenizing imperatives, emerged across the constituent republics of Yugoslavia.[9] This transformation was key to the logic of my argument to become operative.

DIFFERENT REGIONS, DIFFERENT CONTEXTS

Up to this point, the cases I have discussed have all been from the Balkans. Thus, although I have demonstrated that the argument applies in the Balkans all through the modern era, I have yet to show that it applies to other regions of the world. To examine whether my argument can be generalized beyond the Balkans, I focus on People's Republic of China's (PRC's) nation-building policies during the Cold War and on Estonia's post–Cold War policies toward

---

[8] For a thorough treatment of these cases, see Jenne and Mylonas 2011.
[9] Banac 2006; Snyder 2000.

Russian-speakers. Three important conclusions may be drawn from these cases: the relative capacity of the external power versus the host state has a significant impact on the mobilization of the non-core group and the host state's perception of threat; the understanding of the term *assimilation* varies widely across cases and over time, ranging from loyalty to the state without any demands for acculturation all the way to loyalty to the state and complete acculturation, language acquisition, religious conversion, and so forth; and, in line with my argument, regional integration projects often operate as channels that propagate and enforce international human rights norms and ultimately facilitate accommodationist policies.

PRC Nation-Building during the Cold War

Turning to the Cold War context, first, I conduct a comparison between the treatment of the Uyghurs and Tibetans under Mao's[10] rule from 1949 to 1965.[11] Second, I trace PRC policies over time focusing on the Tibetans from 1949 to the present.[12] Finally, I briefly discuss a comparison across the eighteen largest groups in China (see Table 8.1 below).[13]

Tibet and Xinjiang

The first empirical puzzle from Cold War Asia is why the Chinese government cracked down on the Tibetan movement in 1959 but repressed the Uyghur movement later, in 1962. What accounts for this timing given that Han antipathy, cultural differences, and unrest were present in both cases? I find that although the Chinese government was following the 1952 program for regional autonomy in both Xinjiang and Tibet, different patterns of external involvement and interstate relations can help us explain the variation in the timing of nation-building policy shifts in the two regions. In particular, the limited external support that Tibetans received during the 1949–1956 period[14] did not derail the uneasy but functioning coexistence with the Chinese until 1956–1959.[15] A transitional policy of accommodation was pursued while the terminal goal was assimilation.[16]

Beijing allowed Tibetans to run their own affairs through the first half of the 1950s, but not outside of political Tibet. In the latter areas that were not accommodated the Khampas organized revolts. This situation in the context of the Cold War reignited U.S. interest in Tibet, and the CIA began its operations by

---

[10] Mao Zedong or Mao Tse-Tung (1893–1976) was a Han Chinese and the leader of the People's Republic of China from 1949 until his death in 1976.

[11] Jenne and Mylonas 2011.

[12] Mylonas 2008.

[13] Han and Mylonas 2011.

[14] "Supply of arms for Tibet," January 1950, FO 371/84465. "Assistance for Tibet to help combat the Communist Threat," January 1950, FO 371/84451.

[15] For a description of this period, see Goldstein 1989; Shakya 2002; Wang 2002.

[16] The CCP initially accommodated rather than assimilated the Tibetans since PRC capacity at the time was limited. Tibet's location was also an important factor in this choice; see Fravel 2008.

airdropping arms for the rebels and sending agents into Tibet to disrupt Chinese efforts to control the region.[17] However, accommodation policies continued in political Tibet.

U.S. policy toward Tibet was motivated by a desire to contain the influence of Communist China in the region and around the world.[18] Consistent with my argument, the Chinese government faced with an enemy-supported non-core group adopted exclusionary policies toward the Tibetan leadership and resistance. As Fravel put it, "Chinese leaders' knowledge of external support, especially from the United States, no doubt had a strong psychological impact on their sense of China's internal vulnerability to external influence."[19] Mao tightened Beijing's grip over the internal affairs of Tibet, leading the Dalai Lama and his supporters to flee into exile in 1959.

In the case of the Uyghurs – a Muslim Turkic-speaking group living in the northwestern province of Xinjiang[20] – the most significant support came from the Soviet Union.[21] With the Chinese Communist Party having risen to power, Soviet support for Uyghur independence ceased although Uyghur ties with the Soviet Union remained. In 1955, the territory was given the status of Xinjiang Uyghur Autonomous Region. As expected, Sino-Soviet relations greatly influenced the Chinese government's policies toward the Uyghurs. Initially, the relationship was a cooperative one and this led to an accommodationist minority policy. The Soviet Union was involved in the industrialization of the province and the PRC permitted access to Xinjiang's oil and minerals.[22] The Chinese authorities also approved the adoption of a Cyrillic-based Uyghur script in 1954 on the advice of the region's Soviet advisors. Usage of the language in Xinjiang "reached its peak between 1955 and 1958, when it was introduced into a number of schools and employed in academic publications."[23]

As soon as Sino-Soviet relations became confrontational,[24] the Soviets pulled out of the region, began to distribute Soviet passports in the area, and used their influence in the region to destabilize the PRC.[25] For more than twenty years the border between the PRC and the Soviet Union was closed down and guarded by PLA troops.[26] Given this context, my argument predicts exclusionary policies pursued by the PRC toward the Uyghurs. Indeed, the Chinese government implemented a policy of purging pro-Soviet Uyghur elites and engaged in widespread persecution of anyone suspected of having ties to the Soviets. The

---

[17] McGranahan 2010. The United States was not the only power involved but it was the most significant.
[18] Grunfeld 1987; Knaus 1999; Weiner 2007.
[19] 2008: 81.
[20] Dillon 2004; McMillen 1979.
[21] Wheeler 1963.
[22] Millward 2007: 225.
[23] Dwyer 2005: 18–19.
[24] MacFarquhar 1997: 128; Schecter 1963; see also "Communists: One-Third of the Earth," *Time Magazine*, 27 October 1961, vol. 78(17).
[25] Roberts 1998. See also Kamalov 2009: 117.
[26] The USSR also sided with India in the 1962 Sino-Indian War.

crackdown intensified in the spring of 1962, with more than 60,000 Uyghurs and Kazakhs fleeing across the border to the Soviet Union. The newly adopted Cyrillic scripts for the Uyghur language were also replaced by a new writing system that was similar to the Chinese pinyin system.[27]

Keeping many factors relatively constant in both Tibet and Xinjiang, we still find that PRC treated the regions differently at the same point in time – accommodating one minority while repressing the other. Therefore, my argument helps us explain variation in the timing of the shift from accommodation to exclusion in Tibet and Xinjiang and adds another layer to the existing interpretations of these events.

Tibet Over Time

Even when we take a look at the over time variation in the treatment of Tibetans, the fluctuations of repression are better understood when we take into account changes in external support and interstate relations between China and the United States. For instance, following the Cultural Revolution the treatment of Tibetans improved significantly. I argue that this was causally related to the normalization of U.S.–China relations under the Nixon administration in 1972.

The U.S.–PRC rapprochement in 1972 transformed U.S. Cold War strategy and "created a new set of foreign policy conditions that quickly marginalized the U.S. government's 'pragmatic' interest in Tibet."[28] The CIA's final missions in Tibet occurred in 1974 and with Mao's death in 1976 the path was now clear for a return to accommodationist policies. The PRC began encouraging a cultural renaissance in Tibet with the "reopening of monasteries, permission to recruit new monks, greater leeway to use written Tibetan, and the replacement of large numbers of ethnic Chinese cadres with Tibetans."[29] Wang describes this shift:

On December 28, 1978, less than a week after taking power, Deng ... indicated his willingness to start a dialogue with the Dalai Lama.... The 376 participants in the 1959 Rebellion still serving prison sentences were freed. Over 6,000 others who had been released after completing their sentences but were still branded as "rebels" and kept under "supervised reform" had these labels removed.[30]

This cultural revival however was not a policy targeting just Tibet, but it was rather carried out throughout China after the Cultural Revolution. This nation-wide policy was linked more to leadership change within the CCP from Mao to Deng than just PRC's relationship with the United States. Thus the two arguments at this point are observationally equivalent. The way to adjudicate between the two arguments would be to observe how the PRC would react to a new wave of external support for the Tibetans.

Indeed, Western involvement resurfaced in the late 1980s and shifts in Chinese nation-building policies followed suit. The Dalai Lama made an appearance in

[27] Millward 2007: 235–36.
[28] Goldstein 2006: 155; for more on this, see Weiner 2007: 350.
[29] Goldstein 2006: 155.
[30] 2002: 100.

the U.S. Congress in 1987 and proposed some bold steps in front of the U.S. Congressional Human Rights Caucus.[31] Following this speech the first demonstrations in favor of independence since 1959 erupted in Lhasa, Tibet. Things escalated and Han were targeted in retaliation to the crackdown of the Tibetan demonstrations. Clearly, the PRC perceived the Dalai Lama's address as the main reason for this unrest. The fact that this address was given at the U.S. Congress further worried the Chinese government. As a result of this external instigation and apparent U.S. support for Tibetan independence, the accommodationist policy had to be put aside for a more repressive policy. No wonder "the next seventeen months saw an increasingly bloody pattern of disturbances, leading ultimately to the imposition of martial law in March 1989, which remained in effect for 419 days."[32]

My argument is not that the conflict in Tibet or Xinjiang was the mere outcome of interference by interested external powers. It was not. The conflict had its roots in the aversion of the Tibetans and Uyghurs toward Han Chinese domination and self-determination ideas, as well as the interests of local elites to preserve their traditional social structures and religious practices. For example, years before the United States decided to interfere, the Tibetan government had expelled all Chinese as well as Tibetan communists in anticipation of Chinese plans to incorporate Tibet after the end of the Chinese civil war.[33] My argument is that external support by enemy powers of non-core groups that turn against the Communist Chinese state both provided these non-core groups with more resources and triggered a more violent reaction from the People's Republic of China.

My theory helps us explain the timing of the shifts in nation-building policies toward Tibetans and Uyghurs within the context of Cold War competition. It also helps explain the shifts in Beijing's minority policy toward Tibetans over time from assimilation (through accommodation) to exclusion to accommodation and back to assimilation through a mix of repression and colonization. However, in both cases the external power has been a strong state. No doubt there are cases where the external power is relatively weaker than the host state. I have explored this possibility elsewhere,[34] but I think that for the purposes of the argument I developed in this book this issue deserves further discussion. I turn to it in the section that follows.

Subnational Variation

Table 8.1 depicts a two-by-two that captures the variation in interstate relations and the relative strength of the external power when compared to the host state. The main corrective that emerges from studying the eighteen largest non-core groups in China during the first years of Mao's rule is that when we relax the assumption that the host state and the external power are symmetrical, my

[31] Dalai Lama 1987.
[32] Wang 2002: 105.
[33] Goldstein et al. 2004.
[34] Han and Mylonas 2011.

TABLE 8.1. *Nation-Building Policies toward China's largest Non-Core Groups, 1949–1965*

Group's Perceptions of External Power's Strength	Non-Core Group Enjoys External Support		
	Yes		No
	Enemy	Ally or Neutral	
Strong State	Tibetans (U.S. 1959–1965) Uyghurs (USSR 1960–1965) Kazaks (USSR 1960–1965) Group: Mobilization Host State: Exclusion	Tibetans (India 1949–1958) Uyghurs (USSR 1949–1959) Kazaks (USSR 1949–1959) Group: Exit/ Autonomy Host State: Accommodation	Zhuang, Manchu, Yi, Hui, Miao, Tujia, Buyi, Dong, Yao, Bai, Hani, Li Group: No Mobilization Host State: Integration
Weak State	Mongols (MPR 1960–1965) Group: Weak Mobilization Host State: Integration/ Mix	Mongols (MPR 1949–1959) Koreans (DPRK) Dai (Thailand and Burma) Group: No Mobilization Host State: Accommodation/ Mix	

Source: Han and Mylonas 2011.

theory must be slightly modified. Allowing for an asymmetrical relationship, that is, a weak external power supporting a non-core group, greatly influences the non-core group's agency and the level of threat for the host state. Thus, the non-core group is less likely to mobilize against the host state and the latter is also less likely to react violently to any form of mobilization since the threat is low. Allowing for variation in the relative capacity of the external power versus the host state is an important addition to my theory that brings back non-core group's agency to the fore.

In particular, from these eighteen groups, six either had external patrons during the period under study or external kin relations with neighboring countries, while twelve of these groups were either indigenous to China alone or did not enjoy any external support. For example, the Uyghurs and Kazaks have kin relations with Central Asian states. Mongolia is a kin state for the Mongols, as are both North and South Koreas for the Koreans. Non-core groups located in the Southwestern border areas – such as the Miao, Yao, Hani, and Dai – all have external kin in mainland Southeast Asia but did not receive any external support. The Tibetans have extensive relations with groups in Bhutan, Nepal, and India. Finally, as we have seen above, Tibetans and Uyghurs received external support by Great Powers.

This variation often goes unnoticed in studies that focus on prominent groups alone. In this extension of my work, in collaboration with Enze Han, I relaxed the assumption with regard to relatively symmetrical host state–external patron dyad and demonstrated that my argument can help us explain the variation in nation-bulding policies as well as patterns of non-core group mobilization (see Table 8.1).

Estonian Nation-Building in the Post–Cold War Era

Now we can turn to the post–Cold War era and focus on the policies toward the "Russian-speakers" in Estonia[35] with an eye on the role of two important post–World War II developments: the emergence of strong regional integration projects, such as the EU, and the spread of international norms regarding human rights.

Right after Independence, when Russian troops and KGB officers were still in Estonia, the Russian-speaking population was perceived as a potential fifth column and was thus targeted with exclusionary measures. By the mid-1990s, with the withdrawal of the Russian troops as well as a shift in the Russian Diaspora policy, a gradual turn to accommodation began. But it was only after Estonia's EU accession that more clear policies of accommodation for the Russian-speakers emerged. Again, the cleavage between the Estonians and the Russian-speakers is not a recent phenomenon; however, the activation of this cleavage and the consequent nation-building policies pursued – and their timing – were conditional to a great extent on the interstate relations between Estonia and Russia and between Estonia and the EU, which pressured Estonia to accommodate the Russian-speakers.[36] Consistent with my argument, the Russian foreign policy toward its diaspora had a significant impact on the nation-building policies pursued by the Estonian state. Let's take a closer look.

---

[35] For a historical overview of Estonian language and culture, see Raun 1991; Roos 1994; and David Smith 2001 and 2005. For a comprehensive historical account of the Estonian party system and cleavage structure since 1917, see Arter 1996 and Pettai and Kreuzer 1999. For a comparative study of elections in Estonia during the transition period (1989–1993), see Raitviir 1996. For an epitomized version of the process of transition with a focus on the internal competition among Estonian elites, see Pettai and Hallik 2002, Steen and Ruus 2002. Ishiyama and Breuning (1998) put the case of Estonia in a comparative perspective with other cases of ethnopolitical conflict in Western and Eastern Europe. Finally, for very insightful comparative accounts on the question of citizenship policies in the post-soviet Republics, see Brubaker 1992; Barrington 1995; and Smith and Wilson 1997.

[36] Also conditional, by extension, on the interstate relations between Russia and the EU.

TABLE 8.2. *Ethnic Composition of Estonia, 1920–1989*

Year	Estonians (%)	Russians (%)
1920	87.7	8.2
1934	87.8	8.2
1959	74.6	20.1
1979	64.7	27.9
1989	61.5	30.3

Source: Kirch et al. 1993: 174.

During the 1980s, *glasnost* and *Perestroika* changed the opportunity structure for mobilization in the Soviet Republics.[37] Ethnic Estonians organized in both moderate (Popular Front) and more extreme forms (Estonian Citizens Committees). A nationalistic language law was introduced in 1989, and the legal restorationist logic propagated by the Estonian Citizens Committees together with their "grassroots campaign to register citizens of the pre-war republics and their descendants,"[38] were signals of exclusionary intentions toward the Russian-speakers.[39] Most of the latter had migrated to the Baltic republics during the Soviet Era, as part of the central economic planning of the Soviet Union. In this process of migratory flows, Russians were the most numerous ethnic group to migrate in the region. Between 1979 and 1989, the Baltic republics were the destination of 246,000 immigrants. Since the beginning of the twentieth century, the share of the titular population in the total population dropped from 87 percent to 61.5 percent in Estonia (see Table 8.2).

My theory predicts exclusionary policies in the first half of the 1990s. The logic here is that the Estonian ruling elites in their efforts to restore the Estonian State were really suspicious of a sizeable non-core group backed by an enemy power – the Russian Federation (see Table 8.3).[40] Indeed until the withdrawal of the Russian military forces in 1994 the security of Estonia's

[37] Suny 1993.
[38] Pettai and Hallik 2002: 510.
[39] I use the term "Russian-speakers" for lack of a better term. Students of political science studying the Baltics or Estonia in particular tend to take ethnic categories as given. Usually they base their assumption on census data and surveys. However, the former imposes the criteria on the respondents (Goskomstat SSSR 1991) and the later presupposes the existence and salience of certain cleavages as early as the sampling stage (Rose and Maley 1994). This primordial understanding of the "Russian-speakers" is not restricted in journalistic or academic accounts (*Baltic Review*, Ishiyama and Breuning 1998: 79), but also in the legal framework that has been established in Estonia after independence. For more information on the Russian-speaking populations, Russophones, the new diasporas, the Russians Beyond Russia, see Barrington 1995; Berg 1999; Brubaker 1996; Mandelbaum 2000; Melvin 1995.
[40] It is clear that the cleavage dimension that was politicized in Estonia around the period of Restoration (1988–1992) was "ethnicity," in the sense that Estonians were distinguished from all the immigrants that moved in the country after the Soviet annexation. Four identity categories

TABLE 8.3. *Russians Living in Estonia, 1989*

	Total Population	Total Number of Russians	Russians (%)%	Russians Living in Urban Settlements (%)	Russians Fluent in Titular Language (%)
Estonia	1,566,000	475,000	30.3	92	14.9

Source: Kolstø 2000: 201–222.

independence was not guaranteed in the eyes of its ruling elite. Thus the Estonian ruling political elites at the time were revisionist and faced an enemy-backed non-core group.

Indeed, under these conditions, exclusionary policies ensued. After the August 1991 coup several highly exclusionary provisions were introduced in relation to the naturalization process. It was at this point that the ethnic Estonians managed to effectively exclude the Russian-speaking community from the state. The Russian-speakers went from being a majority in the USSR, enjoying privileges in housing and employment, to being a disenfranchised minority in a restored Estonian State. Citizenship in Estonia was restricted to those who or whose parents were citizens of the republic in 1940 (before the annexation of Estonia to the USSR), and examinations in Estonian language were necessary for naturalization. In 1991 (the year of independence), approximately 450,000 non-Estonians,[41] some of whom had lived their entire lives in Estonia, were automatically disenfranchised.[42] Moreover, injustices were recorded during the process of pre–World War II property restitution.

After the Russian troops left Estonia, Estonian authorities took over all Union enterprises and the property of the Estonian Communist Party (together with the archives), and most of the political organizations that used to mobilize Russian-speakers in favor of the Soviet Union (and had supported the August putsch) were outlawed and new Russian organizations were created. At the same time most Russian-speakers were excluded from the first parliamentary and presidential elections. As Khrychikov and Miall put it:

On 21 June 1993, the Estonian government passed the Law on Aliens.... In the context of radical anti-Russian and anti-Soviet rhetoric, in which prominent politicians and leading parties did not hesitate to voice the desirability of expatriation of non-Estonians, the new requirements were interpreted as a first step towards legalized expulsion.... At the same

were arrayed around the latter cleavage dimension: Estonian Citizens (including 75,000 ethnic Russians in 1992), Citizens of the Russian Federation (with resident permits in Estonia), Stateless persons (Undetermined Citizenship, mostly ethnic Russians), Citizens of other States (Ukraine, Byelorussia, etc.).

[41] A vast majority of this group was reported as ethnically Russian in the 1989 census (see Table 8.3), followed by Ukrainian and Byelarussians. That accounts for the characterization of Russian-speakers that has prevailed in the literature.

[42] Berg 2001:14.

time ... President Boris Yeltsin warned that Estonia had forgotten about "geopolitical and demographic realities" and pointed out that "Russia will take steps to defend its national interests in Estonia."[43]

Estonian elites had good reason to worry about the intentions of the powerful backer of the Russian-speakers. In his first legislative act on the issue[44] Yeltsin referred to the same population in very inclusive terms, as "compatriots."[45] Thus, even people belonging to ethnic groups or nationalities that did not speak Russian were considered to be subject to the Russian state policy. The Russian Federation in the early 1990s cultivated the idea among the "compatriots abroad" that they should expect support, within the framework of international law, in the realization of their civil, political, social, and cultural rights.[46]

At this point the Russian-speaking community was clearly backed by the Russian Federation and the exclusionary Estonian programmatic positions with respect to Russian-speakers can actually be construed as a reaction to the threat the latter posed for their national existence. This security logic underlying the decisionmaking process of the Estonian elites is consistent with my argument.

Change in Russian Foreign Policy, End of Exclusionary Policies (1996–2000)
The terminology used in the 1994 presidential decree changed later on – toward the end of 1996 – in the proposal of a new federal law on state policy for the protection and support of the "diaspora of Russia" and the "compatriots of Russia," under discussion in the Duma, the lower house of the Federal Assembly of Russia. Many high officials thought that the inclusiveness of the definition was actually undermining the implementation of state policy.[47]

Gradually, the Russian Federation resorted to policies that aimed at keeping the Russian-speaking populations in their respective regions abroad and using them as an asset in economic matters, while at the same time avoiding an enormous wave of refugees. Consequently, the official position wanted Russians to adapt to the local culture "while retaining their specific cultural identity." According to Aalto this arrangement lasted until the late 1990s.[48]

The Russian government began to increasingly perceive the Baltic states as "transit corridors for Russian export goods – mainly oil and other raw materials – on their way to European markets"; while at the same time Russian think-tanks "started changing their view."[49] Russian foreign policy makers decided to

[43] 2002: 195. For similar points, see Aalto 2003: 574; King and Melvin 1999/2000: 120.
[44] Presidential decree No. 1681 of 11 August 1994, "On the basic directions of state policy of the Russian Federation in relation to the compatriots living abroad."
[45] Presidential decree No. 1681 of 11 August 1994, Article 1, points 1 and 2.
[46] For more on this, see Shevel 2011.
[47] For more aggressive formulations of this thesis by Russian politicians, institutes, and political and nongovernmental organizations, see Kolstø 2000.
[48] 2003: 576.
[49] Ibid.

stop getting involved in the affairs of the Russian-speakers in the Baltic States for economic and geopolitical reasons.

At the same time, Estonia's early invitation to join the EU in 1997 as well as pressure from OSCE and the EU to improve its minority policies made any Russian complaint for violations of the rights of the Russian-speakers less credible. President Putin's statement in 2001 that Estonia's membership in NATO was inevitable completed the new geopolitical arrangement.

The combination of international backing by the West (EU, the United States, and NATO) coupled with the shift in Russian foreign policy that was already in progress paved the way for a new approach by the Estonian state. It could now afford to moderate its exclusionary policies and resort to assimilationist ones. In the context of the EU, however, these policies had to be called "integrationist." The naturalization of Russian-speakers progressed faster and integrationist rather than exclusionary arguments emerged. Consistent with my argument, the Estonian government although hard pressed by the OSCE and the EU did not consider policies of accommodation, such as cultural and linguistic rights, at any point in the 1990s. Thus in the late 1990s and early twenty-first century:

[O]nly 113,764 had received citizenship by naturalization. The Language Law made many jobs less accessible for people without a sufficient command of Estonian. In February 1998, it was toughened to require fluency of everyone working in the service industry or with customers. Members of the Riigikogu (the Estonian parliament) and local councilors were also required to be fluent, a measure that clearly restricted the representation of non-Estonians in state structures. University education was switched to Estonian, resulting in a significant decline in the number of Russian-speakers entering higher education. In 1998, Estonia also adopted a new education policy, which envisaged the closure of Russian upper-secondary schools in 2007.[50]

International Pressure, "Shy Turn" to Accommodation (2001–2008)

Recent government documents proclaim that Estonia is striving to become a multicultural society or, rather, that it has come to terms with its multicultural character. The Estonian government has accepted the responsibility to align the language legislation with international standards and the European Agreement. It has committed to implement concrete measures for the integration of non-citizens and include language training and necessary financial support.[51] This change in policy is not unrelated to subsiding threat perceptions.

Moreover, reluctant to jeopardize their relationship with the EU or NATO, Estonians try to avoid provocations. Similarly, Herd and Löfgren report that accession to the EU and the increased sense of security that this process generated have both served to diminish the security concerns with respect to their Russian-speaking communities.[52] According to the Estonian Ministry of Defense, "Between the years 2000 and 2003, the percentage of Estonians believing in

[50] Khrychikov and Miall 2002: 198.
[51] Berg and Van Meurs 2002: 259.
[52] 2001: 291–292.

the probability of being attacked from another state steadily decreased from 33 to 15."[53]

To be sure, the improvement of Russo-Baltic relations is an important but not the only reason behind this shift toward accommodation. The Council of Europe, EU, and the OSCE have all put pressure on Estonia and have been a significant driving force behind the shift of Estonian nation-building policies toward more accommodation.[54] This pressure, part and parcel of the process of EU integration, is important for the implementation of the relevant domestic policy changes.

CONCLUSION

All in all, my argument explains critical shifts in nation-building policies beyond the interwar Balkans, provides a novel interpretive perspective on a variety of cases, and accounts for complex empirical patterns that existing theories do not. Further probing of the argument is necessary, but finding adequate evidence to conclusively test my theory in each case is challenging. Material on cases beyond the interwar Balkans presented in this chapter is consistent with my argument that a host state's foreign policy goals interact with the interstate relations between the external power supporting a non-core group and the host state to decide the nation-building policies pursued by the latter toward the non-core group in question.

In the process, a number of conclusions were drawn. From the Balkan cases some lessons stand out. First, I qualified a prominent view about the frequency of scapegoating showing that it is rather a special case of false accusation of a non-core group by a host state. Second, I confirmed the importance of one of my scope conditions for the applicability of my argument, namely the ruling elites must be motivated by a homogenizing imperative. Third, my argument applies more generally in the modern Balkans; changes in the international system impact patterns of alliances and thus the planning of nation-building policies as well. From the cases outside the Balkans three insights arise: the role of the relative capacity of the external power versus the host state, the need to find the functional equivalent terms in each case to capture the concept of assimilation, and the importance of regional integration and international human rights norms in the post–World War II era, but especially the post–Cold War era.

Many research questions emerge. For instance, more empirical work is required on instances of scapegoating. This state policy is a special case of false accusation of a non-core group by a host state; however, we have very little

---

[53] Noreen and Sjöstedt 2004: 733.

[54] One concrete sign of accommodation of the Russian-speaking community – besides the declarations on intent in the programs of national integration submitted to Brussels – is Estonia's decision to change the electoral law and allow candidates to run in national elections irrespectively of their level of proficiency in the Estonian language.

systematic work on the conditions under which scapegoating occurs. Scholars may also want to study the role that the relative capacity of the external power versus the host state plays in the politics of nation-building policies. Finally, work on the impact of regional integration and/or international human rights norms on nation-building policies is long overdue. Pursuing these themes further, however, would require another book.

9

Conclusion

I introduced my argument referring to the shift of Ottoman policies toward the Armenians at the turn of the nineteenth century. Within a couple of decades, Ottoman perceptions of Armenians changed dramatically from viewing them as the most loyal *millet* to perceiving them as a threat to the country's territorial integrity. Policies of accommodation that lasted for centuries were followed by mass killings and deportations. What accounts for this puzzling shift of Ottoman perceptions and policies toward Armenians? Why, how, and when does one become a co-ethnic, a minority, or a refugee?

The most prominent explanations for the variation in nation-building policies focus on domestic factors. Often the ethnic politics that result from the salience of different attributes between the core and the non-core group (race, religion, language) are considered the cause of such policy choices.[1] Other scholars suggest that what matters are political ideologies of the ruling elites[2] or the regime type of the host state where the non-core group resides.[3] For others the history of past interactions between the core and the non-core groups[4] or demographic and terrain variables[5] can explain state policies toward non-core groups. All these explanations capture important aspects of the dynamics of nation-building. But they cannot account for the variation in nation-building policies across space and over time without taking into account the international security environment. The dynamic that I have highlighted in both my theory and empirical chapters has gone largely unnoticed.

Explanations that emphasize structural international factors to account for the occurrence of various nation-building policies are important to understanding long-term processes but unfit to account for quick shifts in nation-building policies. For instance, if a non-core group has a national homeland, we should

---

[1] Geertz 1963; Gurr 1993; Horowitz 1985; Kaufman 2001.
[2] Browning and Matthäus 2004.
[3] Brass 1991; Gagnon 1994/1995; Snyder 2000.
[4] Petersen 2001 and 2002.
[5] Fearon and Laitin 2003; Toft 2003.

expect that the group is more likely to mobilize, be emboldened, and ultimately rebel against the host state, thus bringing exclusionary policies upon it.[6] As I have made clear, however, international alliance patterns often trump such dynamics and, importantly, national homelands do not always act as agitators of co-ethnics abroad.

Mann's systemic argument highlights the "dark side of democracy" suggesting – among other things – that the international diffusion of the ideal of popular rule converts *demos* into *ethnos*, which in turn generates "organic nationalism," and it ultimately encourages ethnic cleansing.[7] Such systemic arguments are useful to account for shifting aggregate patterns between historical periods or regions but, again, cannot account for the differences in nation-building policies pursued toward non-core groups that do not fit equally the *ethnos* in each case. Finally, it is unclear what accounts for variation in nation-building policies in authoritarian regimes that are not supposed to be subject to the same dynamics.

Overall, prominent domestic and international explanations either involve processes that change slowly (e.g., modernization) or focus on attributes that can hardly change (e.g., race, ethnicity). But nation-building policies can – and do – shift at a faster pace. I have presented an argument that moves at a pace similar to that of these policies.

Forging a bridge between the comparative politics and international relations literature on this topic, I have argued that a state's choice of nation-building policies toward non-core groups is driven by both its foreign policy goals and its interstate relations. The foreign policy goals of a host state may be revisionist or status quo. Revisionist states are unhappy with the international status quo and their foreign policy goals are focused on overturning it. Status quo states are content with the existing state of affairs and want to preserve it. Interstate relations with the external powers supporting non-core groups can take the form of rivalry or alliance; these in turn are influenced by – but are independent from – international alliance blocs.

A host state's foreign policy goals as well as its perception of non-core groups drive nation-building choices. The presence of external support for a non-core group and the interstate relations between the external power and the host state determine whether the group will be perceived as threatening or not. A non-core group supported by an enemy external power and residing in a revisionist host state is more likely to be excluded than targeted with assimilation or granted minority rights; if a similar group were to reside in a status quo state it would be most likely to be targeted with assimilationist policies. Non-core groups supported by allied states are more likely to be accommodated than assimilated or excluded.

The evidence makes clear that the attributes of non-core groups are secondary in the process I am describing. To be sure, ethnicity matters, but only when activated in the international arena. Similarly, the existence of a homeland is also

---

[6] Brubaker 1996; Jenne 2007; Van Houten 1998.
[7] Mann 2005.

endogenous to interstate relations with the host state, since in my framework an external power chooses when to act as a "homeland" based on these relations.

Nor do I argue that cultural distance arguments are trivial. While it is true that I draw attention to and force into the discussion international factors previously ignored, I do so without seeking to discount or trivialize cultural distance arguments. In fact, religion comes up as statistically significant in my statistical analysis. Moreover, in the empirical chapters, I control for cultural distance to isolate the effect of international factors, not to render it obsolete.

Furthermore, cultural distance arguments may very well be important for the success or failure of certain policies, but not as relevant in the decisionmaking process of core group elites when they plan their nation-building policies. When the core group elites face a culturally similar non-core group that is supported by an enemy power, the cultural similarity will not prevent them from deporting or exterminating the group. For example, in the 1920s the Turkish-speaking Christian Orthodox population was included in the Greco-Turkish population exchange together with the Greek-speaking population of Asia Minor. Loyalty matters more than cultural markers in the age of nationalism.

Here is the appropriate point to clarify one more thing. The focus of my work is not non-core groups that have suffered status reversals but non-core groups perceived by the core group elites as being supported by an external power. It may be true that groups that have experienced status reversal are more likely to rebel than other types of groups;[8] such findings do not contradict my theory. In fact, such findings might be endogenous to my argument since groups that have experienced status reversal might also be more likely to be supported by external powers because of their propensity to rebel and their organizational cohesion.

In Chapters 3–7, I focused on the politics of nation-building in the states that emerged from the gradual decline of the Ottoman Empire in Europe. These cases provided an optimal context in which to study nation-building policies due to the protracted intermingling of peoples, common experiences of past rule, similar modernization trajectories, and a great deal of external involvement, as well as variation in the timing of their state-building experiences. In Chapter 8, I moved out of the southeast corner of Europe, relaxed some of my assumptions from Chapter 2, and illustrated the generalizability but also some of the limitations of my argument. More such tests are necessary to calibrate the theory for today's rapidly changing international system.

THREE CONCEPTUAL MOVES

This book makes three critical conceptual moves: first, from "minority" to "non-core group"; second, from "homeland" to "external power"; and third, from the dichotomous conceptualization of nation-building policies as "inclusion/exclusion" or "violent/non-violent" to "assimilation, accommodation, and exclusion."

---

[8] Horowitz 1985; Petersen 2001 and 2002.

The first move addresses a long-standing problem in nationalism and ethnic politics studies. Calling a "non-core group" a "minority" often implies either a legal status, recognition from the host state, or the existence of a claim by the non-core group. Thus, referring to "non-core groups" as "minorities" carries a wide range of assumptions that are often flawed. In my framework, a minority is a non-core group that has been targeted with accommodationist policies or one aspiring recognition. The term "non-core group" is more adequate since it includes aggregations of people who are conscious of their difference from the dominant national type without necessarily being mobilized around this difference. It does not imply anything about group size, and allows us to view even stereotypical members of the demographic core group as targets of assimilationist policies by the ruling political elites and not necessarily assume their national loyalty. In the initial stages of nation-building even people who fit the criteria of inclusion in the core group are often not conscious of their national identity and in that sense they have to be assimilated through conscription, schooling, and other nationwide policies. The term "minority" obscures these important points.

The second conceptual move facilitates the study of third parties involved in the mobilization process of a "non-core group" without being an "external kin" or "homeland." In my framework the "external power" could be a neighboring state, a great power, a diaspora group, a non-governmental organization, or a combination of these that interferes with the political fate of a non-core group in the host state. The term "homeland" is restrictive and cannot capture the full range of external actors involved.

The third move refers to the conceptualization of nation-building policies. The dichotomies of inclusion versus exclusion or violent versus non-violent policies are common ways of categorizing policies. I hold that they do not capture the full range of the observed variation. A nuanced and robust theory of nation-building must focus equally on violent and non-violent policies pursued by governments engaged in nation-building policies. In order to better capture the options available to nation-builders, I conceptualize nation-building policies by constructing a categorical variable that takes the following values: accommodation, assimilation, and exclusion. I also allow for mixed policies not just as an unintended consequence but as part of a strategy.

Existing conceptualizations put emphasis on explaining the occurrence of the most violent state policies such as genocide, mass killing, or ethnic cleansing. As a result, theories end up over-aggregating the different "peaceful" outcomes under the residual category of "non-violent" or "inclusionary," however, there is an important difference between assimilation and accommodation. Disaggregating policies is key if we want to test mechanisms, address observational equivalence problems, and unearth the logic of nation-building.

METHODOLOGICAL CONTRIBUTIONS

While collecting archival material and secondary sources to test the various explanations against my own argument, I identified a wide range of caveats in the study of nation-building. Scholars who study state-planned nation-building policies face both technical and conceptual problems. To begin with, as discussed in the Appendix to Chapter 4 there is the politics of "counting people." This issue refers to the difficulties and politics involved in three interrelated choices: identifying a group as an "ethnic group" or a "minority," deciding on an estimate of its population, and studying it as a relatively unitary and homogeneous entity. The most common methodological problems resulting are selection bias and overaggregated actors.

Similarly, in Chapter 5 I identified more caveats in the study of nation-building policies. First, we discussed how the time horizon chosen in each study affects the results we get. Second, that governments often pursue mixed policies toward certain non-core groups. Third, we found that sometimes a government will pursue a transitional nation-building policy before it pursues its terminal one. Fourth, it was revealed that external powers' foreign policy priorities and the degree to which alliances are asymmetrical significantly impact the decisionmaking process of host states with respect to nation-building.

Another caveat in the study of nation-building policies involves a "revealed preferences problem" in the social sciences, namely the practice of inferring an actor's intentions by taking statements at face value or just observing the outcomes on the ground. In Chapter 6 I discussed the importance of disentangling the relationship between intentions, policies, implementation, and outcomes in order to understand the process of nation-building.

In the nation-building process, intentions, policy choices, and policy outcomes are definitely linked, yet intentions are not always translated into policy choices, nor do those choices always produce the desired outcome. Moreover, policy choices are sometimes a function of capabilities and not of intentions. Other times, intentions are veiled because of the possibility of external intervention by an international organization or a hegemonic power. Moreover, private interests and biases of state officials, especially at lower levels of the administration, interfere in the planning and implementation of state policies. As a result, many theories are developed and tested on "events" that were unintended consequences or forced outcomes rather than accurate reflections of the administration's intentions. The outcome often is deceptive empirical support for or incorrect falsification of theories.

An archival approach can help us address the revealed-preferences problem. Studying the decisionmaking process that led to nation-building policies helps differentiate between the intentions of the administration toward a particular non-core group and the actual policy that it eventually adopts. One might argue that this is not necessary because what actually matters in politics is the policy that is implemented. However, if we want to understand why state officials choose particular nation-building policies and not others, studying only the observed outcomes will not suffice.

For example, two different non-core groups might be granted the same minority rights, but with a different reasoning behind each case. In practical terms, the reasoning matters because it most likely will inform the policy implementation. In theoretical terms, understanding elites' reasons can help distinguish between rival explanations. For instance, a hypothesis might predict the granting of minority rights to a non-core group, but for completely different reasons than the ones that were behind the actual decision. In this case, although the hypothesis makes the "right" prediction, it does not accurately capture the logic behind the policy.

To drive this point home, let us return to an example from Chapter 6, the granting of minority rights to "Romanians." A Romanian minority was recognized by the Greek administration because Romania was an allied power at the time and Greece needed its support in the diplomatic arena to secure its territorial gains from the Balkan wars; this reasoning is consistent with my argument. The Romanian minority was never thought of as something permanent and it was treated from the beginning as an instrumental concession to be countered on the ground. This case was different from the strategic nature of the initial accommodation of the Muslims in Western Greek Macedonia.

In addition to the important difference between intentions and actual policy choices, a distinction must be made between these policy choices and policy implementation. The importance of this distinction is captured in the case of the "Bulgarian-leaning" Slavs in Western Greek Macedonia. As described previously, Mazarakis recommended the deportation of the entire population, describing this as a more "radical" measure for nationalizing the territory. However, Eliakis dismissed this idea not because he deemed it immoral or unfeasible, but rather because the Greek government had to act as "a civilized liberal polity in the eyes of the international community." A more practical concern of his had to do with the ability of the Greek administration to repopulate these lands. A mass deportation of all the Bulgarian-speakers would have led to a severe depopulation of Macedonia and resulted in economic loss for the state. Instead, the governor ended up proposing the "hard and rough way of proselytizing, through good and expensive administration." Eliakis's position again points to the distinction between intentions and policy choices. A few years later, however, Eliakis admitted that the policy of assimilation had been inefficient because it was poorly implemented. From this example we see how the initial suggestion of deporting a non-core group was transformed into a policy recommendation of targeting the group with assimilationist policies, and how later, the leader responsible for the policy decision admitted its relative failure due to poor implementation.

Both the challenges of the "revealed preferences problem" and the conflation of intentions, policies, implementation, and outcomes hinder the study of state-planned nation-building policies. Chapter 6 stands as a critique to studies in comparative politics and international relations that fail to address these problems but mostly as an invitation for more work in this line.

Another related difficulty I have identified emerges from the principal-agent problems that exist in any administrative system. I discussed these problems in Chapter 7. In their effort to characterize various state policies toward non-core groups scholars often rely on reports by journalists, secondary sources, eyewitnesses, and archives. Often these reports are biased and even archival documents can be forged. But even if they are not, another problem complicates efforts to characterize a state policy: principal-agent problems. The events reported (e.g., massacres, arson, rape, looting) might have taken place, but they might not have been ordered by the central administration. It is difficult to know whether a central policy actually is implemented locally or whether the local elites pursue their own independent policies. The archival material I use in this book provides ample examples of principal-agent problems. In many cases the central administration of the state had both different intentions and policy preferences than its local officials – not to mention its core group members. The result of this incongruence ranged from private discrimination to systematic violation of human rights by local authorities and even the use of violence.

Moreover, while archival material allows us to trace the logic behind the choice of nation-building policies across groups and over time at the elites' level; it does not allow us to assess the effectiveness of the various policies or even the extent and quality of their implementation. The actual implementation of such policies is always mediated by various administrative levels from the mayor to individual police officers – and sometimes even individual citizens.

In Chapter 7, we discussed an illustration of this in the Kingdom of Serbia where British consuls referred to excessive use of violence by the Serbian army. The consul pondered over the locus of agency of these actions. The degree of control of the Serbian administrative apparatus in the newly annexed territories as well as the quality of policy implementation of state policies is still an understudied topic. It remains unclear what percentage of the actions observed on the ground in Kosovo were dictated by Belgrade and what was part of a micro-level story of opportunism on the part of uncoordinated individuals. Trotsky writes about paramilitaries that killed and looted, but whose connection to the official Serbian forces it was not possible to ascertain.[9] According to Stefanović, "the very existence of the paramilitaries was out of question without the consent, encouragement, supply, and toleration of the authorities."[10] With respect to administrators, we do know that they were often selected on the basis of patronage and were not trained at all.

We find similar concerns in a report to the Hellenic Ministry of Foreign Affairs by the Governor-General of Epirus, A. Kalevras, where he writes: "The officer of the police had his own national policy. The local military authorities also had their own national policy, and so did the educational and re-settlement civil servants."[11] Similarly, Repoulis, Minister of the Interior during World War I, was attributing the difficulties the Greek administration faced in assimilating the local population in Macedonia to the fact that the state representatives were not following state policy and laws but rather acted in a capricious manner.

---

[9] Trotsky 1980: 99, 120.

[10] 2005: 475.

[11] Quoted in Divani 1995: 247.

Eliakis was also always concerned about the principal-agent problem. His conviction was that things would have been different if the representatives of the administration in the new lands had been different. Prime Minister Venizelos also did not conceal his frustration with this phenomenon. As the Serbian Minister of Interior reported to the Serbian Ministry of Foreign Affairs:

Venizelos is disappointed by the actions of the Greek authorities. . . . Addressing the Prefect St. Gregoriou, he told him, "You are forgetting that in Greece there is only one policy, the one that requires the preservation of friendly relations with the Serbs, without propagandas, chauvinisms, and provocations. However, you are following a wholly different policy and you will be punished for that."[12]

Also in Turkey we know that certain local officials did go beyond the scope of their orders in the persecution of Armenians and Greeks, illegally confiscating properties and arbitrarily discriminating against particular individuals.

This list of cases and relevant stories is far from exhaustive, but still makes the point that the principal-agent problem affects the study of nation-building policies in a number of ways. To begin with, focusing on local events may give us a misleading picture of the overall policy of a state administration. For example, if we find evidence of systematic police abuse toward the members of a specific non-core group in a locality we are studying, we might be tempted to infer that this was a policy choice coming from the central administration. However, such an inference is often unwarranted. Thus if we want to understand the logic of state-planned nation-building policies we have to make an effort to distinguish central policy from unauthorized actions by local authorities.[13] Certainly, such a distinction might be unnecessary if we are trying to understand the success or failure of certain policies, but it is crucial if we want to discern the logic of central policy planning.

The above challenges impede the study of state-planned nation-building policies. Not addressing them in our research can lead to deceptive empirical support for theories or just wrongheaded theories. This book demonstrates the centrality of archival research and careful process tracing in the effort to overcome these important caveats in the study of nation-building and serves as a call for more interdisciplinary work in the social sciences.

Beyond the discussion of the methodological problems, important questions remain unanswered and require further research. A set of questions revolves around the form that different nation-building policies take. What accounts for the variation in the actual means that a government follows in order to assimilate, accommodate, or exclude a non-core group? Why is one group targeted with violent assimilationist policies while another with non-violent ones? Why are some groups targeted with deportation while others with mass killing? Another set of questions has to do with the nature of the modern state itself in the future. Is the

---

[12] Quoted in Hassiotis 2004: 353.
[13] There are cases of centrally planned tolerance of unauthorized behavior. The motivations for this vary widely.

nation-state model going to survive the parallel pressures coming from regional integration and globalization? What type of state may replace the nation-state?

In our effort to answer these and other research questions, focusing on the meso-level is key. Bridging the macro-level with the micro-level, that is, understanding the structure of the international system in which nation-building takes place at the local level, is crucial. Studies that focus on specific regions or specific ethnic groups would benefit from a more explicit treatment of the international dimensions of the process they are analyzing. The international context affects the preference ordering of host states, external powers that contemplate interference, and non-core group elites alike. Scholars studying the politics of nation-building should also focus more on the perceptions of state officials as well as the influential international players (Great Powers, international organizations, nongovernmental organizations), and try to identify the new cleavage dimensions that are about to be politicized.

At the same time, studies that emphasize the importance of systemic effects but neglect the micro-level processes at work are also problematic. Such studies often fail to identify the right level of analysis for data collection and hypotheses testing. Moreover, they suffer from a "revealed preferences problem" because they frequently make inferences about the actor's motivations based exclusively on public statements or observed behavior. Archival material coupled with historical contextualization is one way to mitigate this problem. A balanced study of nation-building should bridge the micro-level empirical work with the systemic effects of the structure of the international system by providing a theoretical argument at the meso-level, linking the macro- and the micro-levels.

POLICY IMPLICATIONS

What we learn by examining a number of empirical examples is that external involvement in favor of specific unassimilated ethnic groups in other countries significantly impacts – all too often for the worse – the nation-building policies national governments adopt toward these groups. There are thousands of ethnic groups living in roughly 195 countries today,[14] mostly concentrated in post-imperial and post-colonial territories. Understanding the logic of nation-building is therefore crucial to navigating the challenges ethnic diversity poses to the international system. Such an understanding could help decisionmakers in the international community devise incentives to prevent ethnic cleansing, encourage accommodation, or foster national integration.

In particular, three policy implications flow from my analysis. To prevent exclusionary policies we should (1) uphold the principle of state sovereignty and (2) encourage governments that venture to assist non-core groups in enemy host states to be particularly judicious. Finally, if our goal is to increase the probability of accommodation, we should (3) increase interstate alliances through regional integration initiatives and international institutions such as the EU and ASEAN.

[14] Doyle 1998.

1. Self-Determination as a Universal Norm: a Pandora's Box

To prevent exclusionary policies, we should uphold the principle of state sovereignty. The United Nations should only allow the creation of new states in cases where there will not be any non-core groups in the newly independent states or, alternatively, no external power would have an interest in interfering in their internal affairs.

The principle of state sovereignty has guided the international system for more than three hundred years. Since the Peace of Westphalia, modern states have agreed not to interfere with the internal matters of their neighbors, particularly those that concern their religious and more recently ethnic non-core groups. Once a state's borders are in place, international law guarantees their integrity. The unintended consequences of ethnic partitions have typically brought more violence, more interstate conflict, and more self-determination movements. Moreover, major global players such as the United States and Russia are often supporting self-determination movements without much evidence that they have thought through the consequences (intended and unintended ones). In short: the most judicious plan of action is to work with the borders we have, not the borders we want.[15]

Another reason for discouraging self-determination movements is the well-documented phenomenon of "horizontal escalation" of ethnic conflict.[16] We know that events in one state can – and often do – affect the politics in neighboring states. This can happen directly (e.g., through refugee flows) or indirectly (e.g., by "inspiring" a new movement in the neighboring state). There are plenty of such examples in Africa (e.g., Congo, Rwanda, Burundi, Sudan, Chad), in the Balkans (e.g., Albanians from Kosovo moving to former Yugoslav Republic of Macedonia), and in the Middle East (e.g., Kurds from Turkey moving to Iraq). Gleditsch suggests "the international community can alter the prospects for conflict by regulating access to transnational support, mobilization, and the availability of arms."[17] He is right, but such efforts presuppose a consensus over the principles that should guide the international system. Judging from the recent deadlock in the UN Security Council over the situation in Syria, this is in short supply.[18]

As long as hegemonic blocs of the international community continue to reward overly assertive self-determination movements with new states and partition settlements, the leaders of such movements will continue to pursue maximalist goals – and in response, host states will be more likely to pursue exclusionary policies.

---

[15] Meaney and Mylonas 2008.
[16] Lake and Rothchild 1998.
[17] 2007: 305.
[18] For more on the conflict in Syria, see http://www.bbc.co.uk/news/world-middle-east-17258397.

2. Minimize External Involvement

The causes of interethnic conflict are often to be found outside the place in which they are taking place. External involvement by interested powers politicizes differences that had not been as salient before and often triggers exclusionary policies by the host state; an example of this process occurring was the 2008 Georgian War.[19] The best safeguard against exclusionary policies is to preclude the eventuality of a non-core group being perceived as externally supported, especially by an enemy. As long as there are external powers that have an interest in destabilizing or partitioning other states, however, assimilationist and exclusionary policies will persist. Foreign policy decisionmakers ought to be particularly judicious in supporting indigenous movements in other states – China and Iran are two pertinent examples – since their governments might pursue exclusionary policies against enemy-backed non-core groups.

Thus, the decision whether it is a good idea for an external power to support a non-core group or not – in the special case where the host state is an enemy – depends on the relative capabilities between the external power and the host state and the degree of commitment of the former. For instance, if the external power is significantly stronger than the host state and is willing to dedicate all the necessary resources to support a specific non-core group, then external backing may work to the benefit of the non-core group and maybe even force the host state to change its policies. The auxiliary assumption here is that the external power will act quickly enough to avoid any desperate measures used by the host state against the non-core group.[20]

Critics might ask, "What should we do when groups are forcefully repressed by their host state?" From a moral standpoint, the world community has an obligation to protect them.[21] But it is far from clear that – uncritically or self-interestedly – supporting self-determination movements and partitioning existing states is the best policy for protecting the human rights of non-core group members. History shows that government elites are more likely to consider ethnic cleansing as a solution whenever an enemy-backed movement for a new state emerges.

In a recent study, Kuperman and Crawford found that non-core groups often turn to violent means of claim-making in anticipation of external support.[22] Bearing in mind that there are thousands of ethnic groups that are concentrated in post-imperial and post-colonial territories, the explosive potential consequences of failing to address these problems are apparent.

There is an important and ongoing debate over humanitarian military intervention and its unintended consequences for nation-building policies. Intervention in favor of discriminated-against minorities and oppressed peoples is widely seen today – probably more so than ever before – as a coverup for other,

---

[19] For more on this, see Meaney and Mylonas 2008.
[20] Downes 2006.
[21] Bellamy 2009; Hoffmann and Hollkaemper 2012.
[22] 2006; Bob 2005.

more cynical political goals and interests. Regardless of the external powers' actual motivations (ethnic kinship, human rights, or pure geopolitical interest) in supporting non-core groups against host states, the intervening power is likely to trigger exclusionary policies and repression, particularly in a world order where assimilationist policies have been greatly delegitimized.

Moreover, an international system that favors aggressive humanitarian intervention is more likely, all things being equal, to experience rebellions and self-determination movements, since the opportunity structure for non-core groups is more favorable. Even when an intervention is genuinely attempting to address a local conflict and is not part of geopolitical competition, perverse incentives may easily be generated. If the goal is to prevent ethnic cleansing, then third parties should stop "offering rhetorical and military support for armed secessionists and revolutionaries in the name of fighting oppression and defending human rights, whether in Rwanda, Bosnia, Kosovo, East Timor, Iraq or elsewhere unless they are prepared to act quickly and decisively."[23] The future of nation-building policies will correlate closely with the changing international norms of humanitarian intervention.[24]

It is conceivable that a broad shift away from exclusionary policies would occur if there were no longer any non-core groups mobilized by enemy powers. However, external powers interested in destabilizing certain states persist, and with them so do assimilationist and exclusionary policies. This is not to say that the international efforts to check such practices have no impact on the process. However, the classic drivers of international politics appear to still define the politics of ethnicity today, and there is little reason to think this reality will vanish anytime soon.

3. Regional Alliances and Nation-Building Policies

If we envision a multicultural world where ethnic and racial hierarchies will no longer exist and a new model of citizenship will emerge,[25] we should increase interstate alliances through regional integration initiatives and international institutions. There are three presuppositions behind this statement: that states participating in regional integration schemas such as the European Union are less likely to be revisionist, more likely to be in an alliance with their neighboring states, and consequently more likely to accommodate their non-core groups. Overall, I hold that countries in regions that have established stable security configurations are more likely to move toward multicultural arrangements.

For example, the current prevalence of accommodation in Europe is the product of EU integration, which began since the Treaty of Rome was signed in 1957. ASEAN has also had a more limited but similar impact in Southeast

---

[23] Kuperman 2001: viii.
[24] Finnemore 2004.
[25] Joppke 2005; Kymlicka 2012.

Asia. The norm of nonintervention enforced by ASEAN has contributed to the proliferation of accommodationist policies and the prevention of exclusionary ones. Similarly, the deepening of regional alliances through a "Eurasian Union" proposed by Vladimir Putin is likely to lead to less exclusionary policies and the accommodation of Russians in the near abroad as well as allied-supported non-core groups within the Russian Federation.[26]

Looking Ahead: The Structure of the International System

The future of nation-building policies will ultimately depend on the future of the international system, and vice versa. While everyone agrees that the bipolar system that existed during the Cold War belongs to the past, there is less of a consensus as to what has taken its place since the dissolution of the Soviet Union. The United States has been recognized by scholars and journalists alike as the only superpower for all of the 1990s and into the twenty-first century, providing analysts with evidence for a "unipolar moment." However, experts have been increasingly arguing that we live in a "multipolar" or a "nonpolar" world.[27]

Whether multipolar or nonpolar, the international system is definitely not unipolar as it was in the 1990s or bipolar as it was during the Cold War. The United States, China, Russia, the United Kingdom, France, Germany, India, and Japan are the most important poles of the international system. The picture becomes a great deal more complicated once we consider regional powers as well, such as Brazil, Iran, and South Africa. China's change of stance with respect to interference in other countries' affairs, the resurgence of Russia's hegemonic intentions, and U.S. unwillingness to give up its global hegemonic role are hard to reconcile. Without strong and functional international institutions, the rise of competing hegemonic powers may lead to an international system and nation-building policies that approximate those of the interwar period.

---

[26] Putin, Vladimir. "A new integration project for Eurasia: The future in the making," *Izvestia*, 4 October 2011. Available at: http://premier.gov.ru/eng/events/news/16622/.

[27] Haass 2008: 44–56.

Methodological Appendix

A. THE POLITICS OF "COUNTING PEOPLE"

The most daunting problem of studying nation-building is that of deciding which groups should be included in the analysis. The necessary historical research has not progressed enough in this highly politicized field to allow for a clear picture of the situation on the ground in the Balkan states during the period of interest.

The politics surrounding statistics on "national minorities" or "ethnic groups" is an extremely problematic aspect in the study of nation-building. First, whoever is doing the counting often predetermines the results. Second, even if we assume that existing statistics on ethnic composition are accurate, we can never be sure that the categories used in a census were the most salient ones for the people on the ground. For example, depending on which dimension the state census committee chooses to highlight – religious affiliation, mother tongue, regional identity, racial categories, or ethnic origin – it can produce a very different "ethnic structure."

An aggregate approach to issues related to nation-building is precarious and cannot serve as the final word. Using census data to explain nation-building policies is, to an extent, confusing the outcome for the cause. Census data on "ethnicity" are part and parcel of nation-building policies and so are maps and atlases.[1] The obvious case is that of groups that are not represented in census categories and are thus muted.

Take the Ottoman Empire, for example, which granted official status only to religious communities (*millets*). The Ottoman censuses record Muslims, Orthodox Christians, Gregorian Christians, Jews, and, later, Catholics and Protestants. Ottoman statistics provide no information about language, cultural difference, or national consciousness. In the Balkan Peninsula in particular, this meant that Muslim Albanian-speakers, Turkish-speakers, Ladino-speakers (Donmehs – Jewish converts to Islam), and other Muslim groups were all under the broad "Muslim" category. Similarly, all Christian Orthodox people – Slavic-speakers with various national affiliations, Albanian-speakers, Greek-speakers,

---

[1] Black 2002; Wilkinson 1951; Wood 1992.

Vlach-speakers, Sarakatsans, and so forth – were considered members of the Rum *millet*, represented by the Greek-dominated Patriarchate in Istanbul.

The transition from empire to nation-state in the Balkans occurred in the nineteenth and twentieth centuries, and with it a transition in the relevant recorded categories occurred. The same inhabitants of these territories were now aggregated with respect to language or a notion of national consciousness that was, at least initially, vague. This was the face of modernity in the region. Modern states in Western Europe, such as Germany and Great Britain, recorded language use and national origin in their censuses, and the Balkan states followed suit in order to be on equal footing and to try to prove their historical rights on disputed territories. In the hands of the ruling political elites of the Balkan states, the census was part of a broader war for the hearts and minds of the newly incorporated rural populations.

Scholars of nationalism and ethnic conflict have relied on various indices such as the Ethnolinguistic Fractionalization Index,[2] the Politically Relevant Ethnic Groups,[3] Fearon's,[4] Alesina et al.'s,[5] and so forth to capture ethnic diversity. Most studies rely either on census categories or on material produced by the elites of "oppressed" groups. Both sources are inadequate if our research question has to do with state-planned nation-building policies. For example, when we use census data, we are likely to get deflated population estimates of certain non-core groups and no estimates for the ones that are targeted with assimilationist policies. Similarly, if we try to discern the ethnic makeup of a country or a region using material produced by the elites of non-core groups we often encounter propaganda that inflates their numbers. In this latter case, however, what is more disconcerting is that we are not capturing any of the non-core groups whose elites have been successfully co-opted, or any non-core groups with no elites. Selection bias is therefore almost unavoidable.

Another caveat in the study of nation-building policies is that all of these data collection projects I cited above ignore small groupings of people; this occurs in multiple ways. First, most of the times the cutoff point for inclusion in a study of ethnic politics or conflict is 1 percent of a country's population. This means that groups that are relatively small are rarely if ever included in existing models. If a scholar is genuinely interested in including small groups (or even potential groups) he or she is quickly discouraged by the lack of data.[6] But even if we assume that someone has all the censuses of the world for the

---

[2] Atlas Narodov Mira 1964.
[3] Posner 2004.
[4] Fearon 2003.
[5] Alesina et al. 2003.
[6] I should note that the *Ethnic power relations* data set is an attempt to solve this problem (Cederman et al. 2010) and the *Minorities at Risk* project is also working on improving its dataset in this direction (Birnir et al. 2011).

past hundred years down to the individual questionnaire and an army of research assistants to help with coding, even then the biases would persist since the categories used are the ones strategically selected by political elites and not disinterested academics.

The seriousness of this problem depends on the research question of interest. A straightforward way in which ignoring small groups is problematic is to think of the possibility that a country has 30 groups smaller than 1 percent, which cumulatively total 15 to 20 percent of the total population, as compared with a country that has two such groups. The seriousness of such neglect becomes even more apparent when we consider the possibility that this very fragmentation is an outcome of state policy, as the divide and rule pattern discussed in Chapter 5 suggests, rather than a mere fact of the ethnic landscape.

Finally, comparability across countries is further hindered by the fact that statistical bureaus collect data on identity categories that are arrayed around different cleavage dimensions in each country. And, as we know from the empirical record, once the decision concerning the cleavage dimension and the relevant identity categories has been taken, a particular incentive structure is created for individuals on the ground. The result is usually overreporting in favor of the core group.

How can we overcome this situation where available statistics are capturing host states' nation-building policies instead of realities on the ground? One way to avoid this bias is to shun data from conflict-ridden territories until a fair amount of time has passed. Biased estimates and census manipulation are much more likely in contested areas. Focusing on such cases only exacerbates the problem. Detached historical research can put things into perspective. For example, Yugoslavia and Austria both claimed Carinthia for the first half of the twentieth century. According to the Austrian census of 1951, there were only 7,000 Slovenes in the Klagenfurt area of Carinthia, while the Yugoslavs claimed that there were more than 35,000. What accounts for this discrepancy? The Austrian census grouped people by "language used daily" into nine identity categories: "German, Slovene, Windish (a Slovenian dialect), and six combinations of the three."[7] Scholars had no way to tell how many "Slovenes" were living there. Moreover, the population inhabiting Carinthia could be grouped in various different ways depending on the census question. Data from contested territories are unreliable; scholars studying such areas should be upfront about the various sources of bias.

Another solution involves looking at census data that were produced prior to significant political changes in a region. In the case of Southeastern Europe, I overcame several problems with the help of the Ottoman censuses from the nineteenth century, as well as confidential diplomatic reports prior to World War I.

[7] Kostanick 1974: 27.

The ideal solution when studying state-planned nation-building policies, however, is to move our attention to state policymakers and take their perceptions seriously. The ruling political elites, who are central to the planning of nation-building policies, know that they cannot ignore non-core groups. These governmental officials, ministers, and governors write reports and confidential documents concerning groups of people that rarely come up in censuses or newspapers. They are treasures for both building and testing hypotheses. In the empirical chapters of this book, I relied primarily on such sources.

To construct the dataset for the post–World War I Balkans, I initially looked at available censuses (here we find the groups that the state recognized as "minorities"); then I moved on to secondary sources (here we find some excellent books but also a lot of the propaganda); and then to consular reports, and other materials such as memoranda, petitions, and telegrams from the region (here we get a complex but also more comprehensive picture). Once I put together a list of non-core groups, I then coded the nation-building policies pursued toward them by their respective host states.

A list of the secondary sources I used is available in this appendix. I also conducted a coding reliability test consulting academics, human rights activists, and journalists from the region – the names of those who answered full questionnaires are included in my acknowledgments. This final step was especially crucial for the coding of my dependent variable because it forced me to engage alternative interpretations of these historical events. All final judgments remain my own.

B. CODEBOOK

Variable Name	Description	Coding Rule
Policy	Nation-building policy	When the ruling political elites accommodate the non-core group, I assign the value "0"; when they pursue assimilationist policies I assign the value "1"; finally, when they adopt exclusionary measures, I assign the value "2."
Prediction	Theory prediction	When my theory predicts accommodation of the non-core group, I assign the value "0"; when it predicts assimilationist policies I assign the value "1"; finally, when it predicts exclusionary measures, I assign the value "2."

Variable Name	Description	Coding Rule
External	Non-core group has external support (*Configuration I*)	Coded as "1" if the non-core group was supported by any external power, "0" if it was not.
Extally	Non-core group supported by an ally (*Configuration II*)	Coded as "1" if the non-core group was mobilized by an ally, "0" otherwise.
Extenemy	Non-core group supported by an enemy	Coded as "1" if the non-core group was mobilized by an enemy power, "0" otherwise.
Revisionist	Host state – revisionist	Coded as "1" if the host state was revisionist, "0" if it was status quo.
ConfigIII	Enemy-supported group in revisionist host state (*Configuration III*)	Coded as "1" if the non-core group is supported by an enemy and lives in a revisionist host state, "0" otherwise.
ConfigIV	Enemy supported non-core group in status quo host state (*Configuration IV*)	Coded as "1" if the non-core group is supported by an enemy and lives in a status quo, "0" otherwise.
Contiguous	Host state and external power are contiguous states and have each others' co-ethnics	Coded as "1" if a non-core group is supported by an external power that has co-ethnics of the host state within its territory, "0" otherwise.
Status	Status reversal	Coded as "1" if the non-core group enjoyed a higher status in the polity than the core group in the recent past, "0" otherwise.
Homeland	Non-core group has a homeland	Coded as "1" if the non-core group had an external homeland, "0" otherwise.
Reputation	Host state cracks down harshly in order to prevent future uprisings	Coded as "0" if there was less than one secessionist non-core group in the host state, "1" if there were more.
Pop1918	Percentage of the non-core group in the host state	Percentage of the non-core group in the country in 1918.
Groupsize1	Non-core group size larger than 1%	Coded "1" if the non-core group was larger than 1% of the total population of the host state, "0" otherwise.
Groupsize5	Non-core group size larger than 5%	Coded "1" if the non-core group was larger than 5% of the total population of the host state, "0" otherwise.

(continued)

(*continued*)

Variable Name	Description	Coding Rule
Core	Percentage of the core group in the host state	Percentage of the core group in the host state circa 1918.
Non-core	Percentage of non-core groups in the host state	Total percentage of non-core groups in the host state circa 1918.
Concentrated	Most of the non-core group is territorially concentrated	Coded as "1" if the non-core group was territorially concentrated, "0" otherwise.
Language	Language	Coded as "1" if the non-core group had a different language from the core group, "0" otherwise.
Worldrel	World religion	Coded as "1" if the non-core group had a different world religion from the core group, "0" otherwise.
Religion	Different religion	Coded as "1" if the non-core group had a different religious denomination from the core group, "0" otherwise.
Urban	Non-core group primarily urban	Coded as "1" if the non-core group was primarily urban, "0" otherwise.
Rural	Non-core group primarily rural	Coded as "1" if the non-core group was primarily rural, "0" otherwise.
Nomadic	Non-core group primarily nomadic	Coded as "1" if the non-core group was primarily nomadic, "0" otherwise.

Some of the variables included in the codebook are discussed in the cross tabs but are excluded from the regression analysis because they are not statistically significant and/or due to degrees of freedom constraints.

C. NON-CORE GROUPS IN POST–WORLD WAR I BALKANS CIRCA 1919–1923

TABLE A.1. *Non-Core Groups with a Population Smaller Than 1% of the Total Population of the Host State*

Country	Non-Core Group	Prediction	Policy
Albania	Montenegrins/Serbs	2	1
Albania	Turks	1	1
Bulgaria	Armenians	0	0

Country	Non-Core Group	Prediction	Policy
Bulgaria	Gagauz	1	1
Bulgaria	Germans	0	0
Bulgaria	Russians	0	0
Bulgaria	Sarakatsans/Karakatsans	2	2
Bulgaria	Tatars	0	0
Bulgaria	Uniates	1	1
Greece	Chams/Albanian Muslims	0	0
Greece	Gypsies	1	1
Greece	Meglen Vlachs	0	0
Greece	Pomaks	1	0
Greece	"Romanian leaning" Vlachs	0	0
Greece	Romaniote Jews	1	1
Romania	Armenians	0	0
Romania	Czech and Slovak	0	0
Romania	Gagauz	0	0
Romania	Greeks	0	0
Romania	Serbs	0	0
Romania	Tatars	1	1
Romania	Vlachs	1	1
KSCS	Bulgarians (in the border areas)	1	1
KSCS	Czechs	0	0
KSCS	Greeks	0	2
KSCS	Gypsies	0	0
KSCS	Italians	1	1
KSCS	Jews	1	0
KSCS	Slavophone Muslims (South Serbia)	1	1
KSCS	Slovaks	0	0
KSCS	Vlachs	1	1
Turkey	Albanians	1	1
Turkey	Alevis (Tahtajis)	1	1
Turkey	Arabs, Christian Orthodox	1	1
Turkey	Assyro-Chaldean	2	2
Turkey	Bosnian Muslims	1	1

TABLE A.2. *Non-Core Groups with a Population Larger Than 1% and Less Than 5% of the Total Population of the Host State*

Country	Non-Core Group	Prediction	Policy
Albania	Gypsies	1	1
Albania	Slav Macedonians	0	0
Albania	Vlachs	0	0
Bulgaria	Greeks	2	2
Bulgaria	Gypsies	1	0
Bulgaria	Jews	1	0
Bulgaria	Pomaks	1	1
Bulgaria	Romanians	2	2
Bulgaria	Slav Macedonians	1	1
Bulgaria	Vlachs	2	2
Greece	Albanians (Christian)	1	1
Greece	Armenians	0	0
Greece	Catholics	0	0
Greece	Jews (Sephardim)	1	0
Greece	Sarakatsans	1	1
Greece	Slav Macedonians (Exarchate)	1	2
Greece	Slav Macedonians (Patriarchate)	1	1
Greece	Vlachs	1	1
Romania	Bulgarians	1	1
Romania	Germans	1	0
Romania	Roma/Gypsies	0	0
Romania	Russians	0	0
Romania	Ruthenes/ Ukrainians	1	1
Romania	Turks	1	1
KSCS	Albanians	1	1
KSCS	Germans	1	0
KSCS	Hungarians/Magyars	1	0
KSCS	Montenegrins	1	1
KSCS	Romanians/Vlachs/Cincars	0	0
KSCS	Turks	1	1
Turkey	Arabs (Muslim)	1	1
Turkey	Bulgarians	0	0
Turkey	Circassians	1	1
Turkey	Jews	1	0
Turkey	Laz	1	1
Turkey	Yuruks	1	1

TABLE A.3. *Non-Core Groups with a Population Larger Than 5% of the Total Population of the Host State*

Country	Non-Core Group	Prediction	Policy
Albania	Greeks	2	0
Bulgaria	Turks	2	2
Greece	Turks	1	0
Romania	Jews	1	0
Romania	Hungarians/Magyars/Szeklers/Csangos	1	0
Romania	Romanian Uniates	0	0
KSCS	Slav Macedonians	1	1
KSCS	Bosnian Muslims	1	1
KSCS	Slovenes	1	0
KSCS	Croats	1	1
Turkey	Armenians	2	2
Turkey	Kurds	1	1
Turkey	Greeks	2	2

D. WORKS USED FOR CODING

General Southeastern Europe

Adanır, Fikret, and Suraiya Faroqhi. 2002. *The Ottomans and the Balkans: A Discussion of Historiography*. Leiden and Boston: Brill.

Banac, Ivo. 1995. "Nationalism in Southeastern Europe," in Charles A. Kupchan (ed.), *Nationalism and Nationalities in the New Europe*. Ithaca, N.Y.: Cornell University Press, 107–121, 207–208.

Benbassa, Esther, and Aron Rodrigue. 1995. *The Jews of the Balkans: The Judeo-Spanish Community, 15th to 20th Centuries. Jewish Communities of the Modern World*. Oxford and Cambridge, Mass.: Blackwell.

Bianchini, Stefano, and Marco Dogo (eds.). 1998. *The Balkans: National Identities in a Historical Perspective*. Ravenna: Longo Editore.

Biondich, Mark. 2011. *The Balkans: Revolution, War, and Political Violence since 1878*. Oxford: Oxford University Press.

Bowman, Isaiah. 1926 [1921]. *The New World: Problems in Political Geography*. New York: World Book.

Carnegie Endowment for International Peace. 1993. *The Other Balkan Wars*. Washington, D.C.: Carnegie Endowment for International Peace.

Carr, E. H. 1945 [1939]. *The "Twenty Years" Crisis, 1919–1939*. New York: Harper & Row, Publishers.

Castellan, Georges. 1992. *History of the Balkans: From Mohammed the Conqueror to Stalin*. Columbia: New York: Columbia University Press.

Dafnis, Grigorios. 1955. *I Ellas Metaxy dyo Polemon, 1923–1940* [Greece between Two Wars, 1923–1940]. 2 vols. Athens: Ikaros.

Dérens, Jean-Arnault. 2003. "Winners and Losers among the Minority Groups in Former Yugoslavia. Forgotten Peoples of the Balkans," trans. Barry Smerin. *Le Monde diplomatique*. Available at http://mondediplo.com/2003/08/04Derens.

Destani, B. (ed.). 2003. *Ethnic Minorities in the Balkan States: 1860–1971*. Slough, U.K.: Archive Editions.

Dogo, Marco, and Guido Franzinetti (eds.). 2002. *Disrupting and Reshaping: Early Stages of Nation-Building in the Balkans*. Ravenna: Longo Editore.

Durham, M. E. 1905. *The Burden of the Balkans*. London: Nelson.

Elazar, Daniel J., Harriet Pass Friedenreich, Baruch Hazzan, and Adina Weiss Liberles. 1984. *The Balkan Jewish Communities: Yugoslavia, Bulgaria, Greece and Turkey*. The Center for Jewish Community Studies/Jerusalem Center for Public Affairs. Lanham, Md.: University Press of America.

Gewehr, Wesley M. 1931. *The Rise of Nationalism in the Balkans, 1800–1930*. New York: Henry Holt.

Gianaris, Nikolas V. 1996. *Geopolitical and Economic Changes in the Balkan Countries*. Westport, Conn.: Praeger.

Hupchick, Dennis P., and Harold E. Cox. 2001. *The Palgrave Concise Historical Atlas of the Balkans*. New York and Basingstoke: Palgrave Macmillan.

Ilchev, Ivan. 1995. *Rodinata mi prava ili ne! Vunshnopoliticheskata propaganda na balkanskite strain (1821–1923)* [My Motherland, Right or Wrong! The Foreign Political Propaganda of the Balkan States (1821–1923)]. Sofia: Universitetsko izd-vo "Sv. Kliment Okhridski."

Janković, Branimir M. 1988. *The Balkans in International Relations*, trans. Margot Milosavljević and Boško Milosavljević. London: Palgrave Macmillan.

Janowsky, Oscar Isaiah. 1945. *Nationalities and National Minorities (With Special Reference to East-Central Europe)*. New York: Macmillan.

Jelavich, Barbara. 1964. *A Century of Russian Foreign Policy, 1814–1914*. Philadelphia and New York: J. B. Lippincott.

Jelavich, Barbara. 1983. *History of the Balkans: Eighteenth and Nineteenth Centuries*. Vol. 1. Cambridge: Cambridge University Press.

Jelavich, Barbara. 1988 [1983]. *History of the Balkans: Twentieth Century*. Vol. 2. Cambridge: Cambridge University Press.

Jelavich, Barbara. 1991. *Russia's Balkan Entanglements, 1806–1914*. Cambridge: Cambridge University Press.

Jelavich, Charles, and Barbara Jelavich. 1977. *The Establishment of the Balkan National States, 1804–1920*. Seattle and London: University of Washington Press.

Karpat, Kemal. 1973. *An Inquiry into the Social Foundations of Nationalism in the Ottoman State: From Social Estates to Classes, from Millets to Nations*. Research Monograph No. 39, Center of International Studies, Princeton University.

Karpat, Kemal H. 2002. *Studies on Ottoman Social and Political History: Selected Articles and Essays*. Leiden, the Netherlands, and Boston, Mass.: Brill.

Ladas, Spethen P. 1932. *The Exchange of Minorities: Bulgaria, Greece and Turkey*. New York: Macmillan.

Lampe, John R. 2006. *Balkans into Southeastern Europe: A Century of War and Transition*. New York: Palgrave Macmillan.

Lampe, John R., and Marvin R. Jackson. 1982. *Balkan Economic History, 1550–1950: From Imperial Borderlands to Developing Nations*. Bloomington: Indiana University Press.

Macartney, C. A., and A. W. Palmer. 1962. *Independent Eastern Europe: A History.* New York: St. Martin's Press.

Magocsi, Paul Robert. 2002. *Historical Atlas of Central Europe.* Seattle: University of Washington Press.

McCarthy, Justin. 1995. *Death and Exile: The Ethnic Cleansing of Ottoman Muslims 1821–1922.* Princeton, N.J.: Darwin Press.

McGrowan, Bruce. 1981. *Economic Life in Ottoman Empire: Taxation, Trade and the Struggle for Land, 1600–1800.* Cambridge and Paris: Cambridge University Press and Editions de la Maison des Sciences de l'Homme.

Ortakovski, Vladimir. 2000. *Minorities in the Balkans.* Ardsley, N.Y.: Transnational Publishers.

Palairet, Michael. 1997. *The Balkan Economies c. 1800–1914: Evolution without Development.* New York: Cambridge University Press.

Pavlowitch, Stevan K. 1999. *A History of the Balkans, 1804–1945.* New York: Longman.

Pavlowitch, Stevan K. 2000. "Europe and the Balkans in a Historical Perspective, 1804–1945," *Journal of Southern Europe and the Balkans,* 2(2): 141–148.

Pearson, Raymond. 1983. *National Minorities in Eastern Europe, 1848–1945.* London and Basingstoke: Macmillan.

Poulton, Hugh. 1993. *The Balkans: Minorities and States in Conflict.* London: Minority Rights Publications.

Rossos, Andrew. 1981. *Russia and the Balkans: Inter-Balkan Rivalries and Russian Foreign Policy 1908–1914.* Toronto; Buffalo, N.Y.; and London: University of Toronto Press.

Rothschild, Joseph. 1974. *East Central Europe between the Two World Wars.* Seattle and London: University of Washington Press.

Roudometof, Vicrtor. 2001. *Nationalism, Globalization, and Orthodoxy: The Social Origins of Ethnic Conflict in the Balkans.* Westport, Conn.: Greenwood Press.

Seton-Watson, Hugh. 1962 [1945]. *Eastern Europe between the Wars, 1918–1941.* Hamden, Conn.: Archon Books.

Seton-Watson, Hugh. 1975. *The "Sick Heart" of Modern Europe: The Problem of the Danubian Lands.* Seattle and London: University of Washington Press.

Seton-Watson, R. W. 1966 [1917]. *The Rise of Nationality in the Balkans.* New York: Howard Fertig.

Shaw, Stanford J. 1974 [1963]. "The Ottoman View of the Balkans," in Charles Jelavich and Barbara Jelavich (eds.), *The Balkans in Transition: Essays on the Development of Balkan Life and Politics since the Eighteenth Century.* Hamden, Conn.: Archon Books, 56–80.

Skran, Claudena M. 1995. *Refugees in Inter-war Europe: The Emergence of a Regime.* Oxford, New York: Clarendon Press.

Stavrianos, L. S. 2000 [1958]. *The Balkans since 1453.* London: C. Hurst.

Stokes, Gale. 1984. *Nationalism in the Balkans: An Annotated Bibliography.* New York: Garland.

Sugar, Peter F., and Ivo J. Lederer. *Nationalism in Eastern Europe.* Seattle and London: University of Washington Press.

Tounta-Fergadi, Areti. 1994. *Meionotites sta Valkania. Valkanikes Diaskepseis 1930–1934* [Minorities in the Balkans. Balkan Summits 1930–1934]. Thessaloniki: Paratiritis.

Tudjman, Franjo. 1981. *Nationalism in Contemporary Europe.* New York: Columbia University Press.

Várdy, Steven Béla, T. H. Tooley, and Agnes Huszar Várdy. 2003. *Ethnic Cleansing in Twentieth-Century Europe*. New York: Columbia University Press.
Winnifrith, T. J. 1987. *The Vlachs: The History of a Balkan People*. London: Duckworth.

Albania

Austin, Robert. 1996. "Fan Noli, Albania and the Soviet Union," *East European Quarterly*, 30(2): 153–169.
Barnes, J. S. 1918. "The Future of the Albanian State," *The Geographical Journal*, 52(1, July): 12–27.
Clayer, Nathalie. 2007. *Aux origines du nationalisme Albanais: La naissance d'une nation majoritairement musulmane en Europe*. Paris: Karthala.
Clayer, Nathalie. 2008. "Behind the Veil. The Reform of Islam in Inter-War Albania or the Search for A 'Modern' and 'European' Islam," in Nathalie Clayer and Eric Germain (eds.), *Islam in Inter-war Europe*. New York: Columbia University Press, 128–155.
Destani, Beytullah (ed.). 1999. *Albania and Kosovo. Political and Ethnic Boundaries 1867–1946*. Slough, U.K.: Archive Editions.
Elsie, Robert. 1997. *Kosovo: In the Heart of the Powder Keg*. Boulder, Colo.: East European Monographs.
Fischer, Bernd Jürgen. 1984. *King Zog and the Struggle for Stability in Albania*. East European Monographs, no. 159. New York: Columbia University Press.
Great Britain. Foreign Office. Historical Section. 1920. *Albania*. No. 17. London: H. M. Stationery Office.
Marmullaku, Ramadan. 1975. *Albania and the Albanians*, trans. Margot Milosavljević and Boško Milosavljević. London: C. Hurst.
Pearson, Owen. 2004. *Albania and King Zog: Independence, Republic and Monarchy 1908–1939*. New York: I. B. Tauris Publishers.
Schwandner-Sievers, Stephanie, and Bernd Jurgen Fischer (eds.). 2002. *Albanian Identities: Myth and History*. Bloomington and Indianapolis: Indiana University Press.
Skendi, Stavro. 1967. *The Albanian National Awakening 1878–1912*. Princeton, N.J.: Princeton University Press.
Tsitselikis, Konstantinos, and Dimitris Christopoulos (eds.). 2005. *He Helliniki Meionotita tis Alvanias* [The Greek Minority in Albania]. Athens: KEMO Editions.
Vickers, Miranda. 1995. *The Albanians. A Modern History*. London and New York: I. B. Tauris.
Zickel, Raymond, and Walter R. Iwaskiw (eds.). 1994. *Albania: A Country Study*. Washington, D.C.: GPO for the Library of Congress.

Bulgaria

Bell, John D. 1977. *Peasants in Power: Alexander Stamboliski and the Bulgarian Agrarian National Union, 1899–1923*. Princeton, N.J.: Princeton University Press.
Black, Cyril E. 1943. *The Establishment of Constitutional Government in Bulgaria*. Princeton, N.J.: Princeton University Press.
Crampton, R. J. 1993. *A Short History of Modern Bulgaria*. Cambridge: Cambridge University Press.
Daskalov, Roumen. 2004. *The Making of a Nation in the Balkans: Historiography of the Bulgarian Revival*. Budapest: CEU Press.

Dimitrov, Vesselin. 2000. "In Search of a Homogeneous Nation: The Assimilation of Bulgaria's Turkish Minority, 1984–1985," *Journal on Ethnopolitics and Minority Issues in Europe*, 1(4): 1–21.

Dragostinova, Theodora. 2011. *Between Two Motherlands: Nationality and Emigration among the Greeks of Bulgaria, 1900–1949*. Ithaca, N.Y.: Cornell University Press.

Eminov, Ali. 1989. "There Are No Turks in Bulgaria." *International Journal of Turkish Studies*, 4: 203–202.

Eminov, Ali. 1997. *Turkish and Other Muslim Minorities in Bulgaria*. Institute of Muslim Minority Affairs, Book Series No. 6. London: C. Hurst.

Eminov, Ali. 2000. "Turks and Tatars in Bulgaria and the Balkans," *Nationalities Papers*, 28(1): 129–164.

Georgeoff, John. 1981. "Ethnic Minorities in the People's Republic of Bulgaria," in George Ed Klein and Milan Reban (eds.), *The Politics of Ethnicity in Eastern Europe*. New York: Columbia University Press.

Great Britain. Foreign Office. Historical Section. 1920. *Bulgaria*. No. 22. London: H. M. Stationery Office.

Karagiannis, Evangelos. *An Introduction to the Pomak Issue in Bulgaria*. Free University Berlin. Available at: http://www2.nbu.bg/iafr/inandout2.htm.

Kostanick, Huey Louis. 1957. *Turkish Resettlement of Bulgarian Turks, 1950–1953*. Berkeley and Los Angeles: University of California Press.

Krasteva, Anna (ed.). 1998. *Communities and Identities in Bulgaria*. Ravenna: Longo Editor.

McCarthy, Justin. 1995. *Death and Exile: The Ethnic Cleansing of Ottoman Muslims 1821–1922*. Princeton, N.J.: Darwin Press.

Meininger, Thomas A. 1970. *Ignatiev and the Establishment of the Bulgarian Exarchate, 1864–1872*. Madison: State Historical Society of Wisconsin.

Monroe, Will S. 1914. *Bulgaria and Her People*. Boston: Page.

Neuberger, Mary. 1997. *"Shifting Balkan Borders: Muslim Minorities and the Mapping of National Identity in Modern Bulgaria."* Ph.D. dissertation, University of Washington.

Neuberger, Mary. 2004. *The Orient Within: Muslim Minorities and the Negotiation of Nationhood in Modern Bulgaria*. Ithaca, N.Y.: Cornell University Press.

Perry, Duncan M. 1993. *Stefan Stambolov and the Emergence of Modern Bulgaria, 1870–1895*. Durham, N.C., and London: Duke University Press.

Radkova, Roumyana. 1980. "The National Awareness of the Bulgarians during the 18th and Early 19th Centuries." *Bulgarskata Nazia Prez Vuzrazhdaneto*. Sofia: Bulgarian Academy of the Sciences.

Tonev, Velko. 1980. "Nation-forming Processes in Northeastern Bulgaria and Dobroudja." *Bulgarskata Nazia Prez Vezrazhdaneto*. Sofia: Bulgarian Academy of the Sciences.

Greece

Aarbakke, Vemund. 2003. *Ethnic Rivalry and Quest for Macedonia, 1870–1913*. Boulder, Colo.: East European Monographs.

Alexandris, Alexis. 1988. "To Istoriko Plaisio ton Ellinotourkikon Sheseon, 1923–1955" [The Historical Framework of Greek-Turkish Relations, 1923–1954], in *Oi Ellinotourkikes Sheseis, 1923–1987* [Greek-Turkish Relation, 1923–1987]. Athens: Gnosi, 31–172.

Anthogalidou, Theopoula. 1987. *O Rolos tis Ekpaideusis stin Anaparagogi kai Exelixi mias Paradosiakis Koinonias* [The Role of Education in the Reproduction and Evolution of a Traditional Society]. Athens: Themelio.

Bowman, Steven. 2002. "Jews," in Richard Clogg (ed.), *Minorities in Greece: Aspects of a Plural Society*. London: C. Hurst, 64–80.

Carabott, Philip. 1997. "The Politics of Integration and Assimilation vis-à-vis the Slavo-Macedonian Minority of Inter-war Greece: From Parliamentary Inertia to Metaxist Repression," in Peter Mackridge and Eleni Yannakakis (eds.), *Ourselves and Others: The Development of a Greek Macedonian Cultural Identity since 1912*. Oxford and New York: Berg, 59–78.

Carabott, Philip. 2005. *"Aspects of the Hellenization of Greek Macedonia, ca. 1912–ca. 1959," ΚΑΜΠΟΣ: Cambridge Papers in Modern Greek*, No. 13: 21–61.

Christides, Christopher J. 1949. *The Macedonian Camouflage, In the Light of Facts and Figures*. Athens: Hellenic Publishing.

Clogg, Richard. 1981. *Balkan Society in the Age of Greek Independence*. Totowa, N.J.: Barnes & Noble Books.

Clogg, Richard (ed.). 2002. *Minorities in Greece: Aspects of a Plural Society*. London: C. Hurst.

Constantinople (Ecumenical patriarchate). 1993 [1906]. *Episema engrapha peri tes en Makedonia odyneras katastaseos* [Official Documents on the Painful Situation in Macedonia]. Thessaloniki: Kyriakides.

Constantopoulou, Photini (ed.). 1999. *The Foundation of the Modern Greek State. Major Treaties and Conventions (1830–1947)*. Ministry of Foreign Affairs of Greece, Service of Historical Archives. Athens: Kastaniotis.

Dakin, Douglass. 1966. *The Greek Struggle in Macedonia 1897–1913*. Thessaloniki: Institute for Balkan Studies.

Dakin, Douglass. 1972. *The Unification of Greece, 1770–1923*. New York: St. Martin's Press.

Danforth, Loring. 1995. *The Macedonian Conflict: Ethnic Nationalism in a Transnational World*. Princeton, N.J.: Princeton University Press.

Divani, Lena. 1995. *Hellada kai Meionotetes: to systema Diethnous Prostasias ton Ethnon* [Greece and Minorities: The League of Nation's International Protection System]. Athens: Nefeli.

Divani, Lena. 2000. *He Edafike Oloklerose tes Elladas* [The Territorial Integration of Greece]. Athens: Kastaniotis.

Eliakis, Ioannis. 1928. *O Venizelos* [Venizelos], 2nd ed. Athens: George Kallergis.

Eliakis, Ioannis. 1932. *O Venizelos os Dimosiografos* [Venizelos as a Journalist]. Athens: Dimitrakou.

Finlay, George. 1861. *History of the Greek Revolution*. Vols. 1 and 2. Edinburgh and London: W. Blackwood and Sons.

Glavinas, Ioannis. 2010. *O Mousoulmanos ypikoos stis antilipseis ton foreon tis ellinikis dioikisis tin periodo 1912–1922* [The Muslim Citizen in the Views of the Hellenic Administration during the Period 1912–1923]. Paper presented at the 4th Conference of the European Society of Modern Greek Studies, University of Granada, Spain (10–12 September 2010).

Gounaris, Basil G. 1996. "Social Cleavages and National 'Awakening' in Ottoman Macedonia," *East European Quarterly*, 29(4): 409–425.

Great Britain. Foreign Office. Historical Section. 1920a. *Greece*. No. 18. London: H. M. Stationery Office.

Great Britain. Foreign Office. Historical Section. 1920b. *Macedonia*. No. 21. London: H. M. Stationery Office.

Heraclides, Alexis. 2001. *He Ellada ke o Ex Anatolon Kindinos* [Greece and the Eastern Threat]. Athens: Polis.

Human Rights Watch/Helsinki Report. 1994. *Denying Ethnic Identity: The Macedonians of Greece.*

Jong, F. de. 1980. *Names, Religious Denomination and Ethnicity of Settlements in Western Thrace: A Supplement to the "Ortsnamenkonkordanz de Balkanhalbinsel."* Leiden: E. J. Brill.

Karakasidou, Anastasia. 1997. *Fields of Wheat, Hills of Blood: Passages to Nationhood in Greek Macedonia, 1870–1990.* Chicago, Ill., and London: University of Chicago Press.

Kontogiorgi, Elisabeth. 2006. *Population Exchange in Greek Macedonia: The Rural Settlement of Refugees 1922–1930.* Oxford: Clarendon Press.

Livanios, Dimitris. 1999. "'Conquering the Souls': Nationalism and Greek Guerrilla Warfare in Ottoman Macedonia, 1904–1908," *Byzantine and Modern Greek Studies,* 23: 195–221.

Mackridge, Peter, and Eleni Yannakakis (eds.). 1997. *Ourselves and Others: The Development of a Greek Macedonian Cultural Identity since 1912.* Oxford and New York: Berg.

Margaritis, George. 2005. *Anepithimiti Sympatriotes* [Unwanted Compatriots]. Athens: Vivliorama.

Mavrogordatos, George Th. 1983. *Stillborn Republic: Social Coalitions and Party Strategies in Greece, 1922–1936.* Berkeley: University of California Press.

Mazower, Mark. 2004. *Salonica, City of Ghosts.* London: HarperCollins.

Michailidis, Iakovos. 1996. "Minority Rights and Educational Problems in Greek Interwar Macedonia: The Case of the Primer 'Abecedar,'" *Journal of Modern Greek Studies* 14(2): 329–343.

Michailidis, Iakovos. 1998. "The War on Statistics: Traditional Recipes for the Preparation of the Macedonian Salad," *East European Quarterly* 32(1): 9–21.

Nakratzas, George. 1999. *The Close Racial Kinship between the Greeks, Bulgarians and Turks: Macedonia–Thrace.* Thessaloniki: Batavia Publications.

Pallis, Alexander A. 1925. "Racial Migrations in the Balkans during the Years 1912–1924," *Geographical Journal,* 66(4): 315–331.

Sotiriou, Stephanos. 2000. *To Alvaniko Ethniko Zetema* [The Albanian National Issue]. Athens: Pelasgos.

Stefanou, Stefanos (ed.). 1965. *Eleutheriou Venizelou Politikai Ypothikai* [The Political Legacy of Eleftherios Venizelos]. Vol. A. Athens: Rodi.

Stefanou, Stefanos (ed.). 1969. *Eleutheriou Venizelou Politikai Ypothikai* [The Political Legacy of Eleftherios Venizelos]. Vol. B. Athens: Rodi.

Tounta-Fergadi, Areti. 1986a. *Ellino-Voulgarikes Meionotetes: Protokollo Polite-Kalfof 1924–1925* [Greek-Bulgarian Minorities: The Politis-Kalfof Protocol 1924–1925]. Thessaloniki: Institute for Balkan Studies.

Tounta-Fergadi, Areti. 1986b. *Themata Ellinikis Diplomatikis Istorias* [Themes in Greek Diplomatic History]. Athens: Paratiritis.

Veremis, Th., and G. Goulimi (eds.). 1989. *Eleftherios Venizelos: Koinotita, Economia, Politiki stin Epochi tou* [Eleftherios Venizelos: Commuity, Economy and Politics in His Era]. Athens: Gnosi.

Vouri, Sophia. 1992. *Ekpaideuse kai Ethnikismos sta Valkania. He Periptose tis Voreiodytikes Makedonias 1870–1904* [Education and Nationalism in the Balkans. The Case of North-Western Macedonia 1870–1904]. Athens: Paraskinio.

Romania

Fischer-Galati, Stephen. 1969. "Romanian Nationalism," in Peter Sugar and Ivo Lederer (eds.), *Nationalism in Eastern Europe*. Seattle and London: University of Washington Press, pp. 373–395.

Great Britain. Foreign Office. Historical Section. 1920. *Rumania*. No. 23. London: H. M. Stationery Office.

Illyes, Elemer. 1982. *National Minorities in Romania: Change in Transylvania*. Boulder, Colo.: East European Monographs.

Iordachi, Constantin. 2002. *Citizenship, Nation- and State-Building: The Integration of Northern Dobrogea into Romania, 1878–1913*. The Carl Beck Papers in Russian and East European Studies, No. 1607.

Livezeanu, Irina. 2000 [1995]. *Cultural Politics in Greater Romania: Regionalism, Nation-Building, and Ethnic Struggle, 1918–1930*. Ithaca, N.Y., and London: Cornell University Press.

Rothschild, Joseph. 1974. "Romania," in *East Central Europe between the Two World Wars*. Seattle and London: University of Washington Press.

Ottoman Empire/Turkey

Akcam, Taner. 2006. *A Shameful Act: The Armenian Genocide and the Question of Turkish Responsibility*, trans. Paul Bessemer. New York: Henry Holt.

Alexandris, Alexis. 1983. *The Greek Minority of Istanbul and Greek-Turkish Relations, 1918–1974*. Athens: Center for Asia Minor Studies.

Cagaptay, Soner. 2003. "Crafting the Turkish Nation: Kemalism and Turkish Nationalism in the 1930s." Ph.D. dissertation, Yale University.

Cagaptay, Soner. 2006. *Islam, Secularism, and Nationalism in Modern Turkey: Who Is a Turk?* London and New York: Routledge.

Dominian, Lèon. 1917. *The Frontiers of Language and Nationality in Europe*. New York: Henry Holt.

Gingeras, Ryan. 2009. *Sorrowful Shores: Violence, Ethnicity, and the End of the Ottoman Empire, 1912–1923*. Oxford: Oxford University Press.

Great Britain. Foreign Office. Historical Section. 1920a. *Turkey in Asia*. No. 58. London: H.M. Stationery Office.

Great Britain. Foreign Office. Historical Section. 1920b. *Turkey in Europe*. No. 16. London: H.M. Stationery Office.

Kasaba, Reşat (ed.) 2008. *Cambridge History of Turkey*, vol. 4: *Turkey in the Modern World*. Cambridge: Cambridge University Press.

Levene, Mark. 1998. "Creating a Modern 'Zone of Genocide': The Impact of Nation- and State-Formation on Eastern Anatolia, 1878–1923," *Holocaust and Genocide Studies*, 12(3): 393–413.

Lewis, Bernard. 1961. *The Emergence of Modern Turkey*. London: Oxford University Press.

McCarthy, Justin. 1983. *Muslim and Minorities: The Population of Ottoman Anatolia and the End of the Empire*. New York and London: New York University Press.

McCarthy, Justin. 1995. *Death and Exile: The Ethnic Cleansing of Ottoman Muslims, 1821–1922*. Princeton, N.J.: Darwin Press.

McCarthy, Justin. 2001. *The Ottoman Peoples and the End of Empire*. New York: Arnold and Oxford University Press.

Poulton, Hugh. 1997. *Top Hat, Grey Wolf and Crescent: Turkish Nationalism and the Turkish Republic*. London: C. Hurst.

Romano, David. 2006. *The Kurdish Nationalist Movement: Opportunity, Mobilization and Identity*. New York: Cambridge University Press.

Sonyel, Salahi R. 2001. *The Assyrians of Turkey: Victims of Major Power Policy*. Ankara: Turkish Historical Society Printing House.

The Kingdom of Serbs, Croats and Slovenes/The Kingdom of Yugoslavia

Banac, Ivo. 1984. *The National Question in Yugoslavia: Origins, History, Politics*. Ithaca, N.Y., and London: Cornell University Press.

Banac, Ivo. 1993. "Insignia of Identity: Heraldry and the Growth of National Ideologies among the South Slavs," *Ethnic Studies*, 10: 215–237.

Banac, Ivo. 1995. "Zarathustra in Red Croatia: Millan Šufflay and His Theory of Nationhood," in Ivo Banac and Katherine Verdery (eds.), *National Character and National Ideology in Interwar Eastern Europe*. (Russian and East European Publications, No. 13). New Haven, Conn.: Yale Center for International and Area Studies.

Biondich, Mark. 2007. "Vladko Maček and the Croat Political Right, 1928–1941," *Contemporary European History*, 16(2): 203–213.

Curtis, Glenn E. (ed.). 1992. *Yugoslavia: A Country Study*. Federal Research Division, Library of Congress.

Destani, Beytullah (ed.). 1999. *Albania and Kosovo: Political and Ethnic Boundaries 1867–1946*. Archive Editions.

Destani, B. (ed.). 2003. *Ethnic Minorities in the Balkan States: 1860–1971*. Slough, U.K.: Archive Editions Limited.

Djilas, Aleksa. 1991. *The Contested Country: Yugoslav Unity and Communist Revolution, 1919–1953*. Cambridge, Mass.: Harvard University Press.

Djokić, Dejan (ed.). 2003. *Yugoslavis Histories of a Failed Idea, 1918–1992*. London: C. Hurst.

Djokić, Dejan. 2007. *Elusive Compromise: A History of Interwar Yugoslavia*. London: C. Hurst.

Dragnich, Alex N. 1983. *The First Yugoslavia: Search for a Viable Political System*. Stanford, Calif.: Hoover Institution Press.

Edwards, Lovett F. (ed.). 1969. *The Memoirs of Prota Matija Nenadović*. London: Oxford University Press.

Great Britain. Foreign Office. Historical Section. 1920a. *Macedonia*. No. 21. London: H. M. Stationery Office.

Great Britain. Foreign Office. Historical Section. 1920b. *Montenegro*. No. 19. London: H. M. Stationery Office.

Great Britain. Foreign Office. Historical Section. 1920c. *Serbia*. No. 20. London: H. M. Stationery Office.

Grimm, Gerhard. 1984. "Ethnographic Maps of the Kosova Region from 1730–1913," in Arshi Pipa and Sami Repishti (eds.), *Studies on Kosova*. Boulder, Colo.: East European Monographs.

Irvine, Jill A. 1993. *The Croat Question: Partisan Politics in the Formation of the Yugoslav Socialist State*. Boulder, Colo.: Westview Press.

Lampe, John R. 2000. *Yugoslavia as History: Twice There Was a Country*. New York: Cambridge University Press.

Malcolm, Noel. 1998. *Kosovo: A Short History*. New York: HarperPerennial.

Miller, Nicholas John. 1991. "Between Great Serbianism and Yugoslavis Serbian Politics in Croatia, 1903–1914." Ph.D. dissertation, Indiana University.

Mittleman, Earl Niel. 1954. "The Nationality Problem in Yugoslavia: A Survey of Developments, 1921–1953." Ph.D. dissertation, University of Michigan.

Pasic, Najdan. 1973. "Varieties of Nation-Building in the Balkans among the Southern Slavs," In S.N. Eisenstadt and Stein Rokkan (eds.), *Building States and Nations: Analyses by Region*. Vol. 2. Beverly Hills, Calif., and London: Sage Publications, 117–141.

Petranović, Branco. 2002. *The Yugoslav Experience of Serbian National Integration*. New York: Columbia University Press.

Ramet, Sabrina P. 2006. *The Three Yugoslavias: State-Building and Legitimation, 1918–2005*. Bloomington and Indianapolis: Indiana University Press.

Sardamov, Ivelin. 1998. "Mandate of History: War, Ethnic Conflict and Nationalism in the South Slav Balkans." Ph.D. dissertation, University of Notre Dame.

Singleton, Fred. 1985. *A Short History of the Yugoslav Peoples*. Cambridge: Cambridge University Press.

Stathi, Sasa K. 1983. *Yugoslavia kai Tito 1919–1953* [Yugoslavia and Tito 1919–1953]. Athens: Hestia.

Vasiliadis, Nikolaos. 2004. *I Elliniki parousia sti Notia Servia apo tous Valkanikous polemous eos to Mesopolemo* [The Hellenic Presence in South Serbia from the Balkan Wars to the Interwar Period]. Thessaloniki: Anatropi.

Vickers, Miranda. 1998. *Between Serb and Albanian: A History of Kosovo*. London: C. Hurst.

References

Archives

AEV   Archive of Eleftherios Venizelos. Benaki Musuem, Athens
A.P.K.   Archeion Pavlou Kalliga [Pavlos Kalligas Papers],
     The Museum of the Macedonian Struggle, Thessaloniki
AYE   Archive of the Hellenic Ministry of Foreign Affairs, Athens
BNA   British National Archives
DDI   Documenti Diplomatici Italiani
GAK/Florinas   General State Archives of Florina
GAK/Kozanis   General State Archives of Kozani
GAK/Makedonias   General State Archives of Macedonia, Thessaloniki
G.L.   Gennadius Library
ELIA   The Hellenic Literary and Historical Archive

Newspapers

Efimeris ton Valkanion
Eleftheron Vima
Iho tis Makedonias
New York Times

Works Cited

Aalto, Pami. 2003. "Revisiting the Security/Identity Puzzle in Russo-Estonian Relations," *Journal of Peace Research*, 40(5): 573–591.

Aarbakke, Vemund. 2000. "The Muslim Minority of Greek Thrace." Ph.D. dissertation, University of Bergen.

Aarbakke, Vemund. 2003. *Ethnic Rivalry and Quest for Macedonia, 1870–1913*. Boulder, Colo.: East European Monographs.

Aarbakke, Vemund. 2012. "Urban Space and Bulgarian-Greek Antagonism in Thrace, 1870–1912," presented at the The Balkans: From Academic Field to International Politics Workshop, a joint workshop by Ecole Française d'Athènes and British School of Athens, (Athens, 17–19 April). Available at: http://www.bsa.ac.uk/doc_store/IT/IT2012_50.pdf.

Ai Agoreuseis tou Ellinikou Koinovouliou, 1909–1956 [The Greek Parliament Speeches].
    1957. Vol. 3. Athens: Ethnikos Kirix.
Akcam, Taner. 2006. *A Shameful Act: The Armenian Genocide and the Question of
    Turkish Responsibility*, trans. Paul Bessemer. New York: Henry Holt.
Akhund, Nadine. 2009. "Muslim Representation in the Three Ottoman Vilayets of
    Macedonia: Administration and Military Power (1878–1908)," *Journal of Muslim
    Minority Affairs*, 29 (December): 443–54.
Akturk, Sener. 2007. "Continuity and Change in the Regimes of Ethnicity in Austria,
    Germany, USSR/Russia, and Turkey: Varieties of Ethnic Regimes and Hypotheses for
    Change," *Nationalities Papers*, 35(1, March): 23–49.
Akturk, Sener. 2011. "Regimes of Ethnicity: Comparative Analysis of Germany, the Soviet
    Union/Post-Soviet Russia, and Turkey," *World Politics*, 61(1, January): 115–164.
Alba, Richard, and Victor Nee. 1997. "Rethinking Assimilation Theory for a New Era of
    Migration," *International Migration Review*, 31(4): 826–874.
Alba, Richard, and Victor Nee. 2003. *Remaking the American Mainstream: Assimilation
    and Contemporary Immigration*. Cambridge, Mass.: Harvard University Press.
Alesina, Alberto, and Enrico Spolaore. 2003. *The Size of Nations*. Cambridge, Mass.:
    MIT University Press.
Alesina, Alberto, Arnaud Devleeschauwer, William Easterly, Sergio Kurlat, and
    Romain Wacziarg. 2003. "Fractionalization." *Journal of Economic Growth*, 8 June:
    155–194.
Alter, Peter. 1994. *Nationalism*. London: Edward Arnold.
Alvanos, Raymondos. 2005. "Koinonikes sygkrouseis kai politikes symperifores stin
    periohi tis Kastorias, 1922–1949" [Social Conflicts and Political Behaviors in the
    Area of Kastoria, 1922–1949]. Ph.D. dissertation, Aristotle University of Thessaloniki.
Ambrosio, Thomas. 2001. *Irredentis Ethnic Conflict and International Politics*. Wesport,
    Conn., and London: Praeger.
Anagnostou, Dia. 2005. "Nationalist Legacies and European Trajectories in the Balkans:
    Post-Communist Liberalization and Turkish Minority Politics in Bulgaria," *Southeast
    Europe and Black Sea Studies*, 5(1): 87–109.
Anagnostou, Dia. 2007. "Development, Discrimination and Reverse Discrimination: The
    Effects of EU Integration and Regional Change on the Muslims of Southeast Europe,"
    in Aziz Al-Ahmet and Effie Fokas (eds.), *Islam in Europe: Diversity, Identity, and
    Influence*. New York: Cambridge University Press.
Anderson, Benedict. 1983. *Imagined Communities: Reflections on the Origins and
    Spread of Nationalism*. New York: Verso.
Anderson, Charles W., Fred R. von der Mehden, and Crawford Young. 1967. *Issues of
    Political Development*. Englewood Cliffs, N.J.: Prentice-Hall.
Andrić, Ivo. 1997. "Draft on Albania (1939)," in Robert Elsie (ed.), *Kosovo: In the Heart
    of the Powder Keg*. Boulder, Colo.: East European Monographs, 435–448.
Armitage, Andrew. 1995. *Comparing the Policy of Aboriginal Assimilation: Australia,
    Canada, and New Zealand*. Vancouver: University of British Columbia Press.
Armstrong, Hamilton Fish. 1928. "Italy, Jugoslavia and Lilliputia," *Foreign Affairs*, 6(2):
    191–202.
Armstrong, John A. 1982. *Nations before Nationalism*. Chapel Hill: University of North
    Carolina Press.
Aron, Raymond. 1966. "Social Class, Political Class, Ruling Class," in Reinhard Bendix
    and Seymour M. Lipset (eds.), *Class, Status and Power*. New York: Free Press, 201–210.

Arter, David. 1996. *Parties and Democracy in the Post-Soviet Republics: The Case of Estonia*. Aldershot, UK: Darmouth Publishing.

Atlas Narodov Mira. 1964. *Moscow: Miklukho-Maklai Ethnological Institute at the Department of Geodesy and Cartography of the State Geological Committee of the Soviet Union*.

Austin, Robert. 1996. "Fan Noli, Albania and the Soviet Union," *East European Quarterly*, 30(2): 153–169.

Austin, Robert. 2004. "Greater Albania: The Albanian State and the Question of Kosovo, 1912–2001," in John R. Lampe and Mark Mazower, *Ideologies and National Identities: The Case of Twentieth-Century Southeastern Europe*. Budapest: Central European University Press, 235–253.

Azcárate, P. de. 1945. *League of Nations and National Minorities: An Experiment*, trans. Eileen E. Brooke. Washington, D.C.: Carnegie Endowment for International Peace.

Babuna, Aydin. 2000. "The Albanians of Kosovo and Macedonia: Ethnic Identity Superseding Religion," *Nationalities Papers*, 28(1): 67–92.

"Bahrain Hints at Iranian Role over Country's Shia Uprising," 2011. *Guardian*, 21 March. Available at: http://www.guardian.co.uk/world/2011/mar/21/bahrain-iran-role-uprising-shia.

Banac, Ivo. 1984. *The National Question in Yugoslavia: Origins, History, Politics*. Ithaca, N.Y., and London: Cornell University Press.

Banac, Ivo. 1995. "Nationalism in Southeastern Europe," in Charles A. Kupchan (ed.), *Nationalism and Nationalities in the New Europe*. Ithaca, N.Y.: Cornell University Press, 107–121, 207–208.

Banac, Ivo. 2006. "The Politics of National Homogeneity," in Brad K. Blitz (ed.), *War and Change in the Balkans*. Cambridge: Cambridge University Press, 30–43.

Barker, Elisabeth. 1950. *Macedonia: Its Place in Balkan Power Politics*. London and New York: Royal Institute of International Affairs/Oxford University Press.

Barnet, Richard J. 1968. *Intervention and Revolution: America's Confrontation with Insurgent Movements around the World*. New York: New American Library/World Publishing.

Barnett, Michael N. 2011. *Empire of Humanity: A History of Humanitarianism*. Ithaca, N.Y.: Cornell University Press.

Barrington, Lowell. 1995. "The Domestic and International Consequences of Citizenship in the Soviet Successor States," *Europe-Asia Studies*, 47(5): 731–763.

Barros, James. 1970. *The League of Nations and the Great Powers: The Greek-Bulgarian Incident, 1925*. Oxford: Clarendon Press.

Barth, Frederik. 1998 [1969]. *Ethnic Groups and Boundaries*. Prospect Heights, Ill.: Waveland Press.

Bartov, Omer. 1996. *Murder in Our Midst: The Holocaust, Industrial Killing, and Representation*. Oxford: Oxford University Press.

Bataković, Dušan. 1991. *Kosovo i Metohija u srpsko-arbanaškim odnosima* [Kosovo and Metohija in Serb-Albanian Relations]. Priština: Jedinstvo.

Bataković, Dušan. *"Kosovo and Metohija: A Historical Survey."* Available at: http://www.kosovo.net/histkim.html.

Beljo, Ante (ed.). 1992. *Greater Serbia: From Ideology to Aggression*. Zagreb: Croatian Information Centre.

Bellamy, Alex J. 2009. *Responsibility to Protect: The Global Effort to End Mass Atrocities*. Cambridge: Polity Press.

Bendix, Reinhard. 1969. *Nation-Building and Citizenship: Studies of Our Changing Social Order*. Garden City, N.Y.: Anchor Books.

Benhabib, Seyla. 2004. *The Rights of Others*. New York: Cambridge University Press.

Berg, Eiki. 1999. *Estonia's Northeastern Periphery in Politics: Socio-Economic and Ethnic Dimensions*. Tartu: Dissertationes Geographicae Universitatis Tartuensis.

Berg, Eiki. 2001. "Ethnic Mobilization in Flux: Revisiting Peripheriality and Minority Discontent in Estonia," *Space & Polity*, 5(1): 5–26.

Berg, Eiki, and Wim Van Meurs. 2002. "Borders and Orders in Europe: Limits of Nation- and State-Building in Estonia, Macedonia and Moldova," *Journal of Communist Studies and Transition Politics*, 18(4): 51–74.

Bieber, Florian. 2000. "Muslim Identity in the Balkans before the Establishment of Nation States," *Nationalities Papers*, 28(1): 13–28.

Biondich, Mark. 2007. "Vladko Maček and the Croat Political Right, 1928–1941," *Contemporary European History*, 16(2): 203–213.

Birch, Anthony. 1978. "Minority Nationalist Movements and Theories of Political Integration," *World Politics*, 30(3): 325–344.

Birnir, Jóhanna, Jonathan Wilkenfeld, James Fearon, David Laitin, Ted Robert Gurr, Dawn Brancati, Stephen Saideman, and Amy Pate. 2011. "A-MAR (All-Minorities at Risk): Addressing the Selection Bias Issue." Unpublished manuscript.

Bisaku, Gjon, Shtjefën Kurti, and Luigj Gashi. 1997. "The Situation of the Albanian Minority in Yugoslavia. Memorandum presented to the League of Nations (1930)," in Robert Elsie (ed.), *Kosovo: In the Heart of the Powder Keg*. Boulder, Colo.: East European Monographs, 361–399.

Biskupski, Mieczyslaw B. 2000. *The History of Poland*. Westport, Conn.: Greenwood Press.

Black, Jeremy. 2002. *Maps and Politics*. Chicago, Ill.: University of Chicago Press.

Bob, Clifford. 2005. *The Marketing of Rebellion: Insurgents, Media, and International Activism*. New York: Cambridge University Press.

Bodlore-Penlaez, Mikael. 2010. *Atlas des nations sans état en Europe: peuples minoritaires en quête de reconnaissance*. Fouenant: Yoran Embanner.

Bogdanović, Dimitrije. 1986. *Knjiga o Kosovu (Book on Kosovo)*. Belgrade. Available at: http://www.kosovo.net/sk/rastkokosovo/istorija/knjiga_o_kosovu/index.html.

Brailsford, Henry Noel. 1906. *Macedonia: Its Races and Their Future*. London: Metheun.

Brass, Paul. 1991. *Ethnicity and Nationalis Theory and Comparison*. New Delhi and Newbury Park, Calif.: Sage.

Brass, Paul. 1997. *Theft of an Idol*. Princeton, N.J.: Princeton University Press.

Braude, Benjamin, and Bernard Lewis. 2000. *Christians and Jews in the Ottoman Empire: The Functioning of a Plural Society*. New York: Holmes & Meir.

Braudel, Fernand. 1980. *On History*, Chicago, Ill.: University of Chicago Press.

Brown, DeNeen L. 2008. "Canadian Government Apologizes for Abuse of Indigenous People," *Washington Post*, 12 June: A01.

Brown, Michael E. (ed.). 1996. *The International Dimensions of Internal Conflict*. Cambridge, Mass.: MIT Press.

Brown, Michael E. (ed.). 1997. *Nationalism and Ethnic Conflict*. Cambridge, Mass.: MIT Press.

Browning, Christopher R., and Jürgen Matthäus 2004. *The Origins of the Final Solution: The Evolution of Nazi Jewish Policy, September 1939–March 1942*. London: William Heinemann.

Brubaker, Rogers. 1992. *Citizenship and Nationhood in France and Germany*. Cambridge, Mass., and London: Harvard University Press.

Brubaker, Rogers. 1993. "National Minorities, Nationalizing States, and External Homelands in the New Europe. Notes toward a Relational Analysis," *Reihe Politikwissenschaft No. 11*. Institut für Höhere Studien.

Brubaker, Rogers. 1996. *Nationalism Reframed: Nationhood and the National Question in the New Europe*. New York: Cambridge University Press.

Brubaker, Rogers. 1998. "Migrations of Ethnic Unmixing in the 'New Europe,'" *International Migration Review* 32(4, Winter): 1047–1065.

Buchanan, Allen, and Margaret Moore (eds.). 2003. *States, Nations, and Borders: The Ethics of Making Boundaries*. New York: Cambridge University Press.

Bulutgil, Zeynep. 2009. "Territorial Conflict and Ethnic Cleansing." Ph.D. dissertation, University of Chicago.

Burgwyn, H. James. 1997. *Italian Foreign Policy in the Interwar Period, 1918–1940*. Westport, Conn.: Praeger.

Byman, Daniel. 2007. *Understanding Proto-Insurgencies*. National Security Research Division, RAND Corporation.

Byman, Daniel, and Stephen Van Evera. 1998. "Why They Fight: Hypotheses on the Causes of Contemporary Deadly Conflict," *Security Studies*, 7(3): 1–50.

Byman, Daniel, Peter Chalk, Bruce Hoffman, William Rosenau, and David Brannan. 2001. *Trends in Outside Support for Insurgent Movements*. National Security Research Division, RAND Corporation.

Caldwell, Christopher. 2009. *Reflections on the Revolution in Europe: Immigration, Islam, and the West*. New York: Doubleday.

Camilleri, Joseph. 1990. "Rethinking Sovereignty in a Shrinking, Fragmented World," in Robert B. J. Walker and Saul H. Mendlovitz (eds.), *Contending Sovereignties*. Boulder, Colo.: Lynne Rienner, 13–44.

Carabott, Philip. 1997. "The Politics of Integration and Assimilation vis-à-vis the Slavo-Macedonian Minority of Inter-war Greece: From Parliamentary Inertia to Metaxist Repression," in Peter and Eleni Yannakakis (eds.), *Ourselves and Others: The Development of a Greek Macedonian Cultural Identity since 1912*. Mackridge, Oxford, and New York: Berg, 59–78.

Carment, David, Patrick James, and Zeynep Taydas. 2006. *Who Intervenes? Ethnic Conflict and Interstate Crisis*. Columbus: Ohio State University Press.

Carnegie Endowment for International Peace. 1914. *Report of the International Commission to Inquire into the Causes and Conduct of the Balkan Wars*. Washington, D.C.: Carnegie Endowment for International Peace.

Cederman, Lars-Erik, Andreas Wimmer, and B. Min. 2010. "Why Do Ethnic Groups Rebel? New Data and Analysis," *World Politics* 62(1): 87–119.

Chandra, Kanchan (ed.). 2001. "Symposium: Cumulative Findings in the Study of Ethnic Politics," *APSA CP* 12.

Chomsky, Noam. 1985. *Turning the Tide: U.S. Intervention in Central America and the Struggle for Peace*. Boston: South End Press.

Chomsky, Noam. 1993/1994. "Humanitarian Intervention," *Boston Review*, 18: 3–6.

Clark, Bruce. 2006. *Twice a Stranger: The Mass Expulsions That Forged Modern Greece and Turkey*. Cambridge, Mass.: Harvard University Press.

Clayer, Nathalie. 2008. "Behind the Veil: The Reform of Islam in Inter-War Albania or the Search for A 'Modern' and 'European' Islam," in Nathalie Clayer and Eric Germain (eds.), *Islam in Inter-war Europe*. New York: Columbia University Press, 128–155.

Clogg, Richard (ed.). 2002. *Minorities in Greece: Aspects of a Plural Society*. London: C. Hurst.

Comstock, John Lee. 1828. *Greek Revolution: Compiled from Official Documents of the Greek Government*. New York: William W. Reed.

Connor, Walker. 1972. "Nation-Building or Nation-Destroying?" *World Politics*, 24(3): 319–355.

Connor, Walker. 1973. "The Politics of Ethnonationalism," *Journal of International Affairs* 27(1): 1–21.

Coufoudakis, Van. 1976. "United Nations Peacekeeping and Peacemaking and the Cyprus Question," *Western Political Quarterly*, 29(3): 457–473.

Čubrilović, Vaso. 1997. "The Expulsion of the Albanians: Memorandum presented in Belgrade on 7 March 1937," in Robert Elsie (ed.), *Kosovo: In the Heart of the Powder Keg*. Boulder, Colo.: East European Monographs, 400–424.

Curtis, Glenn E. (ed.). 1992. *Yugoslavia: A Country Study*. Federal Research Division, Library of Congress.

Dakin, Douglass. 1966. *The Greek Struggle in Macedonia 1897–1913*. Thessaloniki: Institute for Balkan Studies.

Dalai Lama. 1987. *Five Point Peace Plan*. Address to the U.S. Congressional Human Rights Caucus. Available at: http://www.dalailama.com/messages/tibet/five-point-peace-plan.

Danforth, Loring. 1995. *The Macedonian Conflict: Ethnic Nationalism in a Transnational World*. Princeton, N.J.: Princeton University Press.

Darden, Keith. forthcoming. *Resisting Occupation: Mass Literacy and the Creation of Durable National Loyalties*. New York: Cambridge University Press.

Darden, Keith, and Harris Mylonas. 2012. "The Promethean Dilemma: Third-Party State-Building in Occupied Territories," *Ethnopolitics*, 1 (March): 85–93.

David, Steven R. 1991. *Choosing Sides: Alignment and Realignment in the Third World*. Baltimore, Md.: Johns Hopkins University Press.

Davidson, Jason W. 2002. "The Roots of Revisionism: Fascist Italy, 1922–39," *Security Studies*, 11(4): 125–159.

Davis, David R., and Will H. Moore, 1997. "Ethnicity Matters: Transnational Ethnic Alliances and Foreign Policy Behavior," *International Studies Quarterly*, 41(1): 171–184.

Dérens, Jean-Arnault. 2008. *Le piège du Kosovo*. Paris: Non Lieu.

Deutsch, Karl. 1965. *Nationalism and Social Communication*. Cambridge, Mass.: Technology Press.

Deutsch, Karl W., and William J. Foltz (eds.). 1963. *Nation-Building*. New York: Atherton Press.

Dillon, Michael. 2004. *Xinjiang: China's Muslim Far Northwest*. London and New York: RoutledgeCurzon.

Divani, Lena. 1995. *Hellada kai Meionotetes: to systema Diethnous Prostasias ton Ethnon* [Greece and Minorities: The League of Nation's International Protection System]. Athens: Nefeli.

Djilas, Aleksa. 1991. *The Contested Country: Yugoslav Unity and Communist Revolution, 1919–1953*. Cambridge, Mass.: Harvard University Press.

Djokić, Dejan. 2003. "(Dis)Integrating Yugoslavia: King Alexander and Interwar Yugoslavism," in Dejan Djokić (ed.), *Yugoslavism: Histories of a Failed Idea, 1918–1992*. London: C. Hurst, 136–156.

Djokić, Dejan. 2010. *Nikola Pašić and Ante Trubić: The Kingdom of Serbs, Croats and Slovenes*. London: Haus Publishing.

Dobbins, James, John G. McGinn, Keith Crane, Seth G. Jones, Rollie Lal, Andrew Rathmell, Rachel M. Swanger, and Anga R. Timilsina. 2003. *America's Role in Nation-Building: From Germany to Iraq.* Santa Monica, Calif.: RAND Corporation.

Dobbins, James, Seth G. Jones, Keith Crane, Andrew Rathmell, Brett Steele, Richard Teltschik, and Anga Timilsina. 2005. *The UN's Role in Nation-Building: From the Congo to Iraq.* Santa Monica, Calif.: RAND Corporation.

Dobbins, James, Seth G. Jones, Keith Crane, and Beth Cole DeGrasse. 2007. *The Beginner's Guide to Nation-Building.* Santa Monica, Calif.: RAND Corporation.

Donohoe, J. Patrick. 2004. "Preparing Leaders for Nationbuilding," *Military Review*, 84 (May/June): 24–26.

Doremus, Paul, William W. Keller, and Louis W. Pauly. 1998. *The Myth of the Global Corporation.* Princeton, N.J.: Princeton University Press.

Doyle, Rodger. 1998. "By the Numbers: Ethnic Groups in the World," *Scientific American Magazine*, September.

Downes, Alexander B. 2006. "Desperate Times, Desperate Measures: The Causes of Civilian Victimization in War," *International Security*, 30(4): 152–195.

Downes, Alexander B. 2008. *Targeting Civilians in War.* Ithaca, N.Y.: Cornell University Press.

Dragnich, Alex N. 1974. *Serbia, Nikola Pašić, and Yugoslavia.* New Brunswick, N.J.: Rutgers University Press.

Dragnich, Alex N. 1983. *The First Yugoslavia. Search for a Viable Political System.* Stanford, Calif.: Hoover Institution Press.

Driault, Édouard. 1921. *La question d'orient: depuis ses origines jusqu'a la Paix de Sèvres (1920).* Paris: Alcan.

Dündar, Fuat. 2010. *Crime of Numbers: The Role of Statistics in the Armenian Question (1878–1918).* New Brunswick, N.J., and London: Transaction Publishers.

Durham, M. Edith. 2001. *Albania and the Albanians: Selected Articles and Letters, 1903– 1944,* ed. Bejtullah Destani. London: Center for Albanian Studies and I. B. Tauris.

Dwyer, Arienne M. 2005. *The Xinjiang Conflict: Uyghur Identity, Language Policy, and Political Discourse.* Washington, D.C.: East-West Center Washington.

Eberhardt, Piotr. 2003. *Ethnic Groups and Population Changes in Twentieth-Century Central-Eastern Europe: History, Data, and Analysis.* Armonk, N.Y.: M. E. Sharpe.

Edwards, Lovett F. (ed.). 1969. *The Memoirs of Prota Matija Nenadović.* Oxford: Clarendon Press.

Eisenstadt, S. N., and Stein Rokkan (eds.). 1973. *Building States and Nations: Analyses by Region.* Vol. 2. Beverly Hills, Calif., and London: Sage Publications.

Elbadawi, Ibrahim, and Nicholas Sambanis. 2000. "External Interventions and the Duration of Civil Wars," *Policy Research Working Paper 2433*, Washington, D.C.: The World Bank Development Research Group, Public Economics.

Eliakis, Ioannis. 1940. *He Hestoria Exinta Hronon me eikones kai documenta* [The History of Sixty Years with Pictures and Documents]. Hania, Greece: "Efedrikou Agonos."

Elsie, Robert. 1997. *Kosovo: In the Heart of the Powder Keg.* Boulder, Colo.: East European Monographs.

Emerson, Rupert. 1960. *From Empire to Nation.* Cambridge, Mass.: Harvard University Press.

Eminov, Ali. 1997. *Turkish and Other Muslim Minorities in Bulgaria.* New York: Routeledge.

Evans, James. 2008. *Great Britain and the Creation of Yugoslavia: Negotiating Balkan Nationality and Identity*. London: Tauris Academic Studies.

Evrigenis, Ioannis D. 2008. *Fear of Enemies and Collective Action*. New York: Cambridge University Press.

Fearon, James D. 1998. "Commitment Problems and the Spread of Ethnic Conflict," in David Lake and Donald Rothchild (eds.), *The International Spread of Ethnic Conflict: Fear, Diffusion, and Escalation*. Princeton, N.J.: Princeton University Press, 114–126.

Fearon, James D. 2003. "Ethnic Structure and Cultural Diversity by Country," *Journal of Economic Growth*, 8 (June): 195–222.

Fearon, James D., and David D. Laitin. 2003. "Ethnicity, Insurgency, and Civil War," *American Political Science Review*, 97(1, February): 75–90.

Fearon, James D., and David D. Laitin. 2011. "*Sons of the Soil*, Migrants, and Civil War," *World Development*, 39(2): 199–211.

Fein, Helen. 1993. "Accounting for Genocide after 1945: Theories and Some Findings," *International Journal on Minority and Group Rights*, 1(2): 79–106.

Fichte, Johann Gottlieb. 1968 [1806]. Thirteenth Address, *Addresses to the German Nation*, ed. George A. Kelly. New York: Harper Torchbooks.

Findley, Carter Vaughn. 2010. *Turkey, Islam, Nationalism, and Modernity: A History, 1789–2007*. New Haven, Conn., and London: Yale University Press.

Finnemore, Martha. 2004. *The Purpose of Intervention: Changing Beliefs about the Use of Force*. Ithaca, N.Y., and London: Cornell University Press.

Finney, Patrick B. 1995. "'An Evil for All Concerned': Great Britain and Minority Protection after 1919," *Journal of Contemporary History*, 30(3): 533–551.

Fischer, Bernd J. 2007. "King Zog, Albania's Interwar Dictator," in Bernd J. Fischer (ed.), *Balkan Strongmen: Dictators and Authoritarian Rulers of Southeast Europe*. West Lafayette, Ind.: Purdue University Press, 19–49.

Fleming, Katherine E. 2008. *Greece: A Jewish History*. Princeton, N.J., and Oxford: Princeton University Press.

Fravel, M. Taylor. 2008. *Strong Borders, Secure Nation: Cooperation and Conflict in China's Territorial Disputes*. Princeton, N.J.: Princeton University Press.

Freundlich, Leo. 1997. "Albania's Golgotha: Indictment of the Exterminators of the Albanian People (1913)," in Robert Elsie (ed.), *Kosovo: In the Heart of the Powder Keg*. Boulder, Colo.: East European Monographs, 332–360.

Friedman, Isaiah. 1973. *The Question of Palestine, 1914–1918: British-Jewish-Arab Relations*. New York: Schocken Books.

Friedman, Thomas L. 2000. *The Lexus and the Olive Tree*. New York: Farrar, Straus & Giroux.

Friedman, Thomas L. 2007. *The World Is Flat, 3.0: A Brief History of the Twenty-first Century*. New York: Picador/Farrar, Straus & Giroux.

Friedman, Victor A. 1999. *Linguistic Emblems and Emblematic Languages: On Language as Flag in the Balkans (Kenneth E. Naylor Memorial Lecture Series in South Slavic Linguistics, No. 1)*. Department of Slavic and East European Languages and Literatures, Ohio State University.

Friedman, Victor A. 2001. "Languages and Ethnicity in Balkan Politics: Macedonian, Bulgarian, and Albanian" (Meeting Report No. 215). East European Studies (EES) News, Woodrow Wilson International Center for Scholars. Washington, D.C.: Woodrow Wilson International Center for Scholars. January–February.

Fukuyama, Francis. 2004. "State of the Union: Nation-Building 101," *Atlantic Monthly*, January/February.

Fukuyama, Francis (ed.). 2006. *Nation-Building: Beyond Afghanistan and Iraq*. Baltimore, Md.: Johns Hopkins University Press.

Gaddis, John Lewis. 1997. *We Now Know: Rethinking the Cold War*. New York: Oxford University Press.

Gagnon, V. P. Jr. 1994/1995. "Ethnic Nationalism and International Conflict: The Case of Serbia," *International Security*, 19(3, Winter): 132–168.

Gagnon, V. P. Jr. 2004. *The Myth of Ethnic War: Serbia and Croatia in the 1990s*. Ithaca, N.Y.: Cornell University Press.

Ganster, Paul, and David E. Lorey (eds.). 2005. *Borders and Border Politics in a Globalizing World*. Lanham, Md.: SR Books.

Garašanin, Ilija. 1998 [1844]. *Načertanije*. Beograd: Studio 104.

Gartzke, Erik A., and Kristian Skrede Gleditsch. 2006. "Identity and Conflict: Ties That Bind and Differences That Divide," *European Journal of International Relations*, 12(1): 53–87.

Geertz, Clifford. 1963. "The Integrative Revolution: Primordial Sentiments and Politics in the New States," in Clifford Geertz (ed.), *Old Societies and New States: The Quest for Modernity in Asia and Africa*. New York: Free Press of Glencoe.

Gelber, N. M., D. Florentin, Adolf Friedmann, and G. F. Török. 1955. "An Attempt to Internationalize Salonika, 1912–1913," *Jewish Social Studies*, 17(2): 105–120.

Gellner, Ernest. 1983. *Nations and Nationalism*. Ithaca, N.Y.: Cornell University Press.

General Staff of the Army. 1940. *O Ellinikos Stratos kata tous Valkanikous Polemous tou 1912–1913* [The Greek Army during the Balkan Wars of 1912–1913]. Vol. A. Athens: Army History Directorate.

General Staff of the Army. 1958. *O Ellinikos Stratos kata ton Proton Pagosmion Polemon, 1914–1918* [The Greek Army during World War I, 1914–1918]. Vol. 1. Athens: Army History Directorate.

Gerolymatos, Andre. 2002. *The Balkan Wars: Conquest, Revolution, and Retribution from the Ottoman Era to the Twentieth Century*. New York: Basic Books.

Gerring, John. 2007. *Case Study Research: Principles and Practices*. New York: Cambridge University Press.

Giannoulopoulos, Ioannis. 1999. *I eugenis mas tyflosis. Exoteriki Politiki kai "Ethnika Themata" apo tin Itta tou 1897 eos ti Mikrasiatiki Katastrofi* [Our Noble Blindness. Foreign Policy and "National Issues" from the 1897 Defeat to the Asia Minor Catastrophe]. Athens: Vivliorama.

Giuliano, Elise. 2011. *Constructing Grievance: Ethnic Nationalism in Russia's Republics*. Ithaca, N.Y.: Cornell University Press.

Glavinas, Ioannis. 2008. "*Oi mousoulmanikoi plitismoi stin Ellada (1912–1923): antilipseis kai praktikes tis ellinikis dioikisis, sheseis me hristianous gigeneis kai prosfyges*" [The Muslim Population in Greece (1912–1923): Views and Practices of the Hellenic Administration, Relations with Indigenous Christians and Refugees]. Ph.D. dissertation, Aristotle University of Thessaloniki.

Glazer, Nathan, and Daniel Patrick Moynihan. 1970. *Beyond the Melting Pot*. Cambridge, Mass.: MIT Press.

Glazier, Jack. 1998. *Dispersing the Ghetto: The Relocation of Jewish Immigrants across America*. Ithaca, N.Y.: Cornell University Press.

Gleditsch, Kristian Skrede. 2007. "Transnational Dimensions of Civil War," *Journal of Peace Research*, 44(3): 293–309.

Glenny, Misha. 2001 [1999]. *The Balkans: Nationalism, War, and the Great Powers, 1804–1999*. New York: Penguin Books.

Göçek, Fatma Müge. 1993. "Ethnic Segmentation, Western Education, and Political Outcomes: Nineteenth-Century Ottoman Society," *Poetics Today*, 14(3): 507–538.

Goertz, Gary, and Paul F. Diehl. 1997. "Linking Risky Dyads: An Evaluation of the Relations between Enduring Rivalries," in Gerald Schneider and Patricia A. Weitsman (eds.), *Enforcing Cooperation: Risky States and Intergovernmental Management of Conflict*. London: Macmillan, 132–160.

Goldstein, Melvyn C. 1989. *A History of Modern Tibet, 1913–1951: The Demise of the Lamaist State*. Berkeley: University of California Press.

Goldstein, Melvyn C. 2006. "The United States, Tibet, and the Cold War," *Journal of Cold War Studies*, 8(3): 145–164.

Goldstein, Melvyn C., Dawei Sherap, and William R. Siebenschuh. 2004. *A Tibetan Revolutionary: The Political Life and Times of Bapa Phuntso Wangye*. Berkeley, Los Angeles, and London: University of California Press.

Gordon, Milton. 1964. *Assimilation in American Life: The Role of Race, Religion and National Origins*. New York: Oxford University Press.

Gounaris, Basil G. 1996. "Social Cleavages and National 'Awakening' in Ottoman Macedonia," *East European Quarterly*, 29(4): 409–425.

Gounaris, Basil G. 2005. "Preachers of God and Martyrs of the Nation: The Politics of Murder in Ottoman Macedonia in the Early Twentieth Century," *Balkanologie*, 9(1–2): 31–43

Great Britain. Foreign Office. Historical Section. 1920. *Albania*. No. 17. London: H. M. Stationery Office.

Greenfeld, Liah. 1993. *Nationalism: Five Roads to Modernity*. Cambridge, Mass.: Harvard University Press.

Grigoryan, Arman. 2010. "Third-Party Intervention and the Escalation of State-Minority Conflicts," *International Studies Quarterly*, 54(4, December): 1143–1174.

Grimm, Gerhard. 1984. "Ethnographic Maps of the Kosova Region from 1730–1913," in Arshi Pipa and Sami Repishti (eds.), *Studies on Kosova*. Boulder, Colo.: East European Monographs.

Grunfeld, Tom A. 1987. *The Making of Modern Tibet*. London: Zed Books.

Guibernau, Montserrat. 1999. *Nations without States: Political Communities in a Global Age*. Cambridge: Polity Press.

Gullather, Nick. 2006. *Secret History: The CIA's Classified Account of Its Operations in Guatemala, 1952–1954*. Stanford, Calif.: Stanford University Press.

Gurr, Ted. 1993. *Minorities at Risk: A Global View of Ethnopolitical Conflicts*. Washington, D.C.: United States Institute of Peace.

Haass, Richard. 2008. "The Age of Nonpolarity: What Will Follow U.S. Dominance," *Foreign Affairs*, 87(3): 44–56.

Hadri, Ali. 1995. "The Albanian League of Prizren 1878–1881," *Kosova*, 5: 7–9.

Hajdarpašić, Edin. 2008. "Out of the Ruins of the Ottoman Empire: Reflections on the Ottoman Legacy in South-eastern Europe," *Middle Eastern Studies*, 44(5): 715–734.

Hale, Henry E. 2008. *The Foundations of Ethnic Politics: Separatism of States and Nations in Eurasia and the World*. Cambridge: Cambridge University Press.

Han, Enze, and Harris Mylonas. 2011. "Interstate Relations, Perceptions, and Power Balance: Explaining China's Nation-Building Policies, 1949–1965," paper presented at the 2011 ISA Annual Convention, Montreal, Canada (16–19 March 2011).

Hanioğlu, M. Şükrü. 2001. *Preparation for a Revolution: The Young Turks, 1902–1908*. Oxford: Oxford University Press.

Harff, Barbara. 1987. "The Etiology of Genocides," in Isidor Walliman and Michael N. Dobkowski (eds.), *Genocide and the Modern Age: Etiology and Case Studies of Mass Death*. New York: Greenwood Press, 41–59.

Harff, Barbara. 2003. "No Lessons Learned from the Holocaust? Assessing Risks of Genocide and Political Mass Murder since 1955," *American Political Science Review*, 97(1): 57–73.

Harth, Erica. 2001. *Last Witnesses: Reflections on the Wartime Internment of Japanese Americans*. New York: Palgrave.

Hartmuth, Maximilian. 2008. "De/constructing a 'Legacy in Stone': Of Interpretative and Historiographical Problems Concerning the Ottoman Cultural Heritage in the Balkans," *Middle Eastern Studies*, 44(5): 695–713.

Hassiotis, Loukianos. 2004. *Hellinoservikes Sheseis 1913–1918* [Greek-Serbian Relations 1913–1918]. Thessaloniki: Vanias.

Hassiotis, Loukianos. 2005. "Forcible Relocation from Greek Macedonia during the First World War." Available at: http://www.maccdonian-heritage.gr/Contributions/20030110_HassiotisL.html.

Hausman, Jerry, and Daniel McFadden. 1984. "Specification Tests for the Multinomial Logit Model," *Econometrica*, 52(5): 1219–1240.

Heaton-Armstrong, Captain Duncan. 2005. *The Six Month Kingdom: Albania 1914*, ed. Gervase Belfield, and Bejtullah Destani. London: I. B. Tauris in association with the Centre for Albanian Studies.

Hechter, Michael. 1975. *Internal Colonialism: The Celtic Fringe in British National Development, 1536–1966*. Berkeley and Los Angeles: University of California Press.

Hechter, Michael. 1987. *Principles of Group Solidarity*. Berkeley: University of California Press.

Hechter, Michael. 2000. *Containing Nationalism*. Oxford: Oxford University Press.

Helmreich, Ernst Christian. 1938. *The Diplomacy of the Balkan Wars: 1912–1913*. Cambridge, Mass.: Harvard University Press.

Heraclides, Alexis. 1990. "Secessionist Minorities and External Involvement," *International Organization*, 44(3): 341–378.

Heraclides, Alexis. 1991. *The Self-Determination of Minorities in International Politics*. London: Frank Cass.

Herder, Johann Gottfried. 2004. *Another Philosophy of History and Selected Political Writings*, trans. and ed. Ioannis Evrigenis and Daniel Pellerin. Indianapolis, Ind.: Hackett Publishing.

Hersh, Seymour. 2008. "Preparing the Battlefield: The Bush Administration Steps Up Its Secret Moves against Iran," *The New Yorker*, 7 July.

Hippler, Jochen. 2005. *Nation-Building: A Key Concept for Peaceful Conflict Transformation?* London: Pluto Press.

Hirschon, Renee. 2003. *Crossing the Aegean: An Appraisal of the 1923 Compulsory Population Exchange between Greece and Turkey*. New York: Berghahn Books.

Hobsbawm, Eric. 1990. *Industry and Empire: From 1750 to the Present Day*. London: Penguin.

Hobsbawm, Eric. 1991. *Nations and Nationalism since 1780: Programme, Myth, Reality*. New York: Cambridge University Press.

Hoffmann, Julia, and André Hollkaemper (eds.). 2012. *Responsibility to Protect: From Principle to Practice*. Amsterdam: University of Amsterdam Press.

Hollingshead, August B. 1952. "Trends in Social Stratification: A Case Study," *American Sociological Review*, 17(6): 679–686.

Horowitz, Donald. 1985. *Ethnic Groups in Conflict*. Berkeley: University of California Press.

Horvat, Branko. 1988. *Kosovsko Pitanje*. Zagreb: Globus.

Hovannisian, Richard G. (ed.). 1986. *The Armenian Genocide in Perspective*. New Brunswick, N.J.: Transaction Publishers.

Howard, Marc Morje. 2009. *The Politics of Citizenship in Europe*. Cambridge: Cambridge University Press..

Hroch, Miroslav. 2000 [1985]. *Social Preconditions of National Revival in Europe: A Comparative Analysis of the Social Composition of Patriotic Groups among the Smaller European Nations*. New York: Columbia University Press.

Huntington, Samuel. 1968. *Political Order in Changing Societies*. New Haven, Conn.: Yale University Press.

Ilicak, H. Sükrü. 2011. "Ottoman Perceptions of and Reactions to the Greek War of Independence." Ph.D. dissertation, Harvard University.

Institute of History. 1993. *The Truth on Kosova*. Tirana: Academy of Sciences of the Republic Albania.

Isaacs, Harold. 1975. *Idols of the Tribe*. New York: Harper & Row.

Ishiyama, John T., and Marijke Breuning. 1998. *Ethnopolitics in the New Europe*. Boulder, Colo., and London: Lynne Rienner Publishers.

Jagodić, Miloš. 2009. *Srpsko-albanski odnosi u Kosovskom vilajetu 1878–1912* [Serbo-Albanian Rellations in the Kosovo Vilajet/Area]. Belgrade: Zavod za udžbenike.

Jagodić, Miloš. 2010. *Uredjenje oslobodjenih oblasti Srbije 1912–1914* [The Arrangement of the Liberated Areas of Serbia]. Belgrade: Istorijski institut SANU.

Janjetović, Zoran. 2005. *Deca careva, pastorcad kraljeva: nacionalne manjine u Kraljevini Jugoslaviji 1918–1941* [The Children of the Emperors, the Stepchildren of the Kings: Minorities in the Kingdom of SCS 1918–1941]. Belgrade: Istorijski institut SANU.

Janković, Branimir M. 1988. *The Balkans in International Relations*, trans. Margot and Boško Milosavljević. Basingstoke: Macmillan.

Janowsky, Oscar Isaiah. 1966 [1933]. *The Jews and Minority Rights (1898–1919)*. New York: AMS Press.

Jelavich, Barbara. 1991. *Russia's Balkan Entanglements, 1806–1914*. Cambridge: Cambridge University Press.

Jelavich, Charles, and Barbara Jelavich. 1965. *The Balkans*. Englewood Cliffs, N.J.: Prentice-Hall.

Jelavich, Charles, and Barbara Jelavich. 1977. *The Establishment of the Balkan National States, 1804–1920*. Seattle and London: University of Washington Press.

Jenne, Erin. 2004. "A Bargaining Theory of Minority Demands: Explaining the Dog That Didn't Bite in 1990s Yugoslavia," *International Studies Quarterly* 48(4): 729–754.

Jenne, Erin. 2007. *Ethnic Bargaining: The Paradox of Minority Empowerment*. Ithaca, N.Y.: Cornell University Press.

Jenne, Erin, and Harris Mylonas. 2011. "Fighting the 'Enemy Within': State Responses toward Externally Leveraged Minorities," paper presented at the 2011 annual meeting of the American Political Science Association, Seattle, Washington (1–4 September 2011). Previous versions of this paper were presented at the 2010 Annual Meeting of the American Political Science Association, Washington, D.C. (2–5 September 2010) and the GW Comparative Politics Workshop, Washington, D.C. (10 September 2010).

Joppke, Christian. 2005. *Selecting by Origin: Ethnic Migration in the Liberal State.* Cambridge, Mass.: Harvard University Press.

Kamalov, Ablet. 2009. "Uyghurs in the Central Asian Republics: Past and Present," in Colin Mackerras and Michael Clarke (eds.), *China, Xinjiang and Central Asia: History, Transition and Crossborder Interaction into the 21st Century.* London and New York: Routledge.

Kaplan, Robert. 1993. *Balkan Ghosts: A Journey through History.* New York: St. Martin's Press.

Karadžić, Vuk. 1972 [1860]. *Etnografski spisi* [Ethnographic Handwritings]. Belgrade: Prosveta.

Karakasidou, Anastasia. 1997. *Fields of Wheat, Hills of Blood: Passages to Nationhood in Greek Macedonia, 1870–1990.* Chicago, Ill., and London: University of Chicago Press.

Karavas, Spyros. 2010. *"Makarioi oi katehontes tin gin." Gaioktitikoi Shediasmoi pros Apallotriosi Syneidiseon sti Makedonia, 1880–1909* ["Blessed are they who shall possess the Earth." Land-Ownership Plans for Expropriating Consciences in Macedonia, 1880–1909]. Athens: Vivliorama.

Karavidas, Konstantinos. 1931. *Agrotika: Ereuna epi tis Oikonomikis kai Koinonikis Morfologias en Elladi kai en tais Geitonikais Slavikais Horais* [Agrarian Studies: An Inquiry into the Economic and Social Morphology in Greece and in the Neighboring Slavic Countries]. Athens: Ethnikon Typographeion.

Kasaba, Reşat (ed.) 2008. *Cambridge History of Turkey: Turkey in the Modern World.* Vol. 4. Cambridge: Cambridge University Press.

Katsikas, Stefanos. 2009. "Millets in Nation-States: The Case of Greek and Bulgarian Muslims, 1912–1923," *Nationalities Papers*, 37(2): 177–201.

Kaufman, Stuart J. 2001. *Modern Hatreds: The Symbolic Politics of Ethnic War.* Ithaca, N.Y.: Cornell University Press.

Kaufmann, E., and O. Haklai. 2008. "Dominant Ethnicity: From Minority to Majority," *Nations and Nationalism*, 14(4): 743–767.

Kedourie, Elie. 1993. *Nationalism.* Oxford and Cambridge, Mass.: Wiley-Blackwell.

Kennan, George Frost. 1993. *The Other Balkan Wars.* Washington, D.C.: Carnegie Endowment for International Peace.

Khazanov, Anatoly M., and André Wink (eds.). 2001. *Nomads in the Sedentary World.* London: Curzon Press.

Khrychikov, Sergey, and Hugh Miall. 2002. "Conflict Prevention in Estonia: The Role of the Electoral System," *Security Dialogue*, 33(2): 193–208.

King, Charles. 2008. "The Five-Day War: Managing Moscow after the Georgia Crisis," *Foreign Affairs*, 87: 62–11.

King, Charles, and Neil J. Melvin. 1999/2000. "Diaspora Politics: Ethnic Linkages, Foreign Policy, and Security in Eurasia." *International Security*, 24(3): 108–138.

King, Gary, Michael Tomz, and Jason Wittenberg. 2000. "Making the Most of Statistical Analyses: Improving Interpretation and Presentation," *American Journal of Political Science*, 44(2): 347–361.

Kirch, Aksel, Marika Kirch, and Tarmo Tuisk. 1993. "Russians in the Baltic States: To Be or Not to Be?" *Journal of Baltic Studies*, 24(2): 174

Kitromilides, Paschalis M. 1994. *Enlightenment, Nationalism, Orthodoxy: Studies in the Culture and Political Thought of South-Eastern Europe.* Aldershot and Brookfield, Vt.: Variorum.

Kliot, N. 1989. "Accommodation and Adjustment to Ethnic Demands: The Mediterranean Framework," *Journal of Ethnic Studies*, 17(2): 45–70.

Knaus, John Kenneth. 1999. *Orphans of the Cold War: America and the Tibetan Struggle for Survival*. New York: Public Affairs.

Kocher, Matthew Adam. 2004. "Human Ecology and Civil War." Ph.D. dissertation, University of Chicago.

Kofos, Evangelos. 1964. *Nationalism and Communism in Macedonia*. Thessaloniki: Institute for Balkan Studies.

Kohn, Hans. 1945. *The Idea of Nationalism: A Study in Its Origins and Background*. New York: Macmillan.

Kola, Paulin. 2003. *The Myth of Greater Albania*. New York: New York University Press.

Koliopoulos, John S. 1987. *Brigands with a Cause: Brigandage and Irredentism in Modern. Greece 1821–1912*. New York: Oxford University Press.

Koliopoulos, John S. 2003. *I "peran" Ellas kai oi "alloi" Ellines: To Synhrono Elliniko Ethnos kai oi Eteroglossoi Synoikoi Hristianoi (1800–1912)* [The Greece of "Beyond" and the "Other" Greeks]. Thessaloniki: Vanias.

Kolstø, Pål. 2000. "Interstate Integration in the Post-Soviet Space. The Role of the Russian Diasporas," in Renata Dwan and Oleksandr Pavliuk (eds). *Building Security in the New States of Eurasia: Subregional Cooperation in the Former Soviet space*. Armonk, N.Y.: M.E.Sharpe.

Kondylis, Panayotis. 1985. Introduction, Translation, Notes, in *Marx – Engels: I Ellada, I Tourkia kai to Anatoliko Zitima* [Marx – Engels: Greece, Turkey and the Eastern Question]. Athens: Gnosis.

Kontis, Vasilis. 1994. *Evesthites Isorropies. Ellada kai Alvania ston 200 Aiona* [Sensitive Balances. Greece and Albania in the 20th Century]. Thessaloniki: Paratiritis.

Kontogiorgi, Elisabeth. 2006. *Population Exchange in Greek Macedonia: The Rural Settlement of Refugees 1922–1930*. Oxford: Clarendon Press.

Koppa, Marilena. 1997. *Oi Meionotites sta Meta-Kommounistika Valkania: Politikes toy Kentrou kai Meionotikes Apantiseis* [Minorities in Post-Communist Balkans: Center's Policies and Minority Responses]. Athens: "Nea Synora" – A. A. Livani.

Koppa, Marilena. 2002. *I Sigrotisi ton Kraton sta Valkania, 190s aionas* [The Establishment of States in the Balkans, 19th Century]. Athens: "Nea Synora" – A. A. Livani.

Kostanick, Huey Louis. 1948. "Macedonia: A Study in Political Geography." Ph.D. dissertation, Clark University.

Kostanick, Huey Louis. 1974 [1963]. "The Geopolitics of the Balkans," in Charles Jelavich and Barbara Jelavich (eds.), *The Balkans in Transition: Essays on the Development of Balkan Life and Politics since the Eighteenth Century*. Hamden, Conn.: Archon Books, 1–55.

Kostopoulos, Tasos. 2009. *To "Makedoniko" tis Thrakis* [The "Macedonian Question" of Thrace]. Athens: Vivliorama.

Kovrig, Bennett. 2000. "Partitioned Nation: Hungarian Minorities in Central Europe," in Michael Mandelbaum (ed.), *The New European Diasporas: National Minorities and Conflict in Eastern Europe*. New York: Council on Foreign Relations Press, 19–80.

Krstić-Brano, Branislav. 2004. *Kosovo: Facing the Court of History*. Amherst, N.Y.: Humanity Books.

Kuperman, Alan. 2001. *The Limits of Humanitarian Intervention: Genocide in Rwanda*. Washington, D.C.: Brookings Institution Press.

Kuperman, Alan. 2008. "The Moral Hazard of Humanitarian Intervention: Lessons from the Balkans," *International Studies Quarterly*, 52(1, March): 49–80.

Kuperman, Alan, and Timothy Crawford (eds.). 2006. *Gambling on Humanitarian Intervention: Moral Hazard, Rebellion, and Internal War.* New York: Routledge.

Kymlicka, Will. 1995. *Multicultural Citizenship: A Liberal Theory of Minority Rights.* Oxford and New York: Clarendon Press.

Kymlicka, Will. 2012. *Multiculturalism: Success, Failure, and the Future.* Washington, D.C.: Migration Policy Institute.

Ladas, Stephen P. 1932. *The Exchange of Minorities: Bulgaria, Greece and Turkey.* New York: Macmillan.

Laitin, David. 1986. *Hegemony and Culture: Politics and Religious Change among the Yoruba.* Chicago, Ill., and London: University of Chicago Press.

Laitin, David. 1995. "Marginality: A Microperspective," *Rationality and Society*, 7(1): 31–57.

Laitin, David. 1998. *Identity in Formation: The Russian-Speaking Populations in the Near Abroad.* Ithaca, N.Y.: Cornell University Press.

Laitin, David. 2001. "Secessionist Rebellion in the former Soviet Union." *Comparative Political Studies*, 34(8): 839–861.

Lake, David A., and Donald Rothchild. 1998. *The International Spread of Ethnic Conflict: Fear, Diffusion, and Escalation.* Princeton, N.J.: Princeton University Press.

Lampe, John R. 2000. *Yugoslavia as History: Twice There Was a Country.* New York: Cambridge University Press.

Leon, George B. 1974. *Greece and the Great Powers, 1914–1917.* Thessaloniki: Institute for Balkan Studies.

Levene, Mark. 1993. "Nationalism and Its Alternatives in the International Arena: The Jewish Question at Paris, 1919," *Journal of Contemporary History*, 28: 511–531.

Livanios, Dimitris. 1999. "'Conquering the Souls': Nationalism and Greek Guerrilla Warfare in Ottoman Macedonia, 1904–1908," *Byzantine and Modern Greek Studies*, 23: 195–221.

Livanios, Dimitris. 2008. *The Macedonian Question: Britain and the Southern Balkans: 1939–1949.* Oxford and New York: Oxford University Press.

Llewellyn-Smith, Michael. 1998. *Ionian Vision: Greece in Asia Minor, 1919–1922.* London: Hurst.

Lobell, Steven E., Norin M. Ripsman, and Jeffrey W. Taliaferro (eds.). 2009. *Neoclassical Realism, the State, and Foreign Policy.* Cambridge: Cambridge University Press.

Longworth, Philip. 2007. "Albania and King Zog: Independence, Republic and Monarchy 1908–1939," *Slavonic and East European Review*, 85(1): 160–164.

MacFarquhar, Roderick. 1997. *The Origins of the Cultural Revolution.* New York: Columbia University Press.

Mackie, John L. 1988. *The Cement of the Universe: A Study in Causation.* Oxford: Clarendon Press.

MacMillan, Margaret. 2002. *Paris 1919: Six Months That Changed the World.* Toronto: Random House.

Magocsi, Paul Robert. 2002. *Historical Atlas of Central Europe.* Seattle: University of Washington Press.

Malcolm, Noel. 1998. *Kosovo: A Short History.* New York: HarperPerennial.

Mandelbaum, Michael (ed.). 2000. *The New European Diasporas: National Minorities and Conflict in Eastern Europe.* New York: Council on Foreign Relations Press.

Mango, Andrew. 1999. *Atatürk.* London: John Murray.

Mann, Michael. 2005. *The Dark Side of Democracy: Explaining Ethnic Cleansing.* Cambridge: Cambridge University Press.

Mantouvalou, Katerina, and Harris Mylonas. 2010. "Islam at the EU Border: Explaining the Policies of Greece and Bulgaria toward Muslims in the Past Three Decades," presentation at the Constantine Karamanlis Chair in Hellenic and Southeastern European Studies, Fletcher School of Law and Diplomacy, Cambridge, Mass. (22 April 2010). The paper was also presented at the 21st Symposium of the Modern Greek Studies Association, Vancouver, Canada (15–17 October 2009).

Marmullaku, Ramadan. 1975. *Albania and the Albanians.* London: Archon Books.

Martin, Terry. 2001. *Affirmative Action Empire: Nations and Nationalism in the Soviet Union, 1923–1939.* Ithaca, N.Y.: Cornell University Press.

Marx, Anthony W. 1999. *Making Race and Nation: A Comparison of the United States, South Africa, and Brazil.* Cambridge: Cambridge University Press.

Mavrogordatos, George Th. 1982. *Meletes kai Keimena gia tin Periodo 1909–1940* [Studies and Documents on the Period 1909–1940]. Athens: Sakkoulas.

Mavrogordatos, George Th. 1983. *Stillborn Republic: Social Coalitions and Party Strategies in Greece, 1922–1936.* Berkeley: University of California Press.

Mavrogordatos, George Th. 2003. "Oi Ethnikes Meionotites" [The National Minorities], in Chatziiosif, Christos (ed.), *Historia tis Elladas tou 200u aiwna* [History of Greece of the 20th Century]. Vol. B2. Athens: Vivliorama, 9–35.

Mazower, Mark. 1997. "Minorities and the League of Nations in Interwar Europe," *Daedalus*, 126(2, Human Diversity, Spring): 47–63.

Mazower, Mark. 2001. *The Balkans: From the End of Byzantium to the Present Day.* London: Phoenix Press.

Mazower, Mark. 2004. *Salonica, City of Ghosts.* New York: HarperCollins.

Mazower, Mark. 2009. *No Enchanted Palace: The End of Empire and the Ideological Origins of the United Nations.* Princeton, N.J.: Princeton University Press.

McCarthy, Justin. 1995. *Death and Exile: The Ethnic Cleansing of Ottoman Muslims, 1821–1922.* Princeton, N.J.: Darwin Press.

McGarry, John, and Brendan O'Leary. 1994. "The Political Regulation of National and Ethnic Conflict." *Parliamentary Affairs*, 47(1): 94–115.

McGranahan, Carole. 2010. *Arrested Histories: Tibet, the CIA, and Memories of a Forgotten War.* Durham, N.C., and London: Duke University Press.

McMillen, Donald H. 1979. *Chinese Communist Power and Policy in Xinjiang, 1949–1977.* Boulder, Colo.: Westview Press.

Meaney, Thomas, and Harris Mylonas. 2008. "The Pandora's Box of Sovereignty," *Los Angeles Times*, 13 August.

Mearsheimer, John. 2001. *The Tragedy of Great Power Politics.* New York: W. W. Norton.

Meininger, Thomas A. 1970. *Ignatiev and the Establishment of the Bulgarian Exarchate, 1864–1872: A Study in Personal Diplomacy.* New York: Arno Press.

Melson, Robert. 1986. "Provocation or Nationalis A Critical Inquiry into the Armenian Genocide of 1915," in Richard G. Hovannisian (ed.), *The Armenian Genocide in Perspective.* New Brunswick, N.J.: Transaction Publishers.

Melvin, Neil. 1995. *Russians beyond Russia: The Politics of National Identity.* London: Royal Institute of International Affairs.

Michailidis, Iakovos. 1998. "The War on Statistics: Traditional Recipes for the Preparation of the Macedonian Salad," *East European Quarterly*, 32(1): 9–21.

Michailidis, Iakovos. 2003. *Metakiniseis slavofonon plithysmon. O polemos ton statistikon* [Slavophone Population Novement. The War of Statistics]. Athens: Kritiki.

Michailidis, Iakovos. 2005. "National Identity versus Minority Language: The Greek and Bulgarian Experience in the 20th Century," in Ann Katherine Isaacs (ed.), *Language and Identities in Historical Perspective*. Pisa: Pisa University Press.

Mijatovich, Chedomille. 1917. *The Memoirs of a Balkan Diplomatist*. London: Cassell.

Mikesel, Marvin W., and Alexander B. Murphy. 1991. "A Framework for Comparative Study of Minority-Group Aspirations," *Annals of the Association of American Geographers*, 81(4): 581–604.

Miller, Benjamin. 2007. *States, Nations, and the Great Powers: The Sources of Regional War and Peace*. Cambridge: Cambridge University Press.

Miller, William. 1927. "Albania and Her Protectress," *Foreign Affairs*, 5(3, April): 438–445.

Millward, James A. 2007. *Eurasian Crossroads: A History of Xinjiang*. New York: Columbia University Press.

Minahan, James. 2002. *Encyclopedia of the Stateless Nations: Ethnic and National Groups Around the World*. Vols. 1–4. Westport, Conn.: Greenwood Press.

Molho, Rena. *The Jerusalem of the Balkans: Salonica 1856–1919*. The Jewish Museum of Thessaloniki. Available at: http://www.jmth.gr/web/thejews/pages/pages/history/pages/his.htm.

Mylonas, Harris. 2006. "Peripheries, State Capacity, and Great Power Politics: Accounting for Secession from the Ottoman Empire", paper presented at the 11th Annual World Convention of the Association for the Study of Nationalities, Columbia University (22–25 March).

Mylonas, Harris. 2008. "Assimilation and Its Alternatives: The Making of Co-Nationals, Refugees, and Minorities." Ph.D. Dissertation, Yale University.

Mylonas, Harris. 2010. "Assimilation and Its Alternatives: Caveats in the Study of Nation-Building Policies," in Adria Lawrence and Erica Chenoweth (eds.), *Rethinking Violence: States and Non-state Actors in Conflict*. Cambridge, Mass.: MIT Press.

Mylonas, Harris. 2011. "Balkan Nation-Building Policies: Ottoman Legacy or Replication?" paper presented at the PONARS Eurasia Bishkek workshop (Kyrgyzstan, 11–16 June 2011).

Mylonas, Harris. 2012. "Ottoman, Nationalist, and Communist Legacies in the Balkans," in Stoica Lascu (ed.), *Balkans: Contributions to History, Culture and Civilization*. Constanța, Romania: Ovidius University Press.

Mylonas, Harris, and Nadav Shelef. 2012. "Which Land Is Our Land? Explaining Variation in Border Claims," paper presented at the 17th Annual ASN World Convention, Harriman Institute, Columbia University (April).

Naimark, N. 2001. *Fires of Hatred: Ethnic Cleansing in Twentieth Century Europe*. Cambridge, Mass.: Harvard University Press.

Nikolić, Lazar. 2003. "Ethnic Prejudices and Discrimination: The Case of Kosovo," in Florian Bieber and Zidas Daskalovski (eds.), *Understanding the War in Kosovo*. Portland, Ore.: Frank Cass, 53–76.

Njegoš, Petar Petrović. 1930 [1847]. *The Mountain Wreath: An Historical Happening Towards the Close of the 17th Century*, trans. James W. Wiles. London: Allen & Unwin.

Noreen, Erik, and Roxanna Sjöstedt. 2004. "Estonian Identity Formations and Threat Framing in the Post–Cold War Era Source," *Journal of Peace Research*, 41(6): 733–750.

Pallis, Alexander A. 1925. "Racial Migrations in the Balkans during the Years 1912–1924," *Geographical Journal*, 66(4, October): 315–331.

Panaiotov, Ivan. 1946. *Greeks and Bulgarians: A Historical Outline*. Sofia: Hristo G. Danov Publishers.

Pavlowitch, Stevan K. 1999. *A History of the Balkans, 1804–1945*. London and New York: Longman.

Pavlowitch, Stevan K. 2000. "Europe and the Balkans in a Historical Perspective, 1804–1945," *Journal of Southern Europe and the Balkans*, 2(2): 141–148.

Pearson, Owen. 2004. *Albania and King Zog: Independence, Republic and Monarchy, 1908–1939*. Vol. 1. London and New York: Centre for Albanian Studies in Association with I. B. Tauris.

Pentzopoulos, Dimitri. 1962. *The Balkan Exchange of Minorities and Its Impact upon Greece*. Paris: Mouton.

Perry, Duncan M. 1988. *The Politics of Terror: The Macedonian Revolutionary Movements, 1893–1903*. Durham, N.C., and London: Duke University Press.

Petersen, Roger. 2001. *Resistance and Rebellion: Lessons from Eastern Europe*. Cambridge: Cambridge University Press.

Petersen, Roger. 2002. *Understanding Ethnic Violence: Fear, Hatred, and Resentment in Twentieth-Century Eastern Europe*. Cambridge: Cambridge University Press.

Petranović, Branco. 2002. *The Yugoslav Experience of Serbian National Integration*. New York: Columbia University Press.

Pettai, Vello, and Klara Hallik. 2002. "Understanding Processes of Ethnic Control: Segmentation, Dependency and Cooptation in Post-Communist Estonia," *Nations and Nationalism* 8(4): 505–529.

Pettai, Vello, and Marcus Kreuzer. 1999. "Party Politics in the Baltic States: Social Bases and Institutional Context," *East European Politics and Society*, 13(1): 148–189.

Philliou, Christine. 2008. "The Paradox of Perceptions: Interpreting the Ottoman Past through the National Present," *Middle Eastern Studies*, 44(5): 661–675.

Popović, Janjićije. 1987. *Život Srba na Kosovu, 1812–1912* [Life of the Serbs in Kosovo, 1812–1912]. Belgrade: Književne novine.

Posen, Barry. 1993a. "Nationalism, the Mass Army and Military Power," *International Security*, 18(2): 80–124.

Posen, Barry. 1993b. "The Security Dilemma and Ethnic Conflict," *Survival*, 35(1, Spring): 27–47.

Posner, Daniel N. 2003. "The Colonial Origins of Ethnic Cleavages: The Case of Linguistic Divisions in Zambia," *Comparative Politics*, 35(2): 127–146.

Posner, Daniel. 2004. "Measuring Ethnic Fractionalization in Africa," *American Journal of Political Science*, 48(4): 849–863.

Poulton, Hugh. 2003. "Macedonians and Albanians as Yugoslavs," in Dejan Djokić (ed.), *Yugoslavism: Histories of a Failed Idea, 1918–1992*. London: Hurst, 115–135.

Poulton, Hugh, and Miranda Vickers. 1997. "The Kosovo Albanians: Ethnic Confrontation with the Slav State," in Hugh Poulton and Suha Taji-Farouki (eds.), *Muslim Identity and the Balkan State*. New York: New York University Press.

Protić, Milan St. 2007. "Serbian Radicalism 1881–1903: Political Thought and Practice," *Balcanica*, 38: 173–189.

Psomiades, Harry J. 1968. *Eastern Question: The Last Phase, a Study in Greek-Turkish Diplomacy*. Thessaloniki: Institute for Balkan Studies.

Putin, Vladimir. 2011. "A New Integration Project for Eurasia: The Future in the Making," *Izvestia*, 4 October. Available at: http://premier.gov.ru/eng/events/news/16622/.

Quataert, Donald. 2005 [2000]. *The Ottoman Empire, 1700–1922.* Cambridge: Cambridge University Press.

Rae, Heather. 2002. *State Identities and the Homogenisation of Peoples.* Cambridge: Cambridge University Press.

Raitviir, Tiina. 1996. *Eesti üleminekuperioodi valimiste (1989–1993) võrdlev uurimine* [Elections in Estonia during the Transition Period: A Comparative Study 1989–1993]. Tallinn: Rahvusvaliste ja Sotsiaaluuringute Instituut (Institute of International and Social Studies).

Ramet, Sabrina P. 2006. *The Three Yugoslavias: State-Building and Legitimation, 1918–2005.* Bloomington and Indianapolis: Indiana University Press.

Rathbun, Brian. 2008. "A Rose by Any Other Name: Neoclassical Realism as the Logical and Necessary Extension of Structural Realism," *Security Studies,* 17(2): 80–124.

Raun, Toivo. 1991. "The Re-establishment of Estonian Independence," *Journal of Baltic Studies,* 22(3): 251–258.

Ray, Paramesh. 1973. "Independence of Irrelevant Alternatives," *Econometrica,* 41(5): 987–991.

Regan, Patrick M. 2000. *Civil War and Foreign Powers.* Ann Arbor: University of Michigan Press.

Regan, Patrick M. 2002. "Third-Party Interventions and the Duration of Intrastate Conflicts," *Journal of Conflict Resolution,* 46(1): 55–73.

Renan, Ernest. 1996. "What Is a Nation?" in Geoff Eley and Ronald Grigor Suny (eds.), *Becoming National: A Reader.* New York and Oxford: Oxford University Press, 41–55.

Reynolds, Michael A. 2011. *Shattering Empires: The Clash and Collapse of the Ottoman and Russian Empires 1908–1918.* Cambridge: Cambridge University Press.

Roberts, Sean R. 1998. "The Uighurs of the Kazakhstan Borderlands: Migration and the Nation," *Nationalities Papers* 26(3): 511–530.

Robinson, Greg. 2009. *A Tragedy of Democracy: Japanese Confinement in North America.* New York: Columbia University Press.

Roeder, Philip G. 1991. "Soviet Federalism and Ethnic Mobilization," *World Politics* 43: 196–232.

Roeder, Philip G. 2007. *Where Nation–States Come From: Institutional Change in the Age of Nationalism.* Princeton, N.J.: Princeton University Press.

Ron, James. 2003. *Frontiers and Ghettos: State Violence in Serbia and Israel.* Berkeley: University of California Press.

Roos, Aarand. 1994. *Words for Understanding Ethnic Estonians.* Tallinn: Kommunaalprojekt Ltd.

Rose, Gideon. 1998. "Neoclassical Realism and Theories of Foreign Policy," *World Politics,* 51(1): 144–172.

Rose, Richard, and William Maley. 1994. "Conflict or Compromise in the Baltic States?" RFE/RL Research Report 3 (28).

Rosenau, James N. 1964. *International Aspects of Civil Strife.* Princeton, N.J.: Princeton University Press.

Rotzokos, Nikos. 2007. *Ethnafipnisi kai ethnogenesi. Orlofika kai elliniki istoriografia* [National Awakening and Nation-Building: The Orlov Revolt and Greek Historiography]. Athens: Vivliorama.

Roudometof, Victor. 1996. "Nationalism and Statecraft in Southeastern Europe (1750–1923)." Ph.D. dissertation, University of Pittsburgh.

Roudometof, Victor. 2001. *Nationalism, Globalization, and Orthodoxy: The Social Origins of Ethnic Conflict in the Balkans.* Westport, Conn., and London: Greenwood Press.

Rousseau, Jean-Jacques. 1985 [1772]. *The Government of Poland*, trans. Willmoore Kendall. Indianapolis, Ind.: Hackett.

Sabatos, Charles. 2008. "Slovak Perceptions of the Ottoman Legacy in Eastern Europe," *Middle Eastern Studies*, 44(5): 735–749.

Saideman, Stephen M. 1997. "Explaining the International Relations of Secessionist Conflicts: Vulnerability vs. Ethnic Ties," *International Organization*, 51(4): 721–753.

Saideman, Stephen M. 2002. "Discrimination in International Relations: Analyzing External Support for Ethnic Groups," *Journal of Peace Research*, 39(1): 27–50.

Saideman, Stephen M., and William Ayres. 2000. "Determining the Causes of Irredentism: Logit Analyses of Minorities at Risk Data from the 1980s and 1990s," *Journal of Politics*, 62(4): 1126–1144.

Saideman, Stephen M., and William Ayres. 2008. *For Kin and Country: Xenophobia, Nationalism, and War.* New York: Columbia University Press.

Sajti, Enikô A. 2006. "The Former 'Southlands' in Serbia: 1918–1947," *Hungarian Quarterly*, 181: 111–124.

Salehyan, Idean. 2009. *Rebels without Borders: Transnational Insurgencies in World Politics.* Ithaca, N.Y., and London: Cornell University Press.

Salehyan, Idean, and Kristian Gleditsch. 2006. "Refugees and the Spread of Civil War," *International Organization*, 60(2, April): 335–366.

Sambanis, Nicholas. 2001. "Do Ethnic and Non-ethnic Civil Wars Have the Same Causes? A Theoretical and Empirical Inquiry (Part 1)," *Journal of Conflict Resolution*, 45(3): 259–282.

Sambanis, Nicholas, and Branko Milanovic. 2009. "Explaining the Demand for Sovereignty." Unpublished manuscript.

Sanders, Ronald. 1984. *The High Walls of Jerusalem: A History of the Balfour Declaration and the Birth of the British Mandate for Palestine.* New York: Holt, Rinehart and Winston.

Sassen, Saskia. 1996. *Losing Control? Sovereignty in an Age of Globalization.* New York: Columbia University Press.

Sassen, Saskia. 1998. *Globalization and Its Discontents: Essays on the New Mobility of People and Money.* New York: New Press.

Sassen, Saskia. 2002. *Global Networks, Linked Cities.* New York: Routledge.

Schaeffer, R. K. 2003. *Understanding Globalization: The Social Consequences of Political, Economic, and Environmental Change.* New York: Rowman and Littlefield.

Schecter, Jerrold L. 1963. "Khrushchev's Image Inside China," *China Quarterly*, 14 (April/June): 212–217.

Schweller, Randall. 2004. "Unanswered Threats: A Neoclassical Realist Theory of Underbalancing," *International Security*, 29(2): 159–201.

Schweller, Randall. 2006. *Unanswered Threats: Political Constraints on the Balance of Power.* Princeton, N.J.: Princeton University Press.

Sereni, Angelo Piero. 1941. "The Legal Status of Albania," *American Political Science Review*, 35(2, April): 311–317.

Seton-Watson, Hugh. 1962 [1945]. *Eastern Europe between the Wars, 1918–1941.* Hamden, Conn.: Archon Books.

Shakya, Tsering. 1999. *The Dragon in the Land of Snows: A History of Modern Tibet since 1947*. London: Pimlico.

Shaw, Stanford J. 1974 [1963]. "The Ottoman View of the Balkans," in Charles Jelavich and Barbara Jelavich (eds.), *The Balkans in Transition: Essays on the Development of Balkan Life and Politics since the Eighteenth Century*. Hamden, Conn.: Archon Books, 56–80.

Shevel, Oxana. 2011. *Migration, Refugee Policy, and State Building in Postcommunist Europe*. New York: Cambridge University Press.

Skendi, Stavro. 1967. *The Albanian National Awakening 1878–1912*. Princeton, N.J.: Princeton University Press.

Smith, Anthony. 1986. "State-Making and Nation-Building," in John Hall (ed.), *States in History*. Oxford: Basil Blackwell, 228–263.

Smith, Anthony D. 1991. *National Identity*. London: Penguin.

Smith, David J. 2001. *Estonia: Independence and European Integration*. London and New York: Routledge.

Smith, David J. (ed.). 2005. *The Baltic States and Their Region: New Europe or Old?* Amsterdam and New York: Rodopi B.V.

Smith, Graham, and Andrew Wilson. 1997. "Rethinking Russia's Post-Soviet Diaspora: The Potential for Political Mobilization in Eastern Ukraine and North-east Estonia," *Europe-Asia Studies*, 49(5): 845–864.

Smith, Rogers M. 2001. "Citizenship and the Politics of People-Building," *Citizenship Studies*, 5(1): 73–96.

Smith, Rogers M. 2003. *Stories of Peoplehood: The Politics and Morals of Political Membership*. Cambridge: Cambridge University Press.

Snyder, Glenn. 1991. "Alliances, Balance, and Stability," *International Organization*, 45 (1): 121–142.

Snyder, Jack L. 1991. *Myths of Empire*. Ithaca, N.Y.: Cornell University Press.

Snyder, Jack L. 2000. *From Voting to Violence: Democratization and Nationalist Conflict*. New York: Norton.

Snyder, Jack, and Barbara Walter. 1999. *Civil Wars, Insecurity, and Intervention*. New York: Columbia University Press.

Snyder, Timothy. 2003. *The Reconstruction of Nations: Poland, Ukraine, Lithuania, Belarus, 1569–1999*. New Haven, Conn.: Yale University Press.

Snyder, Timothy. 2008. *The Red Prince: The Secret Lives of a Habsburg Archduke*. New York: Basic Books/Random House.

Snyder, Timothy. 2010. *Bloodlands: Europe between Hitler and Stalin*. New York: Basic Books/Random House.

Sørensen, Jens Stilhoff. 2009. *State Collapse and Reconstruction in the Periphery: Political Economy, Ethnicity and Development in Yugoslavia, Serbia and Kosovo*. Oxford: Berghahn Books.

Sowards, Steven W. 1996. *Twenty-five Lectures on Modern Balkan History: The Balkans in the Age of Nationalism*. Available at: http://www.lib.msu.edu/sowards/balkan.

Spruyt, Hendrik. 1994. *The Sovereign State and Its Competitors*. Princeton, N.J.: Princeton University Press.

Stavrianos, L. S. 1957. "Antecedents to the Balkan Revolutions of the Nineteenth Century," *The Journal of Modern History*, 29(4): 335–348.

Steed, H. Wickham. 1927. "Italy, Yugoslavia and Albania," *Journal of the Royal Institute of International Affairs*, 6(3): 170–178.

Steen, Anton, and Jüri Ruus. 2002. "Change of Regime – Continuity of Elites? The Case of Estonia," *East European Politics and Societies*, 16(1): 223–248.

Stefanidis, Yannis, Vlasis Vlasidis, and Evangelos Kofos (eds.). 2010. *Macedonian Identities through Time: Interdisciplinary Approaches*. Thessaloniki: Epikentro.

Stefanović, Đorđe. 2005. "Seeing the Albanians through Serbian Eyes: The Inventors of the Tradition of Intolerance and Their Critics, 1804–1939," *European History Quarterly*, 35(3): 465–492.

Stein, Leonard. 1961. *Balfour Declaration*. New York: Simon and Schuster.

Stephenson, Carolyn. 2005. "Nation Building," in Guy Burgess and Heidi Burgess (eds.), *Beyond Intractability*. Conflict Research Consortium, University of Colorado. Available at: http://www.beyondintractability.org/essay/nation_building/.

Stern, Laurence. 1975. "Bitter Lessons: How We Failed in Cyprus," *Foreign Policy*, 19: 34–78.

Strange, Susan. 2000. "The Declining Authority of States," in David Held and Anthony McGrew (eds.), *The Global Transformation Reader: An Introduction to the Global Debate*. Cambridge: Polity Press, 148–155.

Straus, Scott. 2006. *The Order of Genocide: Race, Power, and War in Rwanda*. Ithaca, N.Y.: Cornell University Press.

Sugar, Peter. 1977. *Southeastern Europe under Ottoman Rule, 1354–1804*. Seattle and London: University of Washington Press.

Suny, Ronald Grigor. 1993. *The Revenge of the Past: Nationalism, Revolution, and the Collapse of the Soviet Union*. Stanford, Calif.: Stanford University Press.

Suny, Ronald Grigor, and Terry Martin. 2001. *A State of Nations: Empire and Nation-Making in the Age of Lenin and Stalin*. New York: Oxford University Press.

Suny, Ronald Grigor, Fatma Muge Gocek, and Norman M. Naimark (eds.). 2011. *A Question of Genocide: Armenians and Turks at the End of the Ottoman Empire*. Oxford and New York: Oxford University Press.

Swire, Joseph. 1971. *Albania: The Rise of a Kingdom*. London: Allen & Urwin.

Taras, Ray, and Rajat Ganguly. 2002. *Understanding Ethnic Conflict: The International Dimension*, 2nd ed. New York: Longman.

Thyne, Clayton L. 2009. *How International Relations Affect Civil Conflict: Cheap Signals, Costly Consequences*. Lanham, Md.: Rowman & Littlefield.

Tilly, Charles (ed.). 1975. *The Formation of National States in Western Europe*. Princeton, N.J.: Princeton University Press.

Tilly, Charles. 1992. *Coercion, Capital and European States*. Cambridge, Mass., and Oxford: Blackwell Press.

Tilly, Charles. 1994. "States and Nationalism in Europe 1492–1992," *Theory and Society*, 23: 131–146.

Todorov, Nikolai. 1983. *The Balkan City, 1400–1900*. Seattle and London: University of Washington Press.

Todorova, Maria. 1997. *Imagining the Balkans*. New York: Oxford University Press.

Todorović, Desanka. 1979. *Jugoslavija i balkanske drzave 1918–1923* [Yugoslavia and the Balkan States 1918–1923]. Belgrade: Institut za savremenu istoriju.

Toft, Monica Duffy. 2003. *The Geography of Ethnic Violence*. Princeton, N.J.: Princeton University Press.

Tomasevich, Jozo. 1955. *Peasants, Politics, and Economic Change in Yugoslavia*. Stanford, Calif.: Stanford University Press.

Tomz, Michael, Jason Wittenberg, and Gary King. 2003. CLARIFY: Software for Interpreting and Presenting Statistical Results. Version 2.1. Stanford University,

University of Wisconsin, and Harvard University. Available at: http://gking.har vard.edu.

Treisman, Daniel. 1997. "Russia's 'Ethnic Revival': The Separatist Activism of Regional Leaders in a Postcommunist Order," *World Politics*, 49(2): 212–249.

Troch, Pieter. 2010. "Yugoslavism between the World Wars: Indecisive Nation Building," *Nationalities Papers*, 38(2, March): 227–244.

Trotsky, Leon. 1980. *The Balkan Wars, 1912–1913*, trans. Brian Pearce, ed. George Weissman and Duncan Williams. New York: Monad Press.

Troumbeta, Sevasti. 2001. *Kataskevazontas Tautotites gia tous Mousoulmanous tis Thrakis* [Constructing Identities for the Muslims of Thrace]. Athens: Kritiki.

Tsitselikis, Konstantinos. 2007. "The Pending Modernisation of Islam in Greece: From Millet to Minority Status," *Südosteuropa*, 55(4): 354–372.

Tsitselikis, Konstantinos. 2012. *Old and New Islam in Greece: From Historical Minorities to Immigrant Newcomers*. Leiden, the Netherlands, and Boston: Martinus Nijhoff Publishers.

Tucker, Spencer, Laura Matysek Wood, and Justin D. Murphy (eds.). 1999. *The European Powers in the First World War: An Encyclopedia*. New York: Taylor & Francis.

Ülker, Erol. 2005. "Contextualising 'Turkification': Nation-Building in the Late Ottoman Empire, 1908–18," *Nations and Nationalism*, 11(4): 613–636.

Üngör, Ugur Ümit. 2011. *The Making of Modern Turkey Nation and State in Eastern Anatolia, 1913–1950*. Oxford: Oxford University Press.

Valentino, Benjamin. 2004. *Final Solutions: Mass Killing and Genocide in the Twentieth Century*. Ithaca, N.Y.: Cornell University Press.

Van den Berghe, Pierre L. 1981. *The Ethnic Phenomenon*. New York: Elsevier.

Van Evera, Stephen. 1994. "Hypotheses on Nationalism and War," *International Security*, 18(4): 5–39.

van Houten, Pieter. 1998. "The Role of a Minority's Reference State in Ethnic Relations," *Archives Européennes de Sociologie*, 39(Spring): 110–146.

Vasiliadis, Nikolaos. 2004. *I Elliniki parousia sti Notia Servia apo tous Valkanikous polemous eos to Mesopolemo* [The Hellenic Presence in South Serbia from the Balkan Wars to the Interwar Period]. Thessaloniki: Anatropi.

Vasquez, John, and Marie T. Henehan. 2001. "Territorial Disputes and the Probability of War, 1816–1992," *Journal of Peace Research*, 38(2): 123–138.

Venizelos, Eleutherios. 1919. *Greece before the Peace Congress of 1919: A Memorandum Dealing with the Rights of Greece*. New York: Oxford University Press.

Verli, Marenglen. 1995. "Slavic Colonial Policy in the Albanian Territories between the Two World Wars (1918–1941)," *Kosova*, 5: 15–18.

Verli, Marenglen. 1999. "Garašanin's Načertanije: Ideological Basis of Greater Serbia's Program," *Kosova*, 7: 49–55.

Vickers, Miranda. 1998. *Between Serb and Albanian: A History of Kosovo*. London: C. Hurst.

Villari, Luigi. 1956. *Italian Foreign Policy under Mussolini*. New York: Devin-Adair.

Vlasidis, Vlasis. 1998. "Consequences of the Demographic and Social Re-arrangements to the Vlach-speaking Element of Greek Macedonia (1923–1926)," *Revue des Etudes Sud-Est Europeennes, Danube-Balkans-Mer Noire Tome*, 36(1–4): 155–171.

Vouri, Sophia. 1992. *Ekpaideuse kai Ethnikismos sta Valkania. He Periptose tis Voreiodytikes Makedonias 1870–1904* [Education and Nationalism in the Balkans. The Case of North-Western Macedonia 1870–1904]. Athens: Paraskinio.

Vouri, Sophia. 1994. *Piges gia tin Istoria tes Makedonias. Politike kai ekpaideuse 1875–1907* [Sources for the History of Macedonia. Politics and Education 1875–1907]. Athens: Paraskinio.

Vouri, Sophia. 2005. *Oikotrofeia kai ypotrofies ste Makedonia (1903–1913). Tekmiria Istorias* [Boarding Schools and Scholarships in Macedonia (1903–1913). Historial Evidence]. Athens: Gutenberg.

Walt, Stephen. 1985. "Alliance Formation and the Balance of World Power," *International Security*, 9(4): 3–43.

Walt, Stephen. 1987. *The Origins of Alliances*. Ithaca, N.Y.: Cornell University Press.

Walt, Stephen. 1988. "Testing Theories of Alliance Formation: The Case of Southwest Asia," *International Organization*, 42(2): 275–316.

Walt, Stephen. 1997. "Why Alliances Endure or Collapse," *Survival*, 39(1): 156–179.

Walter, Barbara. 2009. *Reputation and Civil War: Why Separatist Conflicts Are So Violent*. New York: Cambridge University Press.

Waltz, Kenneth. 1979. *Theory of International Politics*. New York: McGraw-Hill.

Wang, Lixiong. 2002. "Reflections of Tibet," *New Left Review*, 14 (March/April): 79–111.

Weber, Eugen. 1976. *Peasants into Frenchmen: The Modernization of Rural France, 1870–1914*. Stanford, Calif.: Stanford University Press.

Weber, Katja. 1997. "Hierarchy amidst Anarchy: A Transaction Costs Approach to International Security Cooperation," *International Studies Quarterly*, 41: 321–340.

Weber, Max. 1978. *Economy and Society*. Vol. 1. Trans. and ed. Guenther Roth and Claus Wittich. Berkeley: University of California Press.

Weinberg, Gerhard L. 1995. *Germany, Hitler, and World War II*. New York: Cambridge University Press.

Weiner, Myron. 1971. "The Macedonian Syndrome: An Historical Model of International Relations and Political Development," *World Politics*, 23(4): 665–683.

Weiner, Myron. 1996. "Bad Neighbors, Bad Neighborhoods: An Inquiry into the Causes of Refugee Flows," *International Security*, 17(1): 5–42.

Weiner, Tim. 2007. *Legacy of Ashes: The History of the CIA*. New York: Anchor Books.

Wheeler, Geoffrey. 1963. "Sinkiang and the Soviet Union," *China Quarterly*, 16: 56–61.

Wilkinson, Henry R. 1951. *Maps and Politics: A Review of Ethnographic Cartography of Macedonia*. Liverpool: Liverpool University Press.

Wilson, Thomas M., and Hastings Donnan. 1998. *Border Identities: Nation and State at International Frontiers*. Cambridge: Cambridge University Press.

Wimmer, Andreas. 2002. *Nationalist Exclusion and Ethnic Conflict: Shadows of Modernity*. Cambridge: Cambridge University Press.

Wimmer, Andreas. 2012. *Waves of War: Nationalism, State Formation, and Ethnic Exclusion in the Modern World*. Cambridge: Cambridge University Press.

Wolf, Lucien. 1919. *Notes on the Diplomatic History of the Jewish Question: With Texts of Protocols, Treaty Stipulations and Other Public Acts and Official Documents*. London: Ballantyne.

Wolfers, Arnold. 1962. *Discord and Collaboration: Essays on International Politics*. Baltimore, Md.: Johns Hopkins University Press.

Wood, Denis (with John Fels). 1992. *The Power of Maps*. New York: Guilford Press.

Woodwell, Douglas. 2004. "Unwelcome Neighbors: Shared Ethnicity and International Conflict during the Cold War," *International Studies Quarterly*, 48: 197–223.

Yıldırım, Onur. 2006. *Diplomacy and Displacement: Reconsidering the Turco-Greek Exchange of Populations, 1922–1934.* New York: Routledge.

Yilmaz, Şuhnaz, and İpek K. Yosmaoğlu. 2008. "Fighting the Spectres of the Past: Dilemmas of Ottoman Legacy in the Balkans and the Middle East," *Middle Eastern Studies,* 44(5): 677–693.

Yosmaoğlu-Turner, İpek. 2005. "The Priest's Robe and the Rebel's Rifle: Communal Conflict and the Construction of National Identity in Ottoman Macedonia, 1878–1908." Ph.D. dissertation, Princeton University.

Young, Crawford (ed.). 1993. *The Rising Tide of Cultural Pluralism.* Madison: University of Wisconsin Press.

Zavalani, T. 1969. "Albanian Nationalism," in Peter F. Sugar and Ivo J. Lederer (eds.), *Nationalism in Eastern Europe.* Seattle and London: University of Washington Press, 55–92.

Zickel, Raymond, and Walter R. Iwaskiw (eds.). 1994. *Albania: A Country Study.* Washington, D.C.: GPO for the Library of Congress.

Žižek, Slavoj. 2008. *Violence: Six Sideways Reflections.* London: Profile Books.

Zürcher, Eric J. 2004. *Turkey: A Modern History,* 3rd ed. London: I. B. Tauris.

Author Index

Historical Name Index

Subject Index

Abkhazia, 10
Aboriginals, 28
Accommodation, 1–4, 6, 17–19, 21–48,
71–90, 92, 94, 97–99, 103–106,
110–111, 123–124, 128, 130, 136,
139–140, 144, 155, 158, 166,
174–180, 184–185, 187, 189–190,
192, 195, 198–199
cost of, 23
of non-core groups supported by allies,
10–11, 39
Ottoman form of, 57, 171–172
in the Soviet Union, 31
as a transitional policy, 106
Adriatic, 61, 143, 147, 154
Aegean Sea, 61, 64
African Union (AU), 10
Agreement of Moudania, 140
Albania, 66, 104
Central, 69, 129
Southern, 92, 98, 100–101, 110
vassal state of Italy, 70
Albanians, 64, 69, 94, 105, 127–128,
138–139, 143–164 166–174
Alliances
asymmetric, 30, 110–112,
179, 191
balancing, 25, 46, 47, 101
bandwagoning, 46
international alliance structure, 6, 30,
40, 47, 73, 188
symmetric, 30, 97, 110, 178, 180
Anasselitsa (eparchy), 119, 127

Anschluss, 162
Anti-Venizelist(s) 114
coalition, 117, 125–126
government, 115, 117
in Greek Macedonia, 115
Muslims, 125
party 117, 125
political elites, 126
rule, 68
vote, 125
Apartheid, 22
Armenia, 8
Armenians, 1–2, 9, 121, 187, 194
ASEAN (*see* Association of Southeast
Asian Nations)
Asia Minor, 33, 66, 68, 100, 110, 125,
127, 129, 132, 140, 189
Assimilation, 2–7, 11–12, 17–27, 31,
36, 37–41, 44, 54, 57, 77–112,
128, 130–133, 136–140, 144,
147–148, 153–154, 156, 159–160,
164, 169–173, 175, 178, 184–185,
188, 190, 192, 194, 197–198,
202, 204
through accommodation, 25, 37,
105–110, 128, 137, 140, 175
core group as target of, 27, 190
cost of, 23
as "cultural genocide," 171
escalates into conflict, 45
through internal colonization, 37, 44,
84, 102, 153, 160
linguistic, 59–60, 76–77, 139